Children
of Abraham

God said to Abraham,
"Look up into heaven and count the stars if you can.
Such will your descendants be."
Genesis 15:5

Children
of Abraham

JUDAISM│CHRISTIANITY│ISLAM

F. E. PETERS

PRINCETON UNIVERSITY PRESS
PRINCETON, NEW JERSEY

Library of Congress Cataloging in Publication Data

Peters, F.E. (Francis E.)
  Children of Abraham.

  Includes index.
  1. Judaism—History.   2.   Christianity—History.
  3. Islam—History.   I.   Title.
  BM157.P47   291   81-47941
  ISBN 0-691-07267-1   AACR2
  ISBN 0-691-02030-2 (pbk.)

This book has been composed in Linotron Bembo

Princeton University Press books are printed on acid-free paper and
meet the guidelines for permanence and durability of the Committee on
Production Guidelines for Book Longevity of the Council on Library Resources

Printed in the United States of America by Princeton Academic Press

First Princeton Paperback Printing, 1984

10   9   8   7

For
Edward Peter Fitzsimmons

Contents

Preface

JUDAISM, Christianity, and Islam are all children born of the same Father and reared in the bosom of Abraham. They grew to adulthood in the rich spiritual climate of the Near East, and though they have lived together all of their lives, now in their maturity they stand apart and regard their family resemblances and conditioned differences with astonishment, disbelief, or disdain.

Rich parallels of attitude and institution exist among these three religions that acknowledge, in varying degrees, their evolution one out of the other. They have all engaged at times in reciprocal polemic of great ferocity, and sometimes pursued a more ecumenical course, but neither is the intention here. My purpose is merely to underline both the parallels and the differences, and to connect them to common origins and to a common spiritual and intellectual environment.

I have not attempted to write the history of these three religions; others have rendered that service to each. I have selected certain issues and institutions and laid them out in a manner that would invite comparison. The matter is sometimes complex, and so I have tried to be clear in the text and generous in the footnotes, where the reader is invited to pursue more deeply questions I have only touched upon.

Judaism is the eldest of this family of three, and its extraordinary career stretches thousands of years before the Christian and Muslim eras, when these latter two normally reckon that "history" begins. The present inquiry begins at none of these points but in that period in the Near East marked by obvious changes and new beginnings. Historians who have drawn attention to the period have not always been certain when it began or what to call it. For us the problem is simpler. Since we are beginning with Judaism and are not concerned with the Near East as a whole, our natural point of departure is the Jewish return from their exile in Babylonia and the reestablishment of Jewish cult and community life in Palestine in the sixth century B.C.E.

Where to close is somewhat more arbitrary, since after the seventh century of the Christian era we are discussing not one but three religious communities, each at a somewhat different stage of its growth. I have closed, then, at the somewhat imprecise point at which I judged that the three religions had reached their normative expression, that is, when there were already in place the chief institutions, codes, practices, and spiritual attitudes that in some perceptible manner continue to characterize them today.

Thus this study ends in what we in the West commonly call the "Middle Ages," and so ignores both the European experiences of these religions and the great movements of reform and revival that have occurred in modern times. I can offer in mild defense only my own competence, which extends no further than I have written. It is perhaps far enough. All the issues of reform and all the wellsprings and mechanisms of revival are present in the place and period under consideration. Faith and reason, Scripture and tradition, understanding and enlightenment are all very old adversaries.

I have tried to write a useful book. The matter and reading grows thick where I have thought that common knowledge runs thinnest. I have used a great many transcribed technical terms out of the conviction that the reader of these pages will certainly read further, and I prefer he receive his introduction to this common vice from me than from other, less helpful hands. And to ease the way, they are all defined in a glossary at the end. Books of special interest or more general utility are marked with an asterisk, and paperbacks have been noted with the rubric "pb." All suggestions for future reading are to books in English. Finally, I have reduced all dates to the Christian or Common Era (B.C.E./C.E).

A brief personal note. These reflections are quite literally the product of the Kevorkian Center for Near Eastern Studies of New York University, where the comparative questions and issues raised in the pages that follow are regularly and routinely discussed by faculty colleagues and students alike, and in the same spirit that they are offered here. It is difficult for me to imagine putting them on paper in any other atmosphere. For that I thank those colleagues, students, and others, particularly Baruch Levine and Lawrence Schiffman for their patient *pilpul*; Linda Knezevich, Stuart Miller, Nadine Posner, and Peter Zirnis for their immediate and invaluable help and stimulation; Dan Urman of Beer-sheba University, my first Hebrew teacher, and Edward Peter Fitzsimmons, who first interested me in Torah; Père Anawati, O.P. of Cairo and the Kingdom of God; Rowland Mitchell and Anthony Manero for expanding my education; two Brownes, one Green and one Dean; Peter Paul and Mary.

Children
of Abraham

CHAPTER I

The Scriptures:
Some Preliminary Notions

JUDAISM, Christianity, and Islam are all scriptural religions, that is, they affirm the existence of a divine revelation in written form. "The Sacred Writings," "The Scripture" or "The Book" are practically interchangeable terms among the three, and their adherents can all be identified as "People of the Book," as the Muslims in fact call them. More, these revelations from on high represent God's intervention in history; and, indeed, the same God: the Jews' Yahweh, the Christians' God the Father who is in Heaven, and the Muslims' Allah is one and the same deity, with the same history, the same attributes and, in fact, the same name.[1]

The three Scriptures show marked differences, however. In the Jewish—and Muslim—view, God gave and Moses wrote down a distinct and discrete multipart book, the Law or Torah. But though the Torah holds pride of place in Jewish revelational history, God's direct interventions were in one manner or another continuous between Moses and Ezra, and thus the Jewish Bible is a collective work that includes, under the three headings of Law, Prophets, and the miscellany called Writings, all of God's revelation to His people.[2]

This was certainly the Jewish view in Jesus' day, and there is no reason to think that Jesus regarded Scripture any differently. He in turn produced no new Writings or Book of his own, and so Christian "Scripture" is formally quite dif-

---

[1] In Hebrew, *Elohim*; in the Aramaic of Jesus' time, *Elah*; and in Arabic, *Allah*.

[2] Bible is an English word of Greek origin. The three divisions of the Jewish Scripture are commonly referred to in Hebrew as Tanak, an acronym for Torah (Law), Nebi'im (Prophets) and Ketubim (Writings).

3

ferent from what the Jews thought of as such. The Gospels are accounts of Jesus' words and deeds set down, in approximately a biographical framework, by his followers. In the eyes of Christians, Jesus did not bring a Scripture; he was himself, in his person and message, a revelation, the "Good News." His life and sacrificial death sealed a "New Covenant" that God concluded with His people, and so the Gospels and the accounts of the deeds and thoughts of the early Christian community recorded in the Acts of the Apostles and the letters of various of Jesus' followers came to be regarded by Christians as a New Testament to be set down next to the Old, that recorded and commemorated in the Jewish Bible.

Muhammad may have had only an imperfect understanding of this somewhat complex process. Though he commonly refers to the Jewish revelation as "Tawrah," the Prophet of Islam was certainly aware that there were other Jewish prophets, and so possibly revelations, after Moses. But he never mentions a New Testament; his sole references are to "the gospel," in Arabic *injil*, and he seems to have thought of it as a sacred book that Jesus had brought or written, much as Moses had the Torah.

Muhammad had a strong sense of the prophetic calling and of the line of prophets that had created the Judeo-Christian tradition, and after some brief initial hesitation, he placed himself firmly within that line. He too was a prophet, and now in these latter times, when His earlier revelations had become distorted at the willful and perverse hands of the Jews and Christians, God had given to him, no less than to Moses and Jesus, a revealed Book. Or so it was in its final, codified version. What God Himself had instructed Muhammad to call The Recitation, in Arabic *al-Qur'an*,[3] was in fact a series of messages delivered to Muhammad by the Angel Gabriel over a period of twenty-two years. Each part was

[3] The name "Recitation" suggests that Muhammad was well aware of the liturgical purposes to which the Jews and Christians were putting their versions of God's Word; see Chapter VI below.

already identified as Scripture during the Prophet's lifetime, and the Book was finally closed only with Muhammad's death.

Thus there came into being three Sacred Books, each in some sense the Word of God; each regarded as a complete, final, and authoritative statement regulating the role and conduct of men vis-à-vis their Creator; and each a birthright and charter for a community that had not existed before. And each community lived in the conviction that God had spoken to it for the last time: the Jews, for the first and final time; the Christians, for the second and final time; the Muslims, for the third and final time.

The Bible, New Testament, and Qur'an, though looked upon as emanating from the same source, are very different works. The Bible is a rich and composite blend of religious myth, historical narrative, legal enactments, prophetic admonitions, cautionary tales, and poetry composed over a long span of time.[4] The time span of the New Testament is considerably shorter, a half-century perhaps,[5] but it too has a very mixed content of quasi biography, community history, letters, and, in some versions, an apocalyptic Book of Revelation. The Qur'an, as we have seen, is absolutely contemporary to its revelation, twenty-two years in the lifetime of the Prophet.

There is nothing but God's own Word in the Qur'an, as Muhammad himself could assure the community of believers.[6] In Jewish and Christian circles, however, there were assuredly circulating other writings that had some claim to being God's Word but are not found in the Bible or the New Testament. Both these Scriptures represent, then, a deliberate decision by someone to designate certain works as au-

[4] How long a span is the subject of some debate. The terms of the debate and some current conclusions are outlined in *P. R. Ackroyd and C. F. Evans, eds., *The Cambridge History of the Bible* (Cambridge: Cambridge University Press, 1970), I, 67-112.

[5] See C. F. Evans, ibid., I, 232-283.

[6] Though it is possible that some of what is in our present Qur'an is not in its heavenly prototype; see Chapter IV below.

thentic or canonical Scripture and to exclude others from the canon.[7] That decision was essentially theological, and the exclusion of the noncanonical writings, generally called Apocrypha, from the Jewish or Christian Scriptures does not render them any less interesting or important from a historical point of view. The Books of Maccabees never made it into the Jewish canon, for example, nor the Gnostic gospels into the Christian, but each tells us something of the events and attitudes of the time that produced them.[8]

The Bible was originally composed in Hebrew, with some late passages in Aramaic, and is available in a variety of English translations, either alone or in combination with the New Testament.[9] It is notable that where once sectarian differences among Jews, Catholics, and Protestants created marked discrepancies in their respective translations, the differences have presently narrowed to so few words or passages that it is possible for Jewish and Christian scholars to collaborate on such translation projects as the *Anchor Bible*.[10]

There are in print a few English translations of the Qur'an, also commonly though somewhat less properly spelled Koran. The diction of the Qur'an is extremely elliptical, and any English version of it will, of course, sound far more alien to Western ears long attuned to the familiar rhythms and images of the Bible and the New Testament, but the most readable English translation, and one that catches some of the flavor of the original, is probably A. J. Arberry's *The*

[7] This important consideration is treated at length in *Ackroyd and Evans, *Cambridge History of the Bible*, I, 113-158 (Bible) and 284-307 (New Testament).

[8] There is a good selection of biblical apocrypha in E. J. Goodspeed, *The Apocrypha* (New York: Vintage pb., 1959), to which should be compared M. R. James, *The Apocryphal New Testament* (London: Oxford University Press, 1924); and E. Hennecke and W. Schneemelcher, *New Testament Apocrypha*, 2 vols. (Philadelphia: Westminster Press, 1963, 1965).

[9] For the translation history of both the Jewish and Christian Scriptures, see *Ackroyd and Evans, *Cambridge History of the Bible*, I, 159-198, 308-376.

[10] Garden City: Doubleday and Co., 1964 and ff.

Koran Interpreted.[11] Translation is also interpretation, as Arberry's title already suggests, and the virtue of *The Meaning of the Glorious Koran* by Mohammed Marmaduke Pickthall, an English convert to Islam, is that the translation reflects in fact a traditional Muslim interpretation of the text.[12]

It is more than familiarity that makes both Bible and Gospels better served by their translations than is the Arabic Qur'an. God's message to Muhammad was delivered in the highly charged, affective images of the sacred poet. It is allusive rather than explicit, a great body of warning, command, injunction, and instruction delivered against a background of men and manners as barren to our eyes as the steppe itself. We feel Sinai and Canaan in the Bible; Palestine, its houses, mountains, rivers and lakes, its towns and cities and the men who lived in them are all present in the Gospel narrative. In the Qur'an, however, we search without success for Mecca, for the profane but vividly commercial life of the Quraysh, for Muhammad's family and companions. In its pages there is only a voice, the voice of God alone. When it was heard, it overwhelmed hearts, as it still does in its written form, but it leaves the historian attending vainly, and deafly, for context.

[11] New York: Macmillan pb., 1955.
[12] New York: Mentor pb., 1953.

CHAPTER II

"And in These Latter Days . . ."

THERE are crucial periods in world history, what some historians have called "axial ages." They occur as well in the history of religious communities, when their own internal evolution or external pressures create new forms and different sensibilities. Religious bodies are by their nature conservative, and communities grounded in a historical revelation are necessarily so. New wine must be poured into old flasks and those who drink it must be assured that it is indeed the original vintage. But the wine is assuredly new, if inevitably familiar.

One such period of change is clearly marked in the history of Judaism. Judea after the Exile was a different place from what it had been before, and so too was the world around it. The older parochial empires had disappeared and new ecumenical political forms prevailed, accompanied by new social and economic institutions and a quickening of the intellectual life in the Near East. Judaism too was different, as we can see now with the historian's hindsight. It both clashed and blended with the new world about it, and though it had done this from the beginning, the results were now deeper, more volatile, and far more visible.

Pre-Exilic Judaism had been, perhaps, further up the ladder of religious evolution than the faith of the Philistines, Canaanites, and Phoenicians, and so could resist or assimilate those competitors with relative ease. But the Greeks were not Canaanites and Caesar Augustus was not Hiram of Tyre or even Ashurbanipal. The new rivals of Judaism were at once more attractive and threatening, and possessed intellectual and spiritual resources little understood in a parochial Judea. Judaism did not simply react. It first refracted the incandescent energies of the new age and then slowly brought them into focus in a form that has survived with vigor into our own day.

In the course of that difficult process of self-transformation, Judaism proved remarkably fertile in new perspectives, some of which were finally rejected but proved nonetheless to have a vitality of their own. Christianity immediately and Islam somewhat more obliquely appear in certain lights like Jewish reform movements. At the very least they are growths from the same stock—post-Exilic Judaism—in a generative process that has no parallel in the varieties of human religious experience. We begin by laying out the chief stages of that process and how they are understood by modern historians.

AFTER THE EXILE

When the Persian shah Cyrus permitted the Jews exiled in Babylonia to return to Palestine in 534 C.E. and to restore both the temple cult and some small element of a national identity, a new chapter in the history of Judaism began. There were two obscure centuries of restoration and growth under Persian sovereignty, followed in quick succession by a cultural, religious, and political confrontation with the Greeks, a war of national liberation, the restoration of a long–defunct Jewish monarchy, and finally the annexation of Palestine to the powerful Roman Empire, under whose sovereignty it remained for six centuries.[1]

[1] There are a number of good histories of the period, from E. Bickerman's succinct *From Ezra to the Maccabees* (New York: Schocken pb., 1962) to the definitive and scholarly work of E. Schürer, *The History of the Jewish People in the Age of Jesus Christ*, in a new English translation revised and edited by G. Vermes and F. Millar (Edinburgh: T. and T. Clark, 1973 and in progress). Both authors draw upon a great variety of sources, and some of the literary and inscriptional material can be inspected first-hand in *C. K. Barrett, *The New Testament Background: Selected Documents* (New York: Harper Torchbook, 1961); and, from a different perspective, in M. Stern, *Greek and Latin Authors on Jews and Judaism*, 2 vols. (Jerusalem: Israel Academy of Sciences and Humanities, 1974, 1976) which gives both the original texts

Many of the themes of this complex period in the history of Judaism will appear under various comparative headings in the pages below, and so only some general considerations will be offered here. From the outset, one should speak more properly of the varieties of post-Exilic Judaism than of a single phenomenon. There was, almost from the beginning of this period, both a Palestinian and a Diaspora Judaism, and if our view of the latter is dominated and partially distorted by the immense literary output of one man, Philo of Alexandria, we can make far more precise and radical distinctions in the Palestinian version.

The Biblical Book of Ezra and Nehemiah provides a portrait of a Judaism already facing both Temple and Torah. Ezra himself, who was the chief architect of the post-Exilic restoration, is the perfect type of his age: he was both a priest (*kohen*) and a scribe (*sofer*). This latter is already a new office and function, a man learned in the Scriptures, a teacher certainly, and possibly a judge on matters of the Law.[2]

Though the older priestly and the new clerical Judaism were united in the person and philosophy of Ezra, that cohesion was not permanent. With the inroads of Hellenism and the affluence it brought to the urban centers of the Near East, we can observe the natural evolution of the upper levels of the Jewish priesthood into a class of power and privilege that was drawn into the cultural and political orbit of the new Greek rulers of Palestine, whether they governed from Alexandria in Egypt or Antioch in Syria.

There was resistance to this fashioning of a Hellenized version of the Jew, if not of Judaism. A new leadership arose out of the lower priesthoods and from among those whom

---

and an English translation. The archeological evidence is most conveniently presented in M. Avi-Yonah, ed., *Encyclopedia of Archaeological Excavations in the Holy Land*, 4 vols. (Jerusalem: Oxford University Press, 1975-1978); and J. Finegan, *The Archaeology of the New Testament* (Princeton: Princeton University Press, 1969).

[2] His portrait is sketched in ★G. F. Moore's *Judaism in the First Centuries of the Christian Era* (New York: Schocken pb., 1971), I, 29-36.

the class distinctions of Hellenism had disinherited in their native land. The Maccabees extended social and economic distress into the incendiary area of religion: they equated Hellenism with godlessness, and so brought into their camp all those pious groups (*hasidim*) and clerics of the Law who were genuinely outraged by the new, alien, and irreligious style of the Jewish upper classes.[3]

JEWISH PARTIES AND SECTS

The Jewish revolt against the Greek Seleucids of Syria was a stunning political success—it reconstituted an independent Jewish state in Judea—but its sequel brought to the surface new factional strains in the community. The Maccabees' coalition disintegrated over the twin issues of the Maccabees'— or Hasmoneans, as they were called in their new dynastic role—own progressive Hellenization and their legitimacy as high priests in the restored kingdom. The earlier *hasidim* reappear as Pharisees, a group that was both a party and a sect in that they had a distinct religious position and were at the same time deeply engaged in political activity under the Hasmoneans. Or so we suppose. We are not on very firm ground here, since we must rely for our information on the self-serving narrative of the Books of Maccabees and on the historical works of the Pharisee Josephus, who was writing with a special purpose of his own for a Roman audience. Josephus' *Jewish War*[4] and *Jewish Antiquities*[5] remain, however, our best sources for the period.

The authors of the Books of Maccabees were appealing to the sympathy and support of Jews outside of Palestine as surely as Josephus was attempting to explain the somewhat arcane practices and convictions of his coreligionists to a baf-

---

[3] See F. E. Peters, *The Harvest of Hellenism* (New York: Clarion pb., 1970), pp. 250-269; and V. Tcherikover, *Hellenistic Civilization and the Jews* (New York: Atheneum pb., 1970), pp. 175-234.

[4] Translated by G. A. Williamson (Harmondsworth: Penguin pb., 1959).

[5] English translation in the Loeb Classical Library edition of Josephus.

fled audience of Gentiles, and so neither was much concerned with either historical or theological accuracy when it came to the Pharisees. The Gospels likewise present a number of vignettes, generally unflattering, of Pharisees engaged in controversy with Jesus. The overall result is, not surprisingly, a confused and often contradictory portrait of the group.[6] Making sense out of this mélange has exercised both Jewish and Christian scholars, with sometimes astonishing results: the Pharisees have been regarded as everything from hidebound and frigid legalists to Jewish revivalists and social reformers on a Weberian model.[7]

Recent work on the Pharisees does not encourage one to think that a consensus is about to emerge on the subject, at least until their lineaments are more skillfully and more fully traced in the available rabbinic literature, as Jacob Neusner has begun to do.[8] But if we leave aside their political role in the history of the times, we can conclude with some assurance that the Pharisees were probably the spiritual descendents of the earlier *hasidim* and that they were characterized as a group by: 1. their detailed study of the Torah; 2. their acceptance of an oral legal tradition that enabled them to extend Torah precepts into new areas of behavior; and whose authority also validated 3. their own strict observance of the laws of ritual purity, especially in matters of food. Their observance set the Pharisees off from most of the other contemporary Jews and led to a moral exemplarism and social cohesiveness typified by their meal-fellowship (*habura*).[9]

Linked by both Josephus and the Gospels to the Pharisees

---

[6] See, for example, the rich texts collected by J. Bowker, *Jesus and the Pharisees* (Cambridge: Cambridge University Press, 1973).

[7] J. Neusner has reviewed, with abundant comment, the modern literature on the Pharisees in his *Rabbinic Traditions* (cited in n. 8 below), III, 320-368.

[8] Notably in his *The Rabbinic Traditions about the Pharisees before 70*, 3 vols. (Leiden: E. J. Brill, 1971) and in a great many other papers and addresses.

[9] See Bowker, *Jesus and the Pharisees*, pp. 35-36.

is another, somewhat dimmer group, the Sadducees. Their name may have come from Zadok, a high priest at the time of David—the priestly hierarchy at Qumran was also known as "the Sons of Zadok"—and it seems plausible to identify the Sadducees as supporters of, if not identical with, the priesthood that presided over the Jewish temple liturgies in Jerusalem. They were almost certainly defenders of the legitimacy of the Hasmonean high priesthood, but Josephus was far more concerned to show their legal and theological positions vis-à-vis the Pharisees. The Sadducees were, on his testimony, literal interpreters of the Law who rejected all Pharisaic appeals to the "traditions of the Fathers," and so could be at the same time stricter in their exegesis of scriptural prescriptions and more permissive where the Torah had not explicitly spoken. They were unwilling, for example, to accept, as the Pharisees did, the notion of an afterlife, since it had little or no scriptural attestation.[10]

This portrait of the Sadducees is not a very full likeness, since none of their own writings is preserved, and after the destruction of the Temple in 70 C.E. they had no spiritual progeny in Judaism, save possibly the Karaites, a sect that arose in the eighth century under Islam, and that shared the Sadducees' repudiation of an oral tradition.[11] The same judgment of ignorance once prevailed with respect to a third group linked by Josephus (but strangely absent from the Gospels) to the Pharisees and Sadducees, the Essenes. They are portrayed, in Josephus' usual shorthand fashion, as an ascetic congregation who had separated themselves from the main body of the Jews. They lived in communities, were celibate, and possessed goods in common.[12] Now, however, the Essenes of Josephus, Philo, and others have been tentatively

[10] The general outlines of their positions are drawn in *Moore, *Judaism*, pp. 67-71 and *S. Sandmel, *Judaism and Christian Beginnings* (London: Oxford University Press pb., 1978), pp. 156-158.

[11] See Chapter V below.

[12] Josephus' chief text is translated in *Barrett, *Background*, pp. 124-127.

identified with a group about which we know a great deal, the sectaries at Qumran.

Since 1947, when their community center and writings were discovered at the northwest corner of the Dead Sea, the community at Qumran is better known by direct and contemporary evidence than any other Jewish religious group of its day. Their own writings have been published and translated,[13] and their habitat and way of life studied by many scholars.[14] They were in fact much as Josephus described them, a highly organized community (*yahad*) who lived a life of strict asceticism, some of them as celibates, apart from the rest of the Jews. But what is now clear is the context of this life. The Essenes were a community of priestly dissenters who rejected the authority of the Hasmonean high priesthood in Jerusalem, and so did not participate directly in the Temple liturgy. Instead, they awaited their vindication through a messianic return and a climactic and victorious war against the forces of evil. In the meantime, the community lived in a state of severe ritual purity and of spiritual readiness for the eschatological battle that lay ahead. They were a purified people of a New Covenant who were elected for survival in wicked days.[15]

Apocalyptic and Messianic Judaism

The Dead Sea scrolls show a community living out two themes long familiar from the literary Apocrypha of the post-

[13] G. Vermes, *The Dead Sea Scrolls in English*, 2nd ed. (Harmondsworth: Penguin pb., 1975).

[14] One of the best treatments remains that of F. M. Cross, *The Ancient Library at Qumran* (New York: Anchor pb., 1961). The bibliography on Qumran is by now immense, but two recent books provide most of the necessary guidance to the more detailed studies: J. Fitzmyer, *The Dead Sea Scrolls: Major Publications and Tools for Study* (Missoula, Mont.: Scholars Press, 1975) and G. Vermes, *The Dead Sea Scrolls: Qumran in Perspective* (London: Collins, 1977).

[15] Vermes, *Scrolls*, pp. 34-52, and *Qumran in Perspective*, pp. 163-197.

Exilic period, those of apocalypse and messianic expectations. The scrolls are gloomy documents that decry the
wickedness of the present time, whether that time is to be
associated with the Hasmoneans or the Romans, and it was
probably a similar religious despair in the present that provoked other Jewish authors from Seleucid times onward to
console their brethren with the promise that this was merely
the prelude to a great eschatological catastrophe out of whose
ashes would emerge an Israel Triumphant.

The most common form of these meditations was the
"unveiling" or apocalypse, a vision of the horrors and glories
of the End Time.[16] Their powerful message, though obscured in detail by the authors' preference for allegorical,
parabolic, and symbolic expression, is nevertheless clear. A
new age is close at hand. Its advent will be signaled by political and natural upheavals, but at the term of these cata-
clysmic events the judgment of history will yield to the judgment of God. The righteous will be glorified; the evil
destroyed.[17]

In the apocalyptic visions of Qumran, as well as those of
the anonymous authors of Daniel, Enoch, and other of the
Apocrypha, a central figure of the End Time is that of the
Messiah. This "Anointed One"—*Christos* is simply the Greek
translation of the word—is a priest-king of Davidic descent
who will be God's instrument of restoration. On this there
was general agreement, but a closer inspection of the texts
shows a wide discrepancy of detail. The Apocrypha on the
one hand, some of them pre-Christian and others possibly
the subject of Christian rewriting, and the rabbinic sources
on the other, all of them post-Christian and some of them
certainly reacting to Christian claims, provide very different

[16] *Barrett, *Background*, pp. 227-255 has a representative selection of these
texts gleaned from the Apocrypha.

[17] H. Rowley, *The Relevance of Apocalyptic* (London: Lutterworth, 1963);
D. S. Russell, *The Method and Message of Jewish Apocalyptic* (London, SCM
Press, 1964).

versions of the Messiah.[18] Again, at Qumran there was another, distinctly Essene anticipation of a Messiah.[19]

Some of these differences are doctrinally generated, but even if we confine our attention to unmistakably pre-Christian material, Jewish concepts surrounding the person and mission of the Messiah show considerable variations. The visions and parables of the apocalypse were obviously susceptible to widely differing interpretations. Most of the Messianic passages may suggest, for example, a spiritualizing exegesis, but only if we divorce them, as they frequently divorced themselves, from the historical context of debates about Hasmonean legitimacy, Herodian oppression, and Rome's dashing all hopes for the restoration of an independent Jewish polity. Josephus' frequent references to brigands and insurrectionists who appealed to Messianic expectations, and particularly the career of Bar Kokhba, whose politico-messianic claims were endorsed by as eminent a Pharisee as Rabbi Akiba, are a sufficient clue that the Kingdom of God of Messianic speculation was understood by many as an achievable political goal here below on earth.[20]

JESUS

Where does Jesus of Nazareth belong in this confusion of Jewish sects and parties, spiritual and political ideals and programs? First, it should be remarked that it has only recently become apparent that Jesus belonged anywhere in this Jewish complex. Studies of Jesus were for centuries dominated by doctrinal considerations, and even when the "quest of the historical Jesus," as Albert Schweitzer's famous book de-

---

[18] See, for example, S. Mowinkel, *He That Cometh* (Philadelphia: Abingdon Press, 1956); J. Klausner, *The Messianic Ideal in Israel* (London: Allen and Unwin, 1956); and J. Bonsirven, *Palestinian Judaism at the Time of Jesus* (New York: McGraw-Hill pb., 1965), pp. 175-225.

[19] Vermes, *Scrolls*, pp. 47-52; and *Qumran in Perspective*, pp. 184-186, 194-196.

[20] *Sandmel, *Christian Beginnings*, pp. 205-207.

16

scribed it,[21] had begun in earnest, the overwhelming importance of Jesus' Jewish milieu was not often understood or acknowledged. Parallels and antecedents were vigorously sought elsewhere, particularly in the surrounding and better-known Hellenic tradition.[22]

Schweitzer's quest still goes on,[23] but the more recent emphases are quite different. One obviously new factor is the Dead Sea finds that have not only produced new documents contemporary with Jesus but have refocused attention on the complexities of the Jewish milieu in which Jesus lived and taught. The scrolls have been extensively scrutinized for insights into Christian origins,[24] and interesting light has been shed on a number of questions—on John the Baptist, for example. But the overwhelming lesson of the scrolls for Christianity is that Jesus and his movement can be firmly located as a fairly ordinary type of Jewish reform whose chief emphases were messianic and eschatological in character.

It is by no means a simple matter to separate Jesus from his movement, a project of some importance, since it has long been felt by some that the early community of Jesus' followers shaped and may even have altered his teaching. The grounds for thinking this are two: the origin and form of the Gospels, and the change in the political and religious climate that occurred between Jesus' lifetime and the period when the Gospels were finally redacted.

[21] Published 1906 (New York: Macmillan pb., 1961).

[22] The method was first made popular by Edwin Hatch's *The Influence of Greek Ideas on Christianity*, published in 1889 (New York: Harper Torchbook, 1957).

[23] Two recent examples are C. H. Dodd, *The Founder of Christianity* (New York: Macmillan pb., 1970), and Michael Grant, *Jesus: An Historian's Review of the Gospels* (New York: Scribner's pb., 1977).

[24] By K. Stendahl, ed., *The Scrolls and the New Testament* (New York: Harper and Row, 1956); M. Black, ed., *The Scrolls and Christian Origins* (New York: Scribner's, 1961); J. Daniélou, *The Dead Sea Scrolls and Primitive Christianity* (New York: Mentor Omega pb., 1958); and J. Fitzmyer, *Essays on the Semitic Background of the New Testament* (London: Chapman, 1971), among others.

The first consideration gave birth to the method of "form criticism," which attempts to reconstruct, and so better understand, the modes of expression that shaped the literary material used in the Gospels.[25] One of those modes was "preaching," in Greek *kerygma*, a notion that has become a keystone in the form-critical method. The Gospels are the preaching of believers in the messiahship of Jesus who now understand the meaning of something that had already occurred. The Gospels announce a fulfillment whose understanding reflects backward upon what the historian would prefer to regard as simply events. Those events were, however, so selected, arranged, and glossed by the Christian community of the first century that the intent of Jesus, if not his actual words and deeds, is scarcely retrievable by the modern historian.

On such a view, the historical Jesus has all but disappeared behind the apostolic preaching with its special kind of theological pleading. Not everyone concurs, by any means,[26] and more recently a new consideration has been added, that the Gospel redactors may have rewritten history as much from political as from theological motives.

The Zealots were a politically active party in Palestine that combined religious agitation with guerrilla warfare against both Herod and the Romans in Jesus' day.[27] Jesus certainly had one of their number among his closest followers, and

[25] This has been the approach of the school led by Martin Dibelius, *From Tradition to Gospel* (New York: Scribner's, 1935); Rudolf Bultman, *Form Criticism* (New York: Harper Torchbook, 1962), and *The History of the Synoptic Tradition* (New York: Harper and Row, 1968); and C. H. Dodd, *The Apostolic Preaching and Its Development* (New York: Harper and Row, 1964). The method is still in its infancy as regards talmudic material, but see J. Neusner, *Rabbinic Tradition* (cited n. 8 above), and J. Wansbrough, *Qur'anic Studies* (London: Oxford University Press, 1977).

[26] The problems posed to all parties in the debate are laid out by *R. M. Grant, *A Historical Introduction to the New Testament* (New York: Touchstone pb., 1972), pp. 284-302.

[27] They have been studied by W. Farmer in his *Maccabees, Zealots and Josephus* (New York: Columbia University Press, 1956).

whereas the Gospels transmit that fact without comment or consequence, S.G.F. Brandon has explored the question of Jesus' own involvement in some sort of overt political activity of the Zealot type[28]—the Gospels' own account of his trial and execution are filled with political shadows—and whether it was the failure of this program that prompted the Christians of the generation after 70 c.e. to rewrite the Gospel narratives so as to disassociate themselves from the Jews and at the same time sanitize the role of the Romans in the execution of Jesus.[29]

The Gospels themselves do not much encourage one to regard Jesus as either an Essene or a Zealot. Jesus is portrayed in them as an unmistakable, if sometimes hesitant, messianic claimant—the claim itself would make little or no sense to a Gentile—whose preaching centers around belief in his person and mission and the announcement of the coming kingdom of heaven. He performed miracles to this end, though often with some reluctance, and he predicted his own apprehension, death, and eventual triumph. On the Gospel testimony itself, his own followers were confused about the "kingdom of God," in what it consisted and when it would come to be. Jesus' audience was principally Jews, though occasionally he addressed both Samaritans and Gentiles, to the obvious and understandable distress of the Pharisees. The Jewish response to Jesus ranged from bewilderment to great and public enthusiasm. He obviously made a deep impression on many of his Jewish contemporaries, but the circumstances of his death apparently cooled the ardor of some.[30]

---

[28] *Jesus and the Zealots* (New York: Scribner's, 1967); compare M. Hengel, *Was Jesus a Revolutionist?* (Philadelphia: Fortress Press, 1971).

[29] See S.G.F. Brandon, *The Fall of Jerusalem and the Christian Church* (London: SPCK, 1957).

[30] The problematic of Jesus' life and teachings is succinctly presented by *R. M. Grant, *Introduction*, pp. 284-377. The orientation of Grant's book is plainly Christian, and its design and address have been largely determined by what Christian theologians and New Testament scholars have been writing and thinking about Jesus over the past century.

*S. Sandmel's *Judaism and Christian Beginnings*, cited earlier, approaches

19

The Gospels make no effort to conceal the fact that Jesus was indeed a Jew who, for all his eschatological and messianic preoccupations, shared to a large degree the concerns of the Pharisees who are so harshly criticized in those same texts.[31] To exploit those parallels and retrieve the Jewish Jesus from the narratives of those who were already in the process of rejecting their own Judaism is a delicate task that still awaits its final achievement.[32]

HELLENISTIC JUDAISM

It has long been recognized that the documents of Hellenistic Judaism are an essential part of the New Testament background.[33] Indeed, it is impossible to understand Paul and much else that occurred in the first century without them. Since the fourth century B.C.E., Jews had been living in dispersion (*diaspora*) outside of Palestine and had encountered in the great urban centers of the Mediterranean world the potent force of Hellenism, that complex sum of attitudes, ideology, and style that comprised the Greek and Roman way of regarding the universe, society, man, and God, and whose

Jesus from the historical perspectives of the contemporary Jewish milieu; or so it is professed, but it remains to be demonstrated how and to what degree the writings of second-century rabbis are the appropriate Jewish context for the life of Jesus early in the first, since the century in question witnessed fundamental changes in the course of Jewish life and history.

[31] See Bowker, *Jesus and the Pharisees*, cited above, and A. Finkel, *The Pharisees and the Teacher of Nazareth* (Leiden: E. J. Brill, 1964); D. Daube, *The New Testament and Rabbinic Judaism* (London: Athlone Press, 1956); and M. Smith, *Tannaitic Parallels to the Gospels* (Philadelphia: Society of Biblical Literature, 1951).

[32] It has been attempted by a number of scholars: by J. Klausner, *Jesus of Nazareth* (New York: Macmillan, 1925); D. Flusser, *Jesus* (New York: Herder and Herder, 1969); and most recently by G. Vermes, *Jesus the Jew* (Cleveland: William Collins pb., 1977).

[33] See, for example, *Sandmel, *Christian Beginnings*, pp. 255-302 and *Barrett, *Background*, pp. 173-189 and passim.

cultural conquest of the Near East had quite revolutionary consequences for Judaism, Christianity, and Islam.[34]

The political consequences of that encounter have already been noted as they bear on Jesus' own life and death, and they will be discussed again below. But far more relevant for our present purpose is the religious encounter between Hellenism and Judaism. It has been explored in great detail,[35] though the evidence is heavily weighted toward Egypt, where there was a very large Jewish population in antiquity and whose chief intellectual spokesman in the first century, Philo of Alexandria, has left behind a large and sophisticated literary legacy.[36]

In almost everything he wrote, Philo explored the differences and points of rapport between his own scriptural tradition and the rationalism of Greek philosophy, and so set both the tone and the method for many of the attempts at philosophical-theological discourse over the next centuries, whether in Judaism, Christianity, or Islam.[37]

[34] The conquest is described in detail by Peters, *Harvest of Hellenism*, but equally interesting are some of the resistance patterns studied by S. K. Eddy, *The King Is Dead* (Lincoln: Nebraska University Press, 1961). The political clash of Roman and Jew is a well-known story and is recounted once again by Michael Grant in his *The Jews in the Roman World* (London: Weidenfeld and Nicolson, 1973) and M. Smallwood, *Jews under Roman Rule* (Leiden: E. J. Brill, 1976).

[35] Notably by Martin Hengel, *Judaism and Hellenism*, 2 vols. (London: SCM Press, 1974), and Victor Tcherikover, *Hellenistic Civilization and the Jews* (New York: Atheneum pb., 1970).

[36] A great number of Philo's works have been preserved, more from Christian than Jewish interest in them, and have been translated from their original Greek into English in the volumes of the Loeb Classical Library. There are selections in *Barrett, *Background*, pp. 173-189, and in H. Levy, *Three Jewish Philosophers* (New York: Jewish Publication Society pb., 1960), pp. 7-106.

[37] This at least was the view of H. A. Wolfson in his *Philo*, 2 vols. (Cambridge: Harvard University Press, 1947), but it has by no means found general acceptance. J. Guttmann, *The Philosophies of Judaism* (New York: Schocken pb., 1973), pp. 24-29, and E. R. Goodenough, *Introduction to Philo Judaeus* (New Haven: Yale University Press, 1940), for example, differ profoundly with Wolfson and each other.

One of the crucial issues at stake in the study of Philo is his relationship to the legal thinking and practice in contemporary Palestine. H. A. Wolfson has strenuously argued the connection, but others have maintained with equal ardor that Philo's legal thinking was far more Greek than Jewish.[38] The debate raises the question of the penetration of Pharisaic norms into the Hellenized milieu of the Jewish Diaspora (and this touches closely upon Paul), but of equal concern, particularly for the study of Jesus and early Christianity, is how deeply Hellenism invaded the Jewish life of Palestine.

A detailed case has been made that Greek language and ideas made an overwhelming impression among the economic and intellectual upper classes in Palestine from the fourth century B.C.E. onward, and that Jewish political resistance, though successful on occasion, was far less effective in the long run than the apocalyptic-eschatological stance adopted by most of the opposition parties.[39]

Apocalypse and Torah, the latter now supported by the "tradition of the Fathers," were the two prime weapons invoked by those Palestinian Jews who regarded Hellenism as a fundamental attack on Covenant Judaism. The debate is described in lively terms in the pages of Josephus, whose own cultural Hellenization and religious Pharisaism show how complex the issue was in fact. The Gospels, for their part, present Jesus in a cultural and religious landscape that appears at first glance remarkably free of Hellenic notions and coloring. And yet many of Jesus' miraculous cures betray not only the acceptance of a Hellenic system of magical belief but many of the techniques associated with that system.[40]

[38] Goodenough, *Introduction*, and S. Sandmel, *Philo's Place in Judaism* (New York: Hebrew Union College, 1956).

[39] Earlier studies by S. Lieberman, *Greek in Jewish Palestine* (New York: Hebrew Union College, 1942), and *Hellenism in Jewish Palestine* (New York: Hebrew Union College, 1950) were essentially essays on specific and often unrelated topics, but now the work of Tcherikover and Hengel (n. 35 above) has made possible a more comprehensive view.

[40] See J. M. Hull, *Hellenistic Magic and the Synoptic Tradition* (London, SCM Press, 1974).

And, as we shall see, the very first issue to trouble the nascent Christian community was a conflict between Hellenist and Torah Jews, both of whom had accepted the messiahship of Jesus but whose differing understanding of their own Jewishness was not transcended by that acceptance.

PRIMITIVE CHRISTIANITY:
THE CHURCH FROM THE CIRCUMCISION

The Gospels were written down in Greek for an audience that was already predominantly gentile. But one document included in the New Testament, The Acts of the Apostles, when read in conjunction with Eusebius and other authorities on the early history of the Christian Church, enables us to reconstruct the events that led from the death of a Jewish Messiah to a Gospel for the Gentiles.[41] It was during that period that a momentous event occurred: the foundering of the original body of Christians in Jerusalem and the progressive growth and eventual triumph of a variant "gentile Christianity" whose chief architect was Paul.

Judeo-Christianity is a modern ascription. The ancient authors rather recognized what they called "the Church from the Circumcision," which was centered at Jerusalem and was composed and governed from Jesus' death to 70 C.E. by what Eusebius called "practicing Hebrews," that is, circumcised Jews who continued to observe both the liturgical practices and Torah ideals of contemporary Judaism. There were problems, however. The first arose in connection with the Hellenists' share in the administration of the community's welfare system—there was no question of permitting them to preach the Word. The Hellenists were Greek- rather than Aramaic-speaking Jews, possibly Jews of the Diaspora who had resettled in Palestine. But in the story of one of them, Stephen, we can discern a more fundamental difference than

[41] J. Weiss, *Earliest Christianity*, 2 vols. (New York: Harper Torchbook, 1959).

that of language.[42] Stephen had publicly argued against both the Temple and the oral tradition, and his apologia in Acts is remarkable in that it is a Jewish and not a Christian attack upon Jewish traditions. Stephen was executed, and the Hellenists were forced to leave Jerusalem; the "Hebrew" Christians suffered no harm from the incident.[43]

The immunity from trouble of some Jews who accepted the messiahship of Jesus was doubtless by reason of their reverence of both Temple and Torah—and somewhat more besides, if James, the first head of the Jerusalem community, was at all typical. James, like most of his episcopal successors at Jerusalem "from among the Hebrews," owed his position at least in part to his family connection with Jesus. But he was, in addition, a Jew of not only strict but ascetical observance, and he was revered by the Jews, Christians, and non-Christians alike, as a *zaddik*, a holy man.

The "Hebrew" succession at Jerusalem lasted until 135 C.E., when the community was dispersed by Hadrian's anti-Jewish pogrom, and thereafter the Jerusalem Church was governed by bishops "from the Gentiles." What happened to them after that is difficult to say. By 135 C.E. the body of Christians was chiefly composed of gentile converts, and the Judeo-Christians, those who viewed Jesus as a strictly Jewish Messiah whose coming abrogated neither the Law nor ritual observance, were thrust to the fringes of the Christian movement, where their history and teachings must be painfully excavated out from under judgments of heresy and apostasy.

Some of those judgments may indeed be true, as the forces of action and reaction forced the Judeo-Christians into more and more extreme forms of belief and practice. As a result, we can attempt, as some have already done,[44] cautiously to reconstruct their system of beliefs from what early authorities tell us about a sect called the Ebionites. Were the Ebio-

[42] See M. Simon, *Saint Stephen and the Hellenists in the Primitive Church* (New York: Longmans, Green, 1958).

[43] Weiss, *Earliest Christianity*, I, 165-179.

[44] See H.-J. Schoeps, *Jewish Christianity* (Philadelphia: Fortress Press, 1969).

nites the descendents of the Jerusalem Church from the Circumcision? Possibly so, but it is equally plausible that they grew out of far more esoteric forms of Judaism, and their rejection by the Great Church may have been a result of that latter influence rather than a more general turning from Christianity's Jewish antecedents.

Thus it is difficult to speak of Judeo-Christianity as if it were a single, unitary phenomenon. All Christianity is in some sense Judeo-Christianity in its acceptance and affirmation of the Jewish Scriptures and Jesus as a Messiah, a claim and a title that make no sense outside a Jewish context. It is rather the specific forms of Judeo-Christianity that reflect not only upon ethnic origins, like Eusebius' "Hebrews," but upon doctrinal positions: Ebionites, Elkasaites, and the terms favored by Jewish writers, *minim* and *notzrim*.

The pursuit of the Judeo-Christians is an exercise in both history, with archeology playing an increasingly important role, and the reconstruction of a theology.[45] The latter task would be considerably easier if we possessed what many sources insist was a gospel in general and perhaps exclusive use among the Hebrew Christians, the Gospel of the Hebrews. Failing that, one must resort to other documents; Eusebius and his sources, Barnabas and Justin, various Apocrypha like the Clementine Recognitions, Gnostic writings, and the products of the Aramaic-speaking Christianity of Edessa.

What can be pieced together is the portrait of a community, or communities, that was deeply committed to an apocalyptic and eventually, in some quarters, a gnostic view of history, and a severe asceticism; that stressed the human, Davidic descent of Jesus; that had its own canon of Scripture; that placed a liturgical emphasis on baptism and celebrated

---

[45] L. E. Elliot-Binns, *Galilean Christianity* (London: SCM Press, 1956); S.G.F. Brandon, *The Fall of Jerusalem and the Christian Church* (London: SPCK, 1957); J. Daniélou, *The Theology of Jewish Christianity* (Chicago: Regnery, 1964).

the Resurrection on Passover; that cherished the ideal of ritual purity; and that had a deep-seated hostility toward Paul.[46]

PAUL, AND LAW, AND THE GENTILES

The Judeo-Christian attitude toward Paul arose out of the issue of the admission of Gentiles into the Christian community. According to Acts, the question may have first presented itself in the Hellenists' proselytizing among the "God Fearers," a somewhat shadowy gentile group standing upon the fringes of Judaism. Association with them, and a fortiori with absolute Gentiles, clearly violated the community sense of Christian *habura* and its attendant notions of ritual purity. The issue came to a head in Jerusalem in 48-49 C.E. By then Paul, once a Pharisee of Tarsus and now a new Christian who had been openly preaching the Good News to Gentiles, was at the center of the controversy. Some at Jerusalem, described as believers of the Pharisaic party, insisted that those new converts be circumcised and bound to the observance of the Mosaic Law. The resolution of the dispute, which had been put before James and the Apostles, was a compromise. Paul was permitted to preach to the Gentiles, and his converts would be bound to a modified version, certainly not the Pharisaic ideal, of the Law. Christianity, it appeared, was for the Gentiles as well as the Jews.[47]

Paul left behind a body of letters that were incorporated into the canon of the New Testament,[48] and that provide an extraordinary glimpse of early Christian thought in the intelligence of a deeply original thinker whose own personality shines through almost every line he has written.[49] It was Paul's Jesus who became the Church's Christ, and it was Paul's

---

[46] Many of these same characteristics were present in the Qumran *yahad*; see Fitzmyer, *Essays*, pp. 271-303.

[47] Weiss, *Earliest Christianity*, I, 258-276.

[48] *Grant, *Introduction*, pp. 171-207, with bibliography.

[49] Weiss, *Earliest Christianity*, II, 399-421.

attitude toward the Torah and the Jewish past that shaped Christianity's own.[50]

The heart of Paul's thinking about the Law, Jews, and Gentiles can be found in his Letter to the Romans, with additional interesting comments in Galatians. God was and is the God of all mankind, Jew and Gentile alike. All men lived under sin, but because of their righteousness the Jews were singled out for a special Covenant whose sign and seal was the Law and circumcision. Nevertheless, righteousness preceded the Covenant and circumcision, as is clear from the case of Abraham, who figures in much the same way in Muhammad's argument to the same point. The Jews had a written Law as a consequence of the Covenant; the Gentiles had the Law inscribed in their hearts. Now, however, with the coming of Jesus, whose death redeemed—the image is from the Roman institution of slavery—man from the bondage of sin, the question of the Mosaic Law was not so much abrogated as rendered moot. Henceforward Jews and Gentiles alike will gain acquittal (the famous Pauline "justification") at the bar of divine justice by pleading their faith in Christ. The

[50] Paul's life and work has obviously generated a large bibliography, but only a few works will be noted here. Some of the most interesting are essays by A. D. Nock that have been collected in two volumes entitled *Essays on Religion in the Ancient World*, edited by Zeph Stewart (London: Oxford University Press, 1972). Reference will be made to several of them in the pages that follow, but particular attention is drawn to his "Early Gentile Christianity and Its Hellenistic Background" in *Essays*, I, 49-133, and also published separately (New York: Harper Torchbook, 1964). Nock also devoted an individual study to Paul entitled *Saint Paul* (New York: Harper Torchbook, 1963). Earlier there was W. L. Knox, *St. Paul and the Church of the Gentiles* (Cambridge: Cambridge University Press, 1935), and the pages devoted to Paul in Weiss, *Earliest Christianity*.

The Jewish side of Paul has been explored by J. Klausner, *From Jesus to Paul* (Boston: Beacon Press pb., 1961); W. D. Davies, *Paul and Rabbinic Judaism* (New York: Harper Torchbook, 1967); H.-J. Schoeps, *Paul: The Theology of the Apostle in the Light of Jewish History* (Philadelphia: Westminster Press, 1961); S. Sandmel, *The Genius of Paul: A Study of History* (New York: Schocken, 1970); and E. P. Sanders, *Paul and Palestinian Judaism* (London: SCM Press, 1977).

Mosaic Law had paradoxically formalized sin; men were now free of sin and, consequentially, of the Law.

If this is a Jew's meditation on the past of Judaism, other elements of Paul's thought appear far less familiar. First, it should be recalled that Paul is that rarest of creatures for the historian, a Pharisee of the Diaspora. Hellenized Jews are familiar figures and Palestinian Pharisaism is tolerably well known. But the combination is novel for us. Thus, when we speak of Paul's cosmic version of the Messiah as the Son of God, present with the Father at creation, who descended from the heavenly world of eternity to take flesh in the historical present, though we can locate it comfortably within neither Jewish nor Hellenistic speculation,[51] we may simply be ignorant of how the Hellenized Jewish Diaspora thought about the Messiah to come.

Paul never repudiated his own or others' Jewishness. He preached Jesus the Christ in synagogues all over the eastern Mediterranean, northward to Syria, Anatolia, Greece, and eventually in Rome,[52] and in accord with his principles he preached as well, publicly and willingly, to Gentiles. There is something missing in this religious geography: the spreading of the Good News (*euangelion; evangelium*) to the southwest, to wit, the founding of Christian centers among the many Jewish communities of Egypt. It is possible that this was the primary mission field of the Judeo-Christians, which would make the official silence and historic uncertainty about Christian origins in Egypt somewhat more explicable.[53]

After Paul and the Gospels, Christian writings swell from a thin and often enigmatic trickle[54] to the broad historical

---

[51] Weiss, *Earliest Christianity*, II, 475-495; Vermes, *Jesus the Jew*, pp. 192-222; Nock, *Essays*, II, 928-939.

[52] Weiss, *Earliest Christianity*, II, 707-866; and A. Harnack, *The Mission and Expansion of Christianity in the First Three Centuries* (first published 1908; New York: Harper Torchbook, 1962).

[53] As Brandon, *The Fall of Jerusalem*, pp. 217-248, has argued.

[54] There are selections of these early Christian documents in M. Staniforth, *Early Christian Writings: The Apostolic Fathers* (Harmondsworth: Penguin pb., 1968); H. Musurillo, *The Fathers of the Primitive Church* (New

narrative of Eusebius' *Ecclesiastical History*.[55] The Church as an institution produced its own documents.[56] With this literary material at hand and with considerable help from more recent archeology, it is possible for the modern historian to write a consecutive and detailed history of the Christian community and its spread across the inhabited world.[57]

RABBINIC JUDAISM

The double conquest of Jerusalem in 70 and 135 C.E. radically affected the course of Judaism and set it on its path from "politics to piety," as Jacob Neusner has called it in the title of a recent book.[58] Both Temple and even the dreams of state were gone, and out of the doctrinal and cultic diversity of barely a century earlier survived only the Pharisees. The Temple priesthoods were rendered moot; Hellenistic Judaism and its spirit of accommodation fell into increasing disrepute; militant nationalists were swept away by the Romans, and new messianic claims, whether pacific or militant, fell upon deaf ears.

The Pharisees, as we have seen, are familiar figures from the New Testament and other sources.[59] It was long assumed that it was a simple step from the Pharisees of the first century to the sages of the second and following centuries of the Christian era, who produced the great literary and ethical

York: Mentor Omega pb., 1966); and H. Bettenson, *The Early Christian Fathers* (London: Oxford pb., 1969).

[55] Translated by G. H. Williamson: *Eusebius, A History of the Christian Church* (Harmondsworth: Penguin pb., 1965).

[56] Selected and translated by H. Bettenson, *Documents of the Christian Church* (London: Oxford pb., 1970).

[57] Only two will be cited here: *J. G. Davies, *The Early Christian Church* (Garden City: Doubleday Anchor pb., 1967), and H. Chadwick, *The Early Church* (Harmondsworth: Penguin pb., 1967).

[58] New York: Prentice Hall, 1973.

[59] See Bowker, *Jesus and the Pharisees*, where all the sources are collected and translated.

structure of talmudic Judaism.[60] To more critical eyes, that step is no longer regarded as quite so simple.[61]

If we look back from the perspective of the Talmud, we can note the presence, from the Hasmoneans onward, of an important institution, the Sanhedrin, governed by collegiate heads, the senior Nasi, who served as its president, and the junior Ab Bet Din. It was this body that took responsibility for the moral well-being of the community and adjudicated cases of law and conscience that fell within the general competence of the Mosaic Law.[62]

The later Jewish tradition recollected the holders of these two chief Sanhedrin offices as "pairs" (zugot), but is vague on the details of their functions and rulings until about the time of Jesus, when the zug of Hillel and Shammai filled the offices and developed what were recalled as distinctive attitudes toward interpreting the Law. The "schools" of Hillel and Shammai dominate legal discussions down to 70 C.E., when the Sanhedrin had necessarily to leave Jerusalem and reconstitute itself elsewhere under the leadership of Yohanan ben Zakkai.[63]

These were difficult days for the Jews, and remain so for the modern historian attempting to trace events that are as dim as they are important.[64] Cultic Judaism, which had its unique center in Jerusalem since the days of David and Solomon, was no more after the debacle of 70 C.E., and the leaders of the community, most of whom appear to have been scholars rather than political figures or rich landowners

[60] Such was the assumption, for example, of R. T. Herford, *The Pharisees* (Boston: Beacon Press pb., 1962) and *Moore's Judaism.

[61] See Bowker, *Jesus and the Pharisees*, pp. 1-15, and Neusner, *Rabbinic Traditions*, III, 320-368.

[62] The evolution of this institution has been traced by H. Mantel, *Studies in the History of the Sanhedrin* (Cambridge: Harvard University Press, 1961).

[63] His career has been studied by J. Neusner, *A Life of Yohanan ben Zakkai* (Leiden: E. J. Brill, 1970).

[64] Among these latter, see A. Guttman, *Rabbinic Judaism in the Making* (Detroit: Wayne State University Press, 1970).

at this point, had to rebuild a shattered community upon new foundations.

That new foundation was the Law. It is obviously one of the oldest parts of the structure of Judaism, and since the time of the Exile was being promoted by many, the Pharisees chief among them, as a central concern of the Jew. Now, however, it became the unique standard of Jewish solidarity. Or nearly so. In these new circumstances the Torah was supported, expanded, and explained by another document of growing authority, the Mishna.

The Mishna is a written and somewhat ordered presentation of the rules of conduct and the moral and spiritual teaching that had been hammered out orally by sages in both academy (*bet ha-midrash*) and law court (*bet ha-din*) over the previous generations. Though the redaction of the final version is credited to Judah "the Prince" (*ha-nasi*) (ca. 170-217 C.E.), the Mishna is obviously a composite work that incorporated, under a generous, catholic perspective, what had developed as a kind of consensus within the Jewish community.[65]

Many of the Jewish Diaspora communities were within the Roman Empire, as was remarked above, but there were other important centers in the ancient Babylonia that dated back to the Exile and were still flourishing in the second to sixth centuries C.E.[66] With the redaction of Judah's Mishna, the scholars in these Iraqi schools joined with their colleagues in Galilee in commenting upon this now central text of the new Torah Judaism. Their commentary, written in Aramaic and called *gemara*, was joined to the Hebrew text of the

[65] The Mishna, which was written in Hebrew, has been translated in its entirety into English by H. Danby, *The Mishnah* (London; Oxford University Press, 1933 with many reprints) and has been usefully analyzed by both *Moore, *Judaism*, pp. 150-160, and *H. L. Strack, *Introduction to the Talmud and Midrash* (New York: Jewish Publication Society pb., 1959), pp. 26-64. On its publication, see Lieberman, *Hellenism in Palestine*, pp. 83-99.

[66] Their history under the Iranian dynasties of the Parthians and Sasanians is described in detail by J. Neusner, *A History of the Jews in Babylonia*, 5 vols. (Leiden: E. J. Brill, 1969-1970).

Mishna. Together they form the Talmud: the Mishna with its Galilean *gemara* is called the Jerusalem or Palestinian Talmud; and with its Iraqi *gemara*, the Babylonian Talmud.[67] Together they constitute the heart of rabbinic Judaism.

The legal tradition was always strong in Judaism, as we shall see in discussing the Jewish sense of community, and there was always in post-Exilic Judaism an authoritative body, generally called the Great Sanhedrin, which both legislated and judged. Its head was the Nasi, who both before and after the destruction of the Temple possessed extensive legislative powers in his own right. Even after the Pharisees introduced the notion of an oral legal tradition whose validation went back to Moses, the Nasi did not cease enacting positive legal prescriptions called *gezerot* and *taqqanot*. The first had, in fact, a Pharisaic justification in that such positive enactments provided "a fence for the Torah," that is, by surrounding the Torah with additional prescriptions, they guaranteed the observance of the Torah prescription (*mitzva*). But eventually a *gezera* came to mean any legal enactment that was not a traditional rabbinic legal prescription (*halaka*), whereas the *taqqanot* referred more properly to the creation of new institutions whose purpose it was to improve the conditions of social, economic, and religious life.[68]

The legislative and judicial process was not confined to the Nasi and his court. He could by "ordination" (*semika*) dele-

---

[67] See *L. Ginzberg, *On Jewish Law and Lore* (New York: Atheneum pb., 1970), pp. 3-60. Both Talmuds are discussed in *Strack, *Introduction*, pp. 65-100, and by J. Mielziner, *Introduction to the Talmud* (reprint New York: Block Paperback Co., 1965); J. Neusner, ed., *The Formation of the Talmud* (Leiden: E. J. Brill, 1970); and A. Corre, ed., *Understanding the Talmud* (New York: Ktav pb., 1975).

The technique of text and comment may be observed in the translation of one of the treatises, *Pirke Abot*, "The Wisdom of the Fathers," by J. Goldin, *The Living Talmud* (New York: Mentor pb., 1957). There are selections in *Barrett, *Background*, pp. 139-172, but the richest sampling of the Talmud in English is in C. G. Montefiore and H. Loewe, *A Rabbinic Anthology* (New York: Schocken pb., 1974).

[68] Mantel, *Sanhedrin*, pp. 227-235.

gate his powers to individual rabbis so that they too could adjudicate disputes at law and issue binding enactments.[69] There was no such ordination among the Babylonian Jews, and if some of the early Babylonian rabbis went to Palestine for ordination, the result was to strengthen the authority of the academies (*yeshibot*) where they taught and not that of the Babylonian Exilarch, who was their nominal leader. With the disappearance of the Palestinian Patriarchate in 425 C.E. under Christian pressures,[70] the Babylonian model began to prevail in Palestine as well: the rabbis could adjudicate and legislate on their own authority.

The rabbis were, in Neusner's words, "a relatively small group of religious virtuosi" who administered Jewish law for Jewish communities which were granted a certain degree of self-government by their political sovereigns, the Romans in Palestine and the Sasanians in Iraq.[71] This law, like its later Islamic counterpart, had chiefly to do with personal status, and dealt with matters of marriage, inheritance, and the transfer of property. But the writ of the rabbis did not end there. In legal matters their word was law, but by their carefully cultivated prestige they influenced a broad range of religious and ethical matters.[72]

It is difficult to underestimate the importance of the rabbis for the continuity of the Jewish tradition. Judaism was precisely tradition, the handing down, in both spirit and letter, of the Covenant. The biblical account of that process smoothes over perhaps the enormous difficulties in both establishing and maintaining Jewish continuity. We have, however, graphic

[69] Ibid., pp. 206–221; compare the texts on judicial procedures cited in *Barrett, *Background*, pp. 169–172.

[70] These are described by M. Avi-Yonah, *The Jews of Palestine: A Political History from Bar Kokhba to the Arab Conquest* (Oxford: Basil Blackwell, 1976), pp. 225–229.

[71] *Jews in Babylonia*, III, 200.

[72] The limits of their legal authority have been laid out by Neusner, *Jews in Babylonia*, III, 155–278 under the headings of "The Rabbi as Administrator" and "The Rabbi as Judge," but for the full extent of their interests and impact, one must turn to pp. 279–402 of the same volume and V, 133–216.

evidence of the difficulty when the Bible account ends and the historian can confront unedited testimony to the bewildering variety of Jewish sects and factions that prevailed in Palestine and the Diaspora in the years that followed the Maccabees, the Herods, and the Romans. The collapse of Jewish political expectations and the destruction of the Jews' unique place of liturgical worship were events of extraordinary magnitude in the life of the community. Masada is a modern myth; in the contemporary sources the taste of ashes is almost palpable.

Some Jews turned, as we have seen, to more radical expectations in this world or the next, to zealot nationalists, messianic claimants, to gnostic reflexes of eschatological hope or historical despair, to the attractions of Hellenic assimilation. Not so the rabbis. Quietly, patiently, they rebuilt a shattered Judaism on the foundations of the Law. The historian may cast a doubtful eye on their claim to represent an unwritten tradition going back to Moses himself, but that claim was accepted in the end by the great body of Jews, and the rabbis used its authority to expand, modify, and define the Torah for a new age.

Traditions calcify, and some later reform movements in Judaism have passed that harsh judgment on the Talmud. Whatever the truth of that judgment for the modern Jew, the Talmud, the men who composed it, studied, glossed, reverenced, and prayed over it, the rabbis who lodged it in the heart and practice of Judaism for more than three thousand generations of observant Jews, recreated Judaism. Though no Jew would be likely to put it so, the Talmud is the true New Testament of Judaism, and the rabbis, who quickly lost interest in such figures, were its veritable Messiahs.

MUHAMMAD AND ISLAM

The lives of the Jewish founding fathers unfolded in such remote antiquity that they are by now irretrievable, and even the sages and scholars who contributed to the Talmud are

34

represented by little more than disjointed utterances and judgments that provide flavor and personality but are poor makings for biography. Both Jesus and Muhammad are bathed, however, in a discernible historical light. If their careers are embellished with legend, we can also find in the narratives concerning them the traces of genuine biography: chronology, events, context.

The case of Jesus has already been discussed. For the Muslim, the Qur'an is not a historical document at all but an immediate and unconditioned revelation of God's will for mankind expressed in God's own eternal words. Western scholars have preferred to see in it not God but the reflection of the interior life and religious mission of Muhammad himself (ca. 570-632 C.E.), and from it and somewhat more traditional biographical material have constructed a life of the Prophet of Islam.

One rather common Western approach has placed heavy emphases on the influence of contemporary social and economic conditions upon Muhammad and his message, whereas others have attempted a more directly religious approach to a religious personality.[73] A modern Muslim biographer of the Prophet, although drawing upon the first approach, obviously prefers to come to the Prophet as a religious figure, though with quite different results from those of his Western, non-Muslim counterparts.[74]

The argument and critico-historical method of non-Muslim scholars may be reflections of modern Western attitudes toward reconstructing the past, but the early Muslims too had put together a biography of Muhammad, and out of

[73] The first approach is essentially that of Muhammad's two most widely read Western biographers: W. M. Watt, *Muhammad, Prophet and Statesman* (London: Oxford pb., 1974) and M. Rodinson, *Mohammed* (New York: Random House, 1974). The best of only a few examples of the second approach is Tor Andrae, *Mohammed, the Man and His Faith* (New York: Harper Torchbook, 1960).

[74] See the interesting analysis of the work of a Muslim biographer of the Prophet in Antonie Wessels, *A Modern Arabic Biography of Muhammad* (Leiden: E. J. Brill, 1974).

35

much the same material available to the modern scholar: the Qur'an and the body of traditions (*hadith*; see Chapter IV below) that purported to report the sayings and deeds of the Prophet. Our earliest preserved example of such a biographical construction is the *Life* composed by Ibn Ishaq (d. 767) in Baghdad.[75]

Ibn Ishaq had predecessors, to be sure, in his biographical project on the Prophet, but that his and their work took place a century after Muhammad's death and only when Islam had moved outward from Mecca and Medina into an overwhelmingly Christian milieu has suggested to some that the enterprise was undertaken as a direct response to the Christians' Gospels, despite the obvious difference in theological function of the two men and the two documents. For the Christian, Jesus was the Christ, the Messiah, whose redemptive act and teachings are authoritatively recorded in the Gospels. For the Muslims, Muhammad was a prophet (*nabi*), a human envoy (*rasul*) who delivered God's own words in the Qur'an but whose other words and deeds, though important for the understanding of the Qur'an and the direction of the Muslim community, are not immediate instruments of salvation.[76]

Whereas Jesus was the product of a Jewish environment obscured by our relative ignorance of the contemporary varieties of Judaism, Muhammad came from an Arab commercial and religious center, Mecca, whose cultic practices were those of Semitic paganism, though certain but unspecified Jewish and Christian influences were operating in the near

[75] Available in English translation by Alfred Guillaume, *The Life of Muhammad* (London: Oxford pb., 1967).

[76] This is a theological distinction commonly drawn by Western scholars and Islamic modernists, who may in fact have drawn a far finer line between Qur'anic revelation and the noncanonical "sayings of the Prophet" than Muhammad's own contemporaries did. This is the recent and convincing argument of William Graham, *Divine Word and Prophetic Word in Early Islam* (The Hague: Mouton, 1977).

vicinity.[77] The Qur'an itself is filled with narratives of obvious biblical inspiration and suggestive of either direct Jewish influence or some version of the same mediated through Semitic Christians.[78] Though purely Christian figures such as Jesus are rare, the case for Christian influences at work upon Muhammad and his religious perceptions is not difficult to make.[79]

The founding document of Islam is the Qur'an or Recitation.[80] It is a composite work in which the revelations given by God through the Angel Gabriel to Muhammad over the last twenty-odd years of his life are collected into one hundred fourteen *surahs* or chapters.[81] The *surahs* vary greatly in length and are not arranged in chronological order; indeed, purely chronological considerations might invite one to read the book from its end to its beginning.

Many of the *surahs* that appear to be early ones show a manner and an elevation of style not unlike that of the Jewish prophets as they admonish men to reform, or warn of the judgment of eternity.[82] The later *surahs* are longer and contain detailed regulations for the conduct of the already converted. For the Muslim it is God alone who speaks in the Qur'an; no other voice is heard. Much of the Qur'an is, indeed, about God, in Arabic *Allah*, and man's relationship to

[77] The environment is described by De Lacy O'Leary, *Arabia before Muhammad* (reprint Tampa, AMS Press, 1973), and S. J. Trimingham, *Christianity among the Arabs in Pre-Islamic Times* (London: Longmans, 1978).

[78] See C. Torrey, *The Jewish Foundations of Islam* (1933; New York: Ktav, 1967). S. Baron, *A Social and Religious History of the Jews* (New York: Columbia University Press, 1957), III, 75-93, 262-270; and J. Jomier, *The Bible and the Koran* (Chicago: Regnery pb., 1967).

[79] So R. Bell, *The Origins of Islam and Its Christian Environment* (reprint London, Frank Cass, 1968); on Jesus: G. Parrinder, *Jesus in the Qur'an* (London: Oxford pb., 1977).

[80] For its other names, see *W. M. Watt, *Bell's Introduction to the Qur'an* (Chicago: Aldine, 1970), pp. 101-147.

[81] Ibid., pp. 57-68.

[82] On Qur'anic style, see ibid., pp. 69-85.

Him.[83] But there is also much about prophecy and prophets, the consequences of men's rejecting them in the past and the need to accept Muhammad as a genuine prophet (*nabi*) and envoy (*rasul*) of God.[84]

Systematic study of the Qur'an as a canonical document began in Islam in the late eighth or early ninth century, as we shall see, and Western scholarship has been working on it for somewhat over a century.[85] The question of revelation aside—the secular student of the text, unlike the Muslim, begins with the presumption that it is Muhammad and not Allah speaking in the Qur'an—the techniques and results of medieval and modern scholarship are not very remote from each other. Attention has been paid on both sides to reconstructing the historical circumstances surrounding each *surah*, what the Muslims called "the occasions of revelation," and so in effect writing a life of Muhammad; to arranging the *surahs* in some kind of chronological sequence; and to trying to understand how the collection was put together in its canonical form.[86]

The task has not been simple because of the difficult nature of the Qur'an and because all historical material produced by later Muslims on the first century of Islam is uncertain at best and possibly even spurious.[87] The Bible and the Gospels are filled with many of the same themes and images as the Qur'an, for example, but in the former Books they are surrounded by a body of narrative that provides a context that smoothes the way to comprehension. The Qur'an, on the

[83] See ibid., pp. 148-166; T. Izutsu, *God and Man in the Qur'an* (Tokyo: Keio Institute of Cultural and Linguistic Studies, 1964), and *Ethico-Religious Concepts in the Qur'an* (Montreal: McGill University Press, 1966).

[84] See *Watt, *Bell's Introduction*, pp. 17-30.

[85] The results of both efforts are surveyed ibid., pp. 167-186.

[86] Ibid., pp. 108-120, 40-56.

[87] A recent example of how, by adopting an extremely and perhaps justifiedly skeptical attitude toward the traditional accounts, one may rewrite the earliest history of Islam in a radical manner is provided by P. Crone and M. Cook, *Hagarism: The Making of the Islamic World* (Cambridge: Cambridge University Press, 1977).

other hand, has no narrative framework: God's utterances are totally disassociated from contemporary events. And where the revelation does take the form of a story, in the "Joseph Surah" (Qur'an 12), for example, the narrative is so allusive and disjointed that one can only assume that the Prophet's listeners were already familiar with the matter.

The literary style, which has been characterized as "referential rather than expository,"[88] the ellipses and repetition of themes in the text, are all in strong contrast with the traditional account of its redaction. In Muhammad's lifetime, it was said, the various *surahs* had not been collected, though some of the Prophet's companions and wives had a copy (*mushaf*). The first two Caliphs attempted a collation of all the codices, but it was not until the third Caliph, 'Uthman (644–656 C.E.), that a final redaction was accomplished. 'Uthman's standard text was promulgated and all other copies were ordered to be burned.[89]

Two of the most recent studies of the Qur'an have rejected this long-accepted account of 'Uthman's "edition," though for somewhat different reasons and with very different consequences. John Burton, in his *The Collection of the Qur'an*, has remarked on a discussion in legal circles in the late eighth and early ninth centuries that finally produced a theory that God had "abrogated" certain verses in the Qur'an but left intact the legal enactments that they contained.[90] Thus a distinction was drawn between an archetypal Book of God that contained all of God's utterances and the current ('Uthmanic) copy (*mushaf*), which was incomplete. For this theory, which was actually a defense of current legal practice

[88] J. Wansbrough, *Qur'anic Studies* (Oxford, London: Oxford University Press, 1977), pp. 1, 20.

[89] ★Watt, *Bell's Introduction*, pp. 40–47.

[90] Notably the penalty for stoning for adultery, which was the current practice in Islam in the ninth century but was in direct contradiction with Qur'an 24:2, which prescribed flogging: Burton, *The Collection of the Qur'an* (Cambridge: Cambridge University Press, 1977), pp. 68–85. On the critical issue of "abrogation," see ★Watt, *Bell's Introduction*, pp. 86–89.

against either explicit Qur'anic contradiction or Qur'anic silence, to have any validity, Muhammad had to be disassociated from the actual collection of the Qur'an, as he indeed was in the 'Uthmanic codex tradition. The whole tradition was a lawyers' fiction, Burton has argued; our present copy of the Qur'an is not 'Uthman's edition but Muhammad's own.[91]

John Wansbrough is equally skeptical of the 'Uthmanic "edition." He notes the fact that no one attempts to derive law from the Qur'an or compose legal or textual commentaries upon it until the ninth century.[92] The earliest creed in Islam, the Fiqh Akbar I (Chapter VIII below), does not mention it. The conclusion seems to impose itself: the Qur'an did not exist in its present canonized version until the lawyers had put into place the whole legal structure of "the custom of the Prophet" (Chapter IV below). Nor was it the product of one man or even one place. The Qur'an is a manifestly composite document in which many prophetic utterances have been assembled but neither integrated into a unified whole nor provided with the kind of narrative framework that one finds in the *Lives* of Muhammad.

Both of these works, though professedly speculative, represent radical departures from the received tradition of both Muslim and Western scholarship. Many of the early historical reports in Islam are suspect, as has been said—a fact amply documented in the traditional evolution of Islamic Law (Chapter IV below)—and Burton has simply and for the first time extended that skepticism to reports about the Qur'an. Wansbrough, on the other hand, has brought to bear on the Qur'an the methods of literary analysis that are commonplace in biblical studies but have not heretofore been applied to Muslim Scripture.

These questions are of considerable interest to the historian, and particularly to the secular historian, but of little

[91] Burton, *Collection*, pp. 225-240, for his summary conclusions.
[92] *Qur'anic Studies*, p. 44.

concern to the Muslim. For him the traditional account was the true account, as indeed it may still be, and our own interest here is not in exploring the historicist's ideal of what really happened but rather what was understood to have happened. And what was understood to have happened was that a new prophet had appeared in the Judeo-Christian tradition and had promulgated a new revelation, or rather a new version of revelation, which had as its object not the abrogation of the old Law but its restoration to its original vigor.[93]

The effect of God's earlier revelations was, as Muhammad understood very well, the creation of communities, most notably the Peoples of the Book, the Jews and Christians. The Arabs, now in possession of a "clear Arabic Qur'an" (Qur'an 16:103), had become just such a community (*ummah*). But even during the lifetime of Muhammad, his community achieved such a remarkable degree of political success that it had become in effect a state—a responsibility faced by Judaism and Christianity only at a considerably more advanced stage of their development. Thus Muhammad was not simply God's envoy; he was also, for much of his later life, judge, spiritual guide, and military and political leader, first of a community, then of a city-state, and finally of a burgeoning empire.[94]

At base Islam is submission to the will of God and the recognition of the rights of the Creator over His creation. For one who had so submitted, the *muslim*—however revolutionary the internal spiritual consequences—there were few external, cultic obligations.[95] From the initial profession of faith ("There is no god but The God and Muhammad is His envoy") flowed the obligation of prayer five times daily, with the noon prayer on Friday said in common; of almsgiving in

[93] One example of the "concealment" or "corruption" of Scripture at the hands of the Jews and Christians was their suppression of the verses foretelling the coming of Muhammad: Qur'an 7:157; 61:6.

[94] See F. Gabrieli, *Muhammad and the Conquests of Islam* (New York: McGraw-Hill pb., 1968).

[95] See *Watt, *Bell's Introduction*, pp. 162-166.

the form of a tithe; of fasting and other abstentions in the month of Ramadan; and, if the circumstances were practical, of making a pilgrimage (*hajj*) to the "House of God" at Mecca.[96]

These are mere bones, the ritual obligations of the Muslim, and though they became the point of departure of a vast body of prescription regulating Islamic behavior, they reflect neither the tone nor the urgency of Muhammad's message, and particularly of the earliest revelations. The Meccan *surahs* of the Qur'an have a dramatic eschatological emphasis, expressed now in commercial terms and now in the vivid images of Jewish and Christian apocalyptic. God who created the world will also be its judge. When the Day of Judgment comes, accompanied by chaos and confusion, the Lord of the World will open the accounts of all men and reckon each at his worth. For those who have gravely sinned or hoarded their goods out of meanness of spirit, there awaits a fiery Gehenna of extreme suffering. But the magnanimous man who has submitted his will to God and committed his goods to the needy and the downtrodden will be rewarded in a garden Paradise of luxurious ease and splendor. Indeed, this is why the Prophet was sent, to be a "warner" to mankind that the reckoning was close at hand.

Little can be said here of Islam's enormous and rapid growth from a state to an empire to a civilization.[97] What is of greater

---

[96] The religious antecedents of Islam are clearly manifested in these practices, many of which went back to pre-Islamic times and whose lineage has been analyzed by S. D. Goitein, *Studies in Islamic History and Institutions* (Leiden: E. J. Brill, 1968). Indeed, they reach far back into the history of Semitic religious institutions, as was already recognized by W. Robertson Smith, *The Religion of the Semites: The Fundamental Institutions* (1889; reprint New York: Schocken pb., 1972).

[97] There are full details in *M. G. Hodgson, *The Venture of Islam*, 3 vols. (Chicago: Chicago University Press pb., 1974), and F. E. Peters, *Allah's Commonwealth* (New York: Simon and Schuster, 1973), both with glossaries and complete bibliographies. For the frequently distorted image of that phenomenon entertained by the West, see N. Daniel, *Islam and the West: The Making of an Image* (Edinburgh: Edinburgh University Press, 1962).

concern for the present undertaking is an understanding of Islam as a religion with its own proper spirituality and institutions. In striking contrast to the cases of Judaism and Christianity, Western non-Muslims have been the chief interpreters of Islam to the West. The best results of their labors have stood up to the most serious scholarly scrutiny,[98] but have often been deficient in conveying a sense of either the moral grandeur or the deep-seated piety of the Islamic religion. Many traditional Muslim works on the subject suffer the same defects, aggravated by the wide cultural gap that separates the writer and his modern Western reader. More accessible perhaps, if by no means representative of the views of all contemporary Muslims, is the approach of "modernist" Muslim intellectuals such as Ameer Ali, Fazlur Rahman, and Seyyed Hossein Nasr.[99]

This sketch has been rapid, all too brief, and perhaps even superfluous for those who know these traditions well. It is, in any event, merely preliminary to what follows, where the attitudes and institutions of Jews, Christians, and Muslims will be examined side by side, not so much from the historian's perspective of tracing influences and borrowings, which there certainly were, as with the intent to illuminate how these three affiliated religions approached common issues on the ground that each of them had rendered holy.

[98] See, for example, *H.A.R. Gibb, *Mohammedanism* (London: Oxford University Press pb., 1970).

[99] Ameer Ali, *The Spirit of Islam* (New York: Barnes pb., 1967); Fazlur Rahman, *Islam* (New York: Doubleday Anchor pb., 1968); Seyyed Hossein Nasr, *Ideals and Realities of Islam* (London: Allen and Unwin, 1966).

CHAPTER III

Community and Hierarchy

To this point Judaism, Christianity, and Islam have been spoken of in somewhat general terms and without inquiring into what it was that gave them their unique identity during the period under discussion. To speak of a "religion" is to speak of many things: a system of beliefs or an accepted complex of ritual, for example. But when one looks at how a Jew, a Christian, or a Muslim regarded himself and his coreligionists, it is the sense of community that asserts itself at every turn; Bene Yisrael, *ekklesia*, and *ummah* all speak, each in its own context, of a powerful sense of group solidarity.

BENE YISRAEL AND ERETZ YISRAEL

Despite the confusions and overlappings in the biblical texts, and despite modern scholars' inability to settle upon a chronology for the various pieces that were put together to compose the Bible, there is a unanimity of testimony that the creation of a people called "Israel" (Bene Yisrael) after its supposed tribal ancestor was the result of a covenant (*berit*) concluded between their God Yahweh and a people of His choice. Yahweh had deserved well of this people: He had led them out of bondage in Egypt. They in turn must submit to His will, as subjects to a sovereign. If they do so, they will be rewarded, most notably by the possession of a promised "Land for Israel" (Eretz Yisrael).

Neither the provisions of God's will—the Ten Commandments are scarcely a detailed code of law—nor the exact boundaries of the promised land were spelled out. The working out of the law governing the new Israelite manner of life had to wait upon the conquest of Canaan. Once there was a people called Hebrews—perhaps simply "wanderers," a rather mixed bag of seminomadic peoples—but now it was Israelites who set up cult centers in honor of Yahweh, who was now to be their God to the exclusion of all others, as He had demanded.

In what sense the Israelites were at first one people in Eretz Yisrael it is difficult to say. They were clearly organized along clan lines, and the fact of twelve clans or tribes has suggested to some scholars that the clans were united in a kind of tribal confederation around a central shrine where they would periodically resort to commemorate with ritual the covenant that gave them their identity. By all appearances the confederation was a loose one: there was no single leader and no apparent apparatus of central government. Individuals whom the Israelites generally called "judges" came forward when need or circumstances dictated.

It was only with David (ca. 1000-960 B.C.E.) that one of these "charismatic leaders" united the tribes of the Bene Yisrael into a somewhat unified whole, and only under his successor Solomon (ca. 960-922 B.C.E.) that a centralized and institutionalized monarchy of a familiar Near Eastern type emerged. Cult center and liturgy were by then firmly established in Jerusalem, where Solomon's newly energized commercial enterprises financed the construction of a magnificent temple.

Thus Israel became a state ruled by a hereditary king, but its "constitution" was still God's Covenant. This latter had become increasingly explicit with the passage of time through the growth of a positive law whose provisions reflected Israel's conversion to a sedentary agricultural society. None of this was the king's writ, however, but rather "the Mosaic Law." Thus the evolutionary character of the community's laws was concealed beneath an appeal back to the original Covenant so that all that had occurred thereafter, whether

45

through custom or design, was progressively incorporated into the charter of Scripture.

The Israelite monarchy proved ephemeral. Internal tensions between northern and southern clans shattered the fragile unity, and foreign cults began to make headway against Yahweh. Successive invasions by more powerful external enemies, and finally the carrying off of part of the population into exile in Babylonia left David and Solomon's political achievement in ruins. But the united monarchy and the Mosaic Covenant were not so closely identified that the destruction of the first necessarily signalled the end of the latter. New charismatic leaders, now prophets rather than earlier warrior types, arose in Israel to preach fidelity to the Covenant and through it the identity of Bene Yisrael.

The Babylonian Exile is a mysterious period in the life of the Israelite community, since there are almost no sources to assist the historians. Some of the exiles did return to Judea—how many remained behind we cannot tell, though the number must have been considerable—and restored some semblance of liturgy and some degree of self-government within the rather loose structure of the Persian Empire, of which Judea was now part. By Persian royal decree the Mosaic Law was publicly repromulgated by Ezra, who was, in the new order of things, neither king nor prophet but a priest (*kohen*) and a scribe (*sofer*).

Post-Exilic Judea, with which we are primarily concerned, was, in the first instance, a temple-state under the general sovereignty of the Persian shah and later the Greek kings of Syria. It was ruled by a crown-appointed governor who consulted on local matters with the hereditary High Priest of the Temple and a Council of Elders. But "Judea" was merely an administrative arrangement, and if it had within it the cult center of the Jews and was served by an official Jewish priesthood, there were also offspring of the Covenant in the other Persian provinces into which Palestine and the Transjordan

46

had been divided,[1] as well as even further abroad, in "dispersion" (*diaspora*) in Syria, Egypt, and Babylonia.[2]

The Jewish Diaspora was not an exile, and those who lived outside the Judean temple-state did so by choice and not by constraint. In one sense they regarded themselves as one community, and the single name *Judaioi,* "Judeans," was applied to all, whether living in Judea or not. All Jews were bound to contribute a half shekel to the upkeep of the Temple in Jerusalem, and many made pilgrimage there. In the larger centers of population abroad they constituted a "corporation," a Hellenistic notion that gave official sanction to a semiautonomous community of non-Greeks who had their own internal organization, guaranteed rights and privileges and, very probably, their own formalized religious cult.[3]

The Maccabean-Hasmonean revolt,[4] and the consequent restoration of a Jewish monarchical state in Judea had little effect on the Jewish sense of community except to underline a premise that had already been implicit in the first experiment in monarchy: a Jewish state, as the ancient Near East understood that latter term, was not identical with Covenant Judaism. And much as the prophets had made that point against the kings of an earlier day, so now others came forward to instruct the Hasmoneans. But where earlier charismatic preaching had been the chief weapon of the Covenanters against the monarchists, now the contest about an authentic Jewish life was waged in open political warfare. The Hasmoneans appear to have envisioned a peculiar hybrid state that was demographically Jewish but culturally Hellen-

---

[1] On these divisions, see M. Avi-Yonah, *The Holy Land: A Historical Geography* (Grand Rapids, Mich.: Baker, 1966), pp. 11-31.

[2] V. Tcherikover, *Hellenistic Civilization and the Jews* (New York: Atheneum pb., 1970), pp. 269-295.

[3] Ibid., pp. 296-309.

[4] Described by F. E. Peters, *The Harvest of Hellenism* (New York: Clarion pb., 1970), pp. 250-273, and Tcherikover, *Hellenistic Civilization,* pp. 204-234.

ized; their expansionist policies included the Judaizing of newly occupied lands, while they themselves became progressively more Hellenized in both their mode of government and their personal life styles.[5] Finally, the Hasmonean head of state was both Hellenistic king and Jewish High Priest, the first in the history of Israel to have held such dual authority.

The prophets who opposed secularizing Jewish monarchs of an earlier day were rather isolated figures whose position as revivalilsts and reformers rested upon charismatic foundations. Opposition to the Hasmoneans took the form of parties whose programs created neither revival nor reform in the first instance, but rather schismatic fissures in the Jewish community. The Sadducees, Pharisees, Essenes, and followers of Jesus were sects with sharply differing views about past history, future prospects, and what constituted a Jewish life.[6] The Covenant that had once been concluded with the entire Bene Yisrael was now understood by many as a special covenant observed by a faithful remnant.[7] The political question of a Jewish state had been rendered moot by Roman intervention, and while there were still those willing to die for its restoration, most of the spiritual energies of the community were devoted to constructing new legal, ascetic, and eschatological canons to answer the question, "what is a Jew?"

There were many issues that separated the sects from each other. One of them emerges, however, with singular clarity, that of table-fellowship (habura). At issue was the extension of ritual purity, which everyone was required to observe within the Temple and which was the special hallmark of the priesthood, to the everyday life of the Jew. Those who observe similar rules of purity, and they alone, may eat together, but no others, lest there be a defilement. Though a similar preoccupation can be observed at Qumran and among

[5] Tcherikover, *Hellenistic Civilization*, pp. 243-253.

[6] M. Simon, *Jewish Sects in the Time of Jesus* (Philadelphia: Fortress Press, 1967).

[7] On the covenant at Qumran, see G. Vermes, *The Dead Sea Scrolls: Qumran in Perspective* (London: Collins, 1977), pp. 163-169.

the early Christians, the strict enforcement of this ideal was at the center of the Pharisaic program, and it set them off not only from Gentiles but from many Temple-observant Jews and those who totally ignored questions of ritual purity, though they would surely have identified themselves as Jews.[8]

It was the Pharisaic answer to the question, "what is a Jew?" that prevailed: a Jew was someone who observed the Law, both the written Torah given to Moses, and the unwritten Law, "the tradition of the Fathers," that went back to the same time and had the same sanction, and whose authoritative interpreters were the rabbis who after 135 C.E. were the sole voice of Judaism. Temple and Qumran were gone, and the sectarian followers of Jesus of Nazareth had chosen or been forced to separate themselves from rabbinic Judaism. More, the Romans accepted the Pharisaic disassociation from the insurrection, and chose to deal with the Pharisaic leadership as representatives of the Jewish Covenant, not merely in a religious but also in a political sense.[9] For their part, the Romans regarded the Jews as both an ethnic group (*natio*) and a religious community (*religio*) at whose head stood a single official, the Nasi or Patriarch.

If we review the powers and functions of the Patriarch from Gamaliel II (ca. 80-117 C.E.) down to the abolition of the office in 425 C.E., we see that he not only presided over the chief religious court, the Sanhedrin, but announced the appearance of the new moon, which determined the date of Jewish liturgical festivals, among other things, and he or his delegates (*shelihim*, "apostles") collected funds from Jewish communities all over the Diaspora and determined and pronounced sentences of excommunication.

---

[8] J. Neusner, *The Rabbinic Traditions about the Pharisees before 70* (Leiden: E. J. Brill, 1971), III, 286-300; J. Bowker, *Jesus and the Pharisees* (Cambridge: Cambridge University Press, 1973), pp. 29-38.

[9] J. Neusner, *A Life of Yohanan ben Zakkai* (Leiden: E. J. Brill, 1970), pp. 166-171; H. Mantel, *Studies in the History of the Sanhedrin* (Cambridge: Harvard University Press, 1961), pp. 7-49.

Excommunication or banishment from the community is a corollary of the very notion of community. A study of how and why the process functions in the Jewish and early Christian context is now tolerably well known,[10] and it is possible to take as its starting point the biblical grounds for execution, expulsion, or cursing, the three most common procedures of separation from the community. Though we are not certain how or why they were carried out on a regular basis, the alleged grounds can be reduced to the worship of idols, contempt of God, and sexual, social, and ritual offenses. In post-Exilic times the picture is by no means so clear, probably because sectarian splitting presented so many views and versions—the Pharisaic *habura* and the Qumran *yahad* are only two of the best known—of what constituted the community of the faithful and what constituted deviation from it.

Once the norms of Pharisaic Judaism became, at least ideally, the norms of the entire Jewish community, the focus returns to the picture of excommunication. The earliest evidence is the addition, about 90 C.E., of three clauses to the twelfth of the eighteen benedictions of the synagogue liturgy.[11] These are the so-called "blessing over the heretics" (*birket ha-minim*), which call down destruction upon the Christians (*notzrim*) and "sectarians" (*minim*). There has been considerable debate over whether the *minim* are in fact the Judeo-Christians who had accepted the messiahship of Jesus but continued to frequent the synagogue, or whether they were an entirely distinct group, a sect of Jewish Gnostics, for example. But as Forkman points out, to cast this imprecation in the form of a regular and mandatory synagogue prayer

---

[10] See G. Forkman, *The Limits of Religious Community* (Lund: Gleerup, 1972).

[11] Text in *C. K. Barrett, *The New Testament Background* (New York: Harper Torchbook, 1961), pp. 166-167; cf. *S. Sandmel, *Judaism and Christian Beginnings* (London: Oxford University Press pb., 1978), pp. 149-150; Forkman, *Limits*, pp. 90-91.

made the curse its own effective fulfillment without trial or further process.

Under the rabbis there were other, more formal ways of distancing the offender. They ranged from a reprimand to a temporary ban (*nidduy*) to full expulsion (*herem*) from the community.[12] Many of the grounds are presented as disrespect for the rabbis, but it is probable that this was interpreted in a formal rather than a personal sense, and included failure to observe the rabbis' legal enactments. The Nasi and the courts could impose such bans, of course, but it is interesting to observe that any Jew could do the same if he or she observed a gross infraction of the Law.

The Nasi's political powers were created, in a sense, by the Roman authorities, who chose to deal with him as the official representative of the Jews of the empire, and all the evidence points to general Jewish acceptance of the Nasi's acting as such.[13] He was granted most of the honors accorded to a client king in the Roman Empire, and was granted dispensation from various provisions of the Law to ease his necessary dealings with Gentiles.

At about the same time as the Romans were recognizing the Nasi as Patriarch, a parallel institution, that of the Exilarch (Resh Galuta), was emerging under the Parthian dynasty in Iraq and Iran. Though the origins of the Babylonian office are somewhat obscure, it seems likely that about 70 C.E. the Parthians did formally recognize a single head for the various Jewish communities living in their Iraqi provinces, that the official in question claimed Davidic descent, and that, like his counterpart on the Roman side of the frontier, he had considerable power, including the disposition of a police force.[14] The Parthian Exilarch differed from the Roman Patriarch, however, in having powerful rivals in the

[12] Their terms and modalities are examined in Forkman, *Limits*, pp. 92-105, and Mantel, *Sanhedrin*, pp. 225-227.

[13] Mantel, *Sanhedrin*, pp. 235-253.

[14] J. Neusner, *A History of the Jews in Babylonia* (Leiden: E. J. Brill, 1969), I, 53-61, 103-118; II, 92-95.

Palestinian-trained rabbis who staffed and directed the Babylonian academies (*yeshibot*). The relationship between the Resh Galuta and the rabbinic community in the Iranian Empire was an uneasy one, and jurisdictional and political questions often divided them.[15]

The institution that succeeded both the patriarchate and the gradually disintegrating exilarchate illustrates the triumph within Judaism of the *yeshibot* and their rabbis over all other competitors, social and political. When the Muslims came to power in the Near East in the seventh century C.E., they adopted the same kind of system favored by their predecessors: groups that constituted some kind of religio-social unity outside the Muslim community were treated as semiautonomous entities, which in much later Islamic times came to be called *millets*, and were permitted a considerable degree of self-regulation. Christianity, with its well-established hierarchical structure, presented few problems in this regard, but when the Muslims had to choose a representative of the Jewish community to the centralized caliphate, they turned to the prestigious "eminences" (*geonim*) who headed the two great *yeshibot* of Sura and Pumbeditha. Palestine had its own Gaon, and he too was a rabbi who stood at the head of the Galilean academies.

Judaism under medieval Islam was much what it had been under Christianity, though without many of the religious and political pressures, and in the full enjoyment of the new economic prosperity that came to the Near East in the wake of the Muslim conquest.[16] The Jews who lived in this net-

[15] Ibid., IV, 41-94; V, 73-124.

[16] See S. D. Goitein, *Jews and Arabs: Their Contact Through the Ages* (New York: Schocken pb., 1964) and S. Baron, *Social and Religious History of the Jews* (New York: Columbia University Press, 1957), III, 120-172; IV, pp. 150-230. These are summary accounts, but in the great mass of documents found in the storehouse (*geniza*) of a Cairo synagogue we have a detailed view of almost all phases of Jewish life under Islam from the mid-tenth to the mid-thirteenth centuries; see S. D. Goitein, *A Mediterranean Society: The Jewish Communities of the Arab World as Portrayed in the Documents of the Cairo Geniza*, 3 vols. (Berkeley and Los Angeles: California University Press,

work of communities across the face of the Islamic empire probably felt some kind of ethnic identity—culturally they were eventually Arabized, though Hebrew and Aramaic continued in use as learned and liturgical languages—but their more deeply felt bond was, as it had been for many centuries, a common observance of the Mosaic Law and its Talmudic corollaries, and a longing for Zion.[17] That bond was preserved and fostered by the rabbis. Efforts were made to standardize and simplify for reading purposes the text of the Bible.[18] More, the rabbis had been trained in a common legal tradition, and so accepted on behalf of themselves and their communities the religious and legal authority of the *geonim*. For their part, the *geonim* intervened directly in the lives of the various communities by setting the liturgical lunar calendar and enunciating legal responsa for the resolution of disputes that could not be settled locally.[19]

THE CHRISTIAN CHURCH

The earliest Christian community was not unlike a Pharisaic *habura* or a Qumran *yahad*. Like the former, it had a formal table-fellowship with a common meal (*agape*), though

1967-1978). For the later life of these same communities, see H. Z. Hirschberg, "The Oriental Jewish Communities" in A. J. Arberry, ed., *Religions in the Middle East* (Cambridge: Cambridge University Press, 1969), I, 119-225, and N. Stillman, *The Jews of Arab Lands* (New York: Jewish Publication Society, 1979).

[17] See, for example, Judah Halevi (d. 1141), the Spanish physician, poet, and scholar who marshals in his Kuzari (see Chapter VIII below) arguments drawn from the natural sciences to demonstrate the superiority of Palestine as the home of prophecy: I. Heinemann, trans., in *Three Jewish Philosophers* (Utica: Meridien pb., 1961), pp. 64-70.

[18] See G. Lampe, ed., *The Cambridge History of the Bible* (Cambridge: Cambridge University Press, 1970), II, 1-26.

[19] Adherence to a common liturgical calendar is a common measure of orthodoxy; see the case of Qumran described in Vermes, *Qumran in Perspective*, pp. 176-178, and the Christian dispute over the date of the celebration of Easter in *J. G. Davies, *The Early Christian Church* (Garden City: Doubleday Anchor pb., 1967), pp. 121-122.

the Eucharistic communion was already at a considerable symbolic and liturgical remove from the Pharisaic *habura*. And like the Qumran *yahad*, it was a community united in eschatological expectation. The Christians held common prayer services on the model of a synagogue liturgy, and there was a familiar Jewish program of philanthropy to take care of widows and orphans. Jesus' immediate disciples stood at the head of the community, and at *their* head stood James, "the brother of the Lord."

As is clear from the Acts of the Apostles, James did not act alone at Jerusalem, as a later bishop might; he was a first among peers. But it is equally clear that he was in a real sense the head of the congregation (*ekklesia*) there, and that he was succeeded in that office by other of Jesus' relations, all of them practicing Jews of strict Temple observance. Elsewhere other congregations came into being, often in connection with Jewish synagogue communities in the Diaspora, and there were appointed "elders" (*presbyteroi*) to govern them.

From the beginning, Jesus' followers had to face the question of their own Jewishness. Hellenized and Pharisaic Jews made poor bedfellows and worse tablemates, inside or outside the Christian community, but Jesus' own exaltation of the act of faith in himself over a strict observance of the Law raised even larger issues. Jesus, who did not observe a marked degree of ritual purity, might fit ill into a strict Christian *habura*, but Gentiles would scarcely fit at all. Some accommodation had to be worked out, at least for a time, but Paul for one refused to surrender the issue to pragmatic solutions.

Paul's attitude toward the Jewish Law must be placed inside the context of his thinking about the Church. In Jesus' own words, a New Covenant had been sealed by his death and resurrection; a new Chosen People, a new Bene Yisrael had been elected—a notion strongly underlined in the Letter to the Hebrews, which was included in the New Testament canon.[20]

---

[20] This letter has been observed at length by Hans Küng in his *The Church* (New York: Doubleday Image pb., 1976), pp. 147-200.

The original *berit* (Covenant) had been accompanied by laws governing the behavior of God's people, laws regulating purity and sacrifice. The New Covenant had no need of such laws, in Paul's view. Jesus now dwelt in the body itself, transforming it from within. Each Christian was his own temple and his own priest: the new sacrifice was eucharistic.[21]

Paul gave elaborate directions for the regulation of discipline within the Christian communities with which he was in contact. But this guidance was based on his own claims to be an Apostle; more generally the governance of individual congregations fell to the "elders" of that congregation, and to one of them who, like James at Jerusalem, was a collegiate first among equals. Already at the end of the first century, in the letters of Ignatius, for example, that *primus inter pares* was taking on a special status as "overseer" (*episkopos*) or bishop, who was coming to be recognized as the single "successor of the Apostles" and so the bearer and interpreter of the authentic Christian tradition.[22] But whereas the ordination (*semika*) of their Jewish counterparts appears to have been a simple act of delegation, the Christians' "laying on of hands" or ordination of the priestly presbyters, and par excellence of the bishops, was a charismatic act. Bishops were ordained by other bishops as part of the Apostolic succession; presbyters were ordained by the bishops of their own communities, whose delegates they were in the performance of liturgical functions.

With the spread of the new beliefs and the appearance of Christian communities both within and without the Roman Empire, the individual parts of the Great Church began to arrange themselves, as neither Judaism nor Islam was to do, in an organic and hierarchical system. The local government of the bishop had sound precedent in the early practice of the Church, and the passage of the Christian message at first created no great discrepancies in the practice of the local

[21] Ibid., pp. 465–495.
[22] Ibid., pp. 510–528.

churches that constituted the Great Church. But the simple relationship between the bishop and his community yielded to considerably more complex arrangements once Constantine had embraced the Great Church as his own.[23]

The social, political, and economic consequences of the emperor's conversion constrained the local churches to fashion for themselves, and for the Great Church, an organizational structure congruent with their new responsibilities. In some instances, existing institutions were adapted, some of them going back to Apostolic times; in others, totally new offices were created. And in almost every instance the model followed by the Church was the parallel institution of the Roman Empire. The bishops within a single region began to conform to the hierarchical municipal pattern of that region: metropolis, cities, towns, and even villages had bishops at their head, but the bishop of the metropolis or provincial capital—he was later called an archbishop—had precedence and jurisdiction over the others.[24]

Theoretically all bishops were equal in the light of the Apostolic succession, but some were clearly more equal than others in the light of Roman provincial organization. The arrangement did not yet do much violence to historical reality; the Church had in fact spread from Jerusalem through large metropolitan centers such as Alexandria, Antioch, and Rome. But Rome was the most equal of all. It had a true claim to the Apostolic succession in Peter and Paul, who early carried the Gospel there; it was, moreover, no mere provincial capital but the head of the empire. The evidence is unmistakable that the bishop of Rome was indeed accorded a kind of primacy of honor among his episcopal and archepiscopal peers.[25]

The question of absolute primacy never arose in the early

[23] See A.H.M. Jones, *Constantine and the Conversion of Europe* (New York: Collier pb., 1962).

[24] A.H.M. Jones, *The Later Roman Empire*, 3 vols. (Oxford: Blackwell, 1964), II, 874-894.

[25] *Davies, *Christian Church*, pp. 124, 180-181.

Church. The presence of many venerable and flourishing centers of Christianity, each ruled by a bishop who stood in a direct and equal line of descent from the Apostolic tradition would have rendered such claims nonsense. Absolute primacy arose only when multiplicity had been reduced to polarity, when Rome and Constantinople, where Constantine had transferred the imperial capital in 330 C.E., each stood alone at the head of a separate spiritual, cultural, and political tradition. Rome did intervene in the affairs of other churches from the beginning; no one protested, and there are even examples of the Roman church being appealed to in certain cases. It is only in the fourth century that the bishops of Rome, who bore, like the bishop of Alexandria, the unofficial title of "Pope," began to insist on their de jure right of final jurisdiction based on Peter's position vis-à-vis the other Apostles.[26]

This particular line of argumentation found its definitive expression in the sermons of Leo, bishop of Rome between 440-461 C.E., who claimed, on his Petrine authority, universal jurisdiction. The Council of Chalcedon in 451 C.E., although accepting Leo's doctrinal formulation of a solution to the theological problem of Monophysitism, did not accept the Petrine argument. Its twenty-eighth canon spelled out the message in unmistakable terms: the emperor and the Senate were now in Constantinople, which now had equal privileges with the Old Rome, and ranked second after it in protocol order. Rome, which supplied the theology of the council, did not put its name to Canon 28; the eastern bishops did. Rome and its natural rival on the Bosphorus were only beginning their poisonous struggle. Their first formal rupture occurred as early as 484 C.E., and over the succeeding centuries the relationship between Latin Pope and Greek Patriarch went from bitterness to bitterness.[27]

[26] *H. Bettenson, *Documents of the Christian Church* (London: Oxford pb., 1970), pp. 111-116.

[27] B. J. Kidd, *The Roman Primacy to A.D. 461* (London: SPCK, 1936); W.H.C. Frend, *The Rise of the Monophysite Movement* (Cambridge: Cam-

The Christian "tradition," as will be seen, was clear-cut in its ideological base but rather ill-defined in its content. New converts might be required to present it in the summary form of a "creed" at their baptism. Many of these latter were simple statements, no more complex than the Muslim profession of faith, but adequate to set the Christian off from his pagan contemporaries. They by no means exhausted the Apostolic tradition, which was being energetically explored by Christians who no longer came from Jewish backgrounds, where behavior in accordance with prescribed norms was the most common measurement of community association, but from a Hellenized Gentile milieu with its own highly developed theology.

Views of the tradition were everywhere put forward, and judgments about the congruence of such views with the understood limits of that tradition was the responsibility of the bishops. But what seemed within the limits of a commonly received tradition in one church did not always seem to be so in another community, and the question had to be taken up in a wider context. Bishops gathered in synods, much like the one held early on in Jerusalem to settle the gentile question. After the issue had been debated and resolved, the decisions of the bishops were recorded in the official "acts" of these provincial or regional synods, and were followed by a set of anathemas imposing excommunication—normally exclusion from the sacramental life of the Church—upon those who held to the contrary.[28]

What was being constructed by these synods was a more and more detailed definition of the Apostolic tradition, which was accompanied by increasingly sophisticated creeds that were no longer simple baptismal formulas but could be applied as a test for orthodoxy and heresy. The term of the

bridge University Press, 1972), pp. 145-147, 181-183; S. Runciman, *The Eastern Schism* (London: Oxford University Press, 1955); F. Dvornik in J. M. Hussey, ed., *The Cambridge Medieval History* (Cambridge: Cambridge University Press, 1966), IV/1, pp. 431-472.

[28] *Davies, *Christian Church*, p. 280.

process came with the summoning by the new Christian emperor Constantine of an Ecumenical Council of Nicea in 325 C.E. At it the bishops of the Great Church were asked to deal with a theological issue that affected the entire community of Christians. The Ecumenical Council of Nicea produced a creed that addressed itself not merely to the general outlines of the Christian tradition but to the specific issues raised by Arius and his teachings.[29]

Christianity had, then, two means of defining itself on an ongoing basis: the individual bishop's charismatic and Apostolic oversight of his own congregation, and a conciliar or synodal instrument that could speak authoritatively to more general questions through a form of consensus. The positive consequence of the employment of these instruments was dogma; the negative, heresy.[30] Heresy did not begin with Nicea, of course. Jesus had foreseen it for his followers, and the pages of Paul's letters are filled with instructions and warnings against preachers of false gospels; Eusebius traced all heresy back to Simon Magus, a contemporary of Peter. What the early conciliar movement did was to institutionalize the episcopal magisterium and, by formally defining dogma, so institutionalize heresy.

Within the post-Exilic period, Judaism proceeded from temple-state to monarchy to a religious community with ethnic associations but no political identity save the shadowy *millet* status granted it by the Roman, Sasanian, and Islamic empires and exercised through the office of Nasi, Resh Galuta, or Gaon. Christianity came into existence near the apocalyptic end of Jewish statehood and grew to maturity in the same environment and with much the same status as rabbinic Judaism. Christians were at first confused with Jews by the Romans, but once the distinction was made in Rome, the Christian Church, which had neither precedent nor the ap-

[29] Two versions in *Bettenson, *Documents*, pp. 36-37; cf. *Davies, *Christian Church*, pp. 262-264.

[30] W. Bauer, *Orthodoxy and Heresy* (Philadelphia: Fortress Press, 1971); H. Turner, *The Pattern of Christian Truth*, (London: SPCK, 1954).

propriate ethnic characteristics, could not even aspire to mil-lethood.

The spiritual climate of the times, which A. D. Nock and E. R. Dodds have brilliantly portrayed, was perhaps ripe for a religious revival.[31] But it was also a period in which the masters of the Roman Empire were suffering their own po-litical anxieties, which they blamed on religious causes, with the Christians as their target. Between 177 and 312 C.E., the Church underwent a series of persecutions that have been described in detail by W.H.C. Frend, *Martyrdom and Perse-cution in the Early Church*.[32] According to Frend, the Church's accommodation with the political power came far earlier in the East than in the Western Church, a division of attitude that he already finds in post-Exilic Judaism. In Palestine, the Maccabean movement had created an atmosphere of deep distrust of secular authority, which would be resolved only in apocalypse of the End Time; in the Diaspora, where Jew had perforce to adapt to Greek, there flourished the more optimistic hope of conversion.

Judaism surrendered this hope after 70 C.E., but it bore remarkable fruits for the Christians, who maintained it per-haps as early as 260 C.E., when, despite continual persecu-tions, the balance began to tip toward Christianity.[33] But the end of the persecutions brought the Church directly into the embrace of an emperor who was openly friendly to Christi-anity; who lavished gifts on the Church and immunities on its ministers; and who turned Rome into a Holy City and Palestine into a Holy Land. The simple evangelical prescrip-tion to render their appropriate dues to Caesar and to God was obviously of little use in a society in which Caesar con-sidered himself an instrument of God, an "equal of the Apos-tles." Beginning with Constantine himself, the emperors could

[31] Nock, *Conversion* (London: Oxford University Press pb., 1961); Dodds, *Pagan and Christian in an Age of Anxiety* (New York: Norton pb., 1965).

[32] New York: New York University Press, 1967; documents in *Betten-son, *Documents*, pp. 10-22.

[33] Frend, *Martyrdom*, pp. 324-350.

and did intervene in ecclesiastical affairs. They summoned ecumenical councils at which they themselves presided, published dogmatic formulae, supervised the good order of the clergy, created new bishoprics, filled and emptied existing ones, and in general exercised a considerable degree of authority in the Church.[34]

The Church for its part could intervene in the affairs of state on the same high level. Religious figures had been influential with emperors before Constantine, but once the emperor became Christian he was subject not only to the spiritual authority of the bishop of Constantinople or Rome, but to the divinely sanctioned laws of the Church as well. The Christianization of the empire, for all the loyalty the Christians demonstrated for both the prince and the principate, was the single most effective curb on the growing absolutism of the Roman Emperor.[35] Emperors were branded as heretics, excommunicated, and successfully opposed on occasion by both the episcopate and that other source of power in the Church, the monastic establishment.[36]

ISLAMIC UMMAH AND THE DAR AL-ISLAM

Christianity had three centuries to brace for the shock of finding itself the part proprietor of a Christian Roman Empire. Islam was from its inception both a religious and a political association; Muhammad was his own Constantine. In 622 C.E. he accepted an invitation to leave his native Mecca, where he was the charismatic leader of a small conventicle of believers, and to emigrate to Medina as the ruler of a

[34] F. Dvornik, *Early Christian and Byzantine Political Philosophy*, 2 vols. (Washington, D.C.: Dumbarton Oaks, 1966), and J. Hussey, ed., *The Cambridge Medieval History*, IV/2 (Cambridge: Cambridge University Press, 1964), 7-13, 104-106.

[35] K. M. Setton, *The Christian Attitude toward the Emperor in the Fourth Century* (New York: Columbia University Press, 1941) and R. M. Grant, *Early Christianity and Society* (New York: Harper and Row, 1977), pp. 13-43.

[36] See Chapter IV below.

faction-ridden community of Arabs and Jews. This was a crucial period in Muhammad's life, and the years following his "emigration" (*hijrah*; Eng., hegira) were spent in trying to forge some kind of community (*ummah*) in accordance with his religious principles and the political realities of the situation.[37] The first *ummah* at Medina was not yet a fully Islamic association—both Jews and pagan Arabs were included—but as Muhammad's political fortunes began to prosper, religious considerations came to the fore. The Jewish tribes of Medina were purged from the coalition, and the pagans were dragged willy-nilly into it; the *ummah* became a community of believers who accepted the dominion of Allah and both the prophethood and the leadership of Muhammad.

These were not artificial associations. Muhammad's role as a prophet (*nabi*) within a community that he himself had summoned into being necessarily included the functions of legislator, executive, and military commander of the *ummah*.[38] God's revelations continued to spill from his lips. Now they were not only threats and warnings to nonbelievers, but more often legislative enactments regulating community life, and particularly the relations of one Muslim with another.

Muhammad no more appointed a successor than Jesus had. In the case of Christianity, immediate eschatological expectations made that seem a natural course of events, but there is no trace of such expectations in Islam, and the *ummah* undertook to guarantee its own political survival by choosing someone to lead its members. They reverted to a type of tribal selection, and the choice of the senior Muslims was designated "Successor (*khalifah*; Eng., Caliph) of the Envoy of God." He was no such thing, of course—the prophetic line was ended by Muhammad's own declaration—but from the manner in which the earliest Caliphs acted we can get

---

[37] M. Rodinson, *Mohammed* (New York: Random House, 1974), pp. 148-214 and W. M. Watt, *Muhammad at Medina* (London: Oxford University Press, 1956); *M. Hodgson, *The Venture of Islam* (Chicago: Chicago University Press pb., 1974), I, pp. 172-199.

[38] Rodinson, *Mohammed*, pp. 215-292.

some very imprecise idea of what were thought to be the powers of that office.

The Caliph was, in fact, chief executive of the *ummah*. He appointed and removed political subordinates. He decided military strategy and was commander (*amir*) of the armies of Islam. He was the chief judge and chief fiscal officer of the new regime. Most of the Caliph's military, judicial, and fiscal responsibilities were soon delegated to others, however; the community was actually a number of armies on the march far from the centers of power, and though decisions might be made in the name of the Caliph, they were increasingly made by others.

The Caliph and his delegates might decide, but they could not or did not legislate. They now had the closed and completed Qur'an, and they could not add to that text which, like Jewish law, addressed itself in great detail to matters of personal status, but was mute on the political governance of what was rapidly becoming an immense empire. The Caliph and his delegates resorted instead to a great many devices to shape their purpose: tribal practices, local customs, pragmatic necessities, and, to some extent, whatever precedents the practice of the Prophet suggested to them. There is no suggestion, on the other hand, that the Caliph regarded himself or was regarded by others as the possessor of special spiritual powers. He was the head of the *ummah*, and though the *ummah* was based entirely on a shared acceptance of Islam, the Caliph was not a religious leader but the leader of a religion.

It was the Caliphs, the earliest ones at any rate, who had to face a problem that Muhammad himself had forestalled only with the greatest difficulty during his lifetime. There was a tension in the community from the beginning between the notion of Islam as a universal religion that claimed the allegiance of all men, and that of the Arabs as a final version of the "Chosen People." The phrase is Judaism's own, of course, and speaks to God's election of Israel as a fellow in His covenant. Muhammad's own perspective was perhaps

63

somewhat different. He knew, from his own understanding of history, that previous revelations had constituted their recipients a community, an *ummah*. It had been true of the Jews and Christians and now, in the final act of the drama of revelation, it would be so with the Arabs.

If this revelation of a "clear Arabic Qur'an" through an Arab prophet to Arabs of western Arabia was calculated to create a sense of unity among those peoples, the project cannot be judged entirely a success. Muhammad had problems with tribal rivalries in his own day, between the mighty and the low in the complex hierarchy of tribes and clans that dominated not only his native Mecca but most of the Bedouin population of the peninsula. Boasting and vilification were common pre-Islamic instruments for establishing and maintaining that order, and though Muhammad decreed that the only aristocracy in Islam was that constituted by piety and merit, the tribal divisions of Arab society long outlived his efforts to suppress them in the name of either a single Arab *ummah* or of a universal religion for all mankind.[39]

With the death of the Prophet, the *ummah* rapidly began to disintegrate, and it was only through the most strenuous military efforts of his first successor, Abu Bakr (Caliph 632-634 C.E.), that Islam was reimposed upon the tribes across Arabia who had read the death of the Prophet as the death-knell of Islam, and declared their secession from the community. What followed was more subtle and perhaps more insidious in the long run. The enormous wealth that came to the community as booty and tribute was distributed according to a system devised by the second Caliph, Umar (Caliph 634-644 C.E.). It recognized and rewarded the merit of early conversion and a concomitant willingness to bear arms against the enemies of Islam, but in institutionalizing this system of rewards and pensions, Umar restored the distribution rights to tribal chieftains, permitted it to be done

[39] I. Goldziher, *Muslim Studies* (1898); revised translation by S. M. Stern (London: George Allen and Unwin, 1967), I, 45-97.

along tribal lines, and to be effected in the new Islamic garrison towns whose social organization was precisely tribal.[40]

The consequences of these purely administrative decisions were twofold, and each was far-reaching in its social impact. They preserved and perhaps reenforced the old pre-Islamic tribal rivalries, which continued to disturb the equilibrium of the Islamic body politic for at least a century afterward; and they conspired to create a distinction between Arab and non-Arab within the bosom of Islam. That distinction always existed, of course, save in that pre-Babel world when all mankind was one (Qur'an 10:19; 2:213), but it had a particular significance in an essentially tribal society where identity and its consequent social and political protections were claimed on the basis of birth. There are ways of associating with tribal societies even if one is not born into them, but one of the most common, fictive adoption and its resultant patron-client relationship, provides the *cliens* with status of a decidely inferior quality. What the *cliens* was to vestigial Roman tribalism, the *mawla* was to Arab tribal societies: a freed slave, protected but dependent. The concept was convenient enough to extend to the non-Arab converts to an Islamic society that had institutionalized itself into a Arab tribal one. It is not certain that Muhammad intended an egalitarian community; what emerged was a society where both tribal and ethnic rivalries died a very slowly lingering death.[41]

The caliphate, though an obvious pragmatic success, did not exhaust the possibilities of leadership in early Islam. There was among some Muslims the concept of the head of the community as a prayer-leader (Imam) or an eschatological chief or Mahdi, literally "The Guided One." The latter has been invoked from time to time in Islamic history as a challenge to the Caliph or a magnet around which to energize Muslim political action, but its successes have been short-

[40] The events and issues of the caliphates of Abu Bakr and Umar are described in M. A. Shaban, *Islamic History, A.D. 600-750: A New Interpretation* (Cambridge: Cambridge University Press, 1971), pp. 16-59.

[41] Goldziher, *Muslim Studies*, I, 98-136.

lived, and the figure of the Mahdi receded, like that of the Messiah in rabbinic Judaism, into an indefinite future.

The ideal of an Imam has had a very different history. In the nonsacramental and nonpriestly system that is Islam, leadership in prayer must soon have become what it was in synagogue Judaism, a kind of honor that could be bestowed upon any Muslim. Not so, said others: the imamate implied moral rectitude, and the Imam par excellence, the head of the entire community, must be the most moral of Muslims. This view had a brief vogue as the thrusting point of what W. M. Watt has called "the charismatic community" of the Kharijites, who held that salvation consists in membership in this new "communion of saints" that is Islam, and whose members were distinguishable only by their virtue and not by their clan or tribal associations.[42]

Another view of the imamate was put forward by the "partisans" (shi'ah) of 'Ali (Caliph 556-661 C.E.), Muhammad's nephew and son-in-law, who was the fourth Caliph of Islam. In its finished version, the Shi'ite vision of Islam regarded the imamate as a spiritual and religious office whereby a special charisma was transmitted through designated descendents of 'Ali down to the point in the tenth century C.E. when the historical Imam vanished, only to return in his eschatological role as Mahdi.[43]

These struggles about the nature of the Islamic community and its leadership, which were first described by Julius Wellhausen in his *Religio-Political Factions in Early Islam*,[44] are complicated by the fact that they chiefly appear in heresiographies as theological sects, whereas in fact they were

[42] *Hodgson, *Venture*, I, 256-258; W. M. Watt, *The Formative Period of Islamic Thought* (Chicago: Aldine, 1973), pp. 34-37; see E. Salem, *Political Theory and Institutions of the Khawarij* (Baltimore: Johns Hopkins University Press, 1956).

[43] Watt, *Formative Period*, pp. 36-62, 271-278; S. H. Jafri, *Origins and Early Development of Shi'a Islam* (London: Longmans, 1978).

[44] 1901; reprint New York: American Elsevier pb., 1975; cf. *H.A.R. Gibb, *Mohammedanism* (London: Oxford University Press pb., 1970), pp. 81-85.

deeply enmeshed in the politics of their time. By the time they were described as religious heresies, the majority of Muslims had settled into a view of themselves as "people of custom (*sunnah*) and the community (*jama'ah*)," frequently shortened to "Sunnis," a self-designation that Hodgson succinctly defined as "the majority of Muslims which accepts the authority of the whole first generation of Muslims and the validity of the historical community."[45] Those who undermined that community unity were guilty of "innovation," Islam's closest approximation to the notion of heresy, because they appealed away from history, now canonized as custom or tradition (*sunnah*), to special and particularist views.

The point at issue here is who shall rule the community. The Sunnis were willing to accept the verdict of history as reflected in the choices of that "whole first generation" of Muhammad's contemporaries and their immediate successors. The Shi'ites argued against history in asserting the preeminence of 'Ali, but in so doing they were forced, to one degree or another, to attack the consensual wisdom of the "Companions of the Prophet" from whom all the Prophetic *sunnah* ultimately derived. Disappointed by history, the Shi'ites turned where some Jewish groups may also have resorted, to a Gnostic wisdom, a kind of particularist and underground *sunnah* transmitted, generation after generation, by infallible Imams of the 'Alid house or by their delegates.[46] In fully developed Shi'ism, which found its most lasting base by connecting itself with Persian nationalism, the entire range of Gnostic ideas is on display: the exaltation of wisdom (*hikmah*) over science ('*ilm*); a view of historical events as reflection of cosmic reality; and a concealed (*batin*) as opposed to an "open" (*zahir*) interpretation of Scripture. It was simply a matter of time before Shi'ite Gnosticism found its siblings within Sufism and philosophy.[47]

---

[45] *★Venture*, I, 517.

[46] On Gnosticism, see Chapter VII below.

[47] On Sufism, see Chapter VII below, and on philosophy, Chapter VIII below.

Though the question of the caliphate or imamate was critical in early Islam, and was often debated precisely as such, there were others who took up the larger question of membership in the *ummah*.[48] One form of the issue was the distinction between *iman*, or faith, and *islam*, the act of submission to God. Both terms are used in the Qur'an, though Muhammad more often designated members of his community as "believers" or "the faithful" (*mu'minun*) than as "Muslims" (*muslimun*). As a matter of actual fact, however, membership in the community depended directly and exclusively, except in the case of the Kharijites, upon making an initial profession of faith (*shahadah*)—There is no god but The God and Muhammad is His Envoy—and a consequent sharing of community prayer and contribution of the alms-tithe.[49]

In this form the *shahadah* is purely a verbal formulation and leaves open the questions of interior intention and of the relative importance to be placed on interior faith and external good works. The Kharijites had placed a great emphasis upon the latter: whoever did not act like a Muslim was in fact not a Muslim, and should be treated accordingly. If the Kharijites were thereby willing to exclude the sinner (*fasiq*) as well as the disbeliever (*kafir*) from their midst, there were others such as Abu Hanifah who regarded faith (*iman*) as something separate from the moral activity of the individual Muslim.[50]

Neither view prevailed in the end. Abu Hanifah's definition of faith as "confessing with the tongue, believing with the mind, and knowing with the heart" was generally accepted as applicable to membership in the community of believers (*mu'minun*) whose profession rendered them subject

[48] Watt, *Formative Period*, pp. 119-143.

[49] On the *shahadah*, see A. J. Wensinck, *The Muslim Creed* (1932; reprint London: Frank Cass, 1965), pp. 1-16, and for later versions of the Muslim creed, Chapter VIII below.

[50] Wensinck, *Muslim Creed*, pp. 36-57; on the moral laxity that logically flowed from this position, see Watt, *Formative Period*, pp. 136-138.

to the Islamic Law.[51] All agreed, moreover, that the one un-
forgivable sin of polytheism (*shirk*) excluded one from that
community. As regards other grave sins such as murder and
fornication, eternal punishment in the afterlife was probable
but not inevitable. The sinner could only hope in God's
goodness and the Prophet's intercession; for their part, the
other Muslims here below must suspend judgment.

This agreeably tolerant attitude of suspending judgment
on the moral conduct of one's neighbor had some extremely
disagreeable political implications that were, in fact, the chief
point in the discussion. Postponement of judgment effectively removed the religious and moral issue from the political life of the Islamic empire. Its acceptance marked another
stage in the secularization of the caliphate, whose tenants could
no longer be challenged on the grounds of their personal
morality. The predestination argument led in the same direction—de facto was in fact de Deo. The predestination vs. free
will argument drifted off in another direction, into the meta-
physical thicket of atoms, accidents, and "acquisition," but
the "postponement" thesis held because it represented some
kind of ill-shaped Muslim consensus that custom and the
community were more important than tossing dead sinners
into hell and live ones out of office or out of the community.

If the lines among Muslims were interpreted generously,
the distinction between submission (*islam*) and disbelief (*kufr*)
was strenuously maintained. This was an absolute antago-
nism that cut across another distinction, that between the
Abode of Islam (Dar al-Islam), the geographical area under
Muslim political control, and the Abode of War (Dar al-Harb),
where the *ummah* did not prevail. Infidels could not be tolerated within the Dar al-Islam: they had either to accept Islam or perish. Their presence outside the Abode of Islam
created the moral imperative of holy war (*jihad*). It was the
only just form of war in Muslim legal theory, but it did not

[51] Wensinck, *Muslim Creed*, pp. 131-138; Watt, *Formative Period*, pp. 140-
141.

necessarily imply violence: the *jihad* might be waged with words as well as with the sword.[52]

There is an anomaly here. After the initial conquests of Islam, a good part of the Abode of War was under the control not of infidels but of Christian powers. Neither Jews nor Christians were infidels in Muslim eyes. They, and somewhat tardily the Zoroastrians of Iran, fell into the category of Peoples of the Book, that is, possessors of authentic Scripture that contained, albeit in humanly distorted form, a genuine divine revelation. They were under no compulsion to convert to Islam, and though they suffered certain minor— and variable—disabilities within the Dar al-Islam, they were protected by a special covenant with the Muslim community that guaranteed their lives, property, and the free exercise of their religious duties.[53]

The paradox of a ruler who possessed no direct religious powers governing a community whose common bond was the acceptance of Islam found its palliative in the growth of a body of Islamic Law that, from the ninth century onward, the Caliphs had to accept as normative.[54] The Law was administered, as Muslim affairs had been from the beginning, by a judge or *qadi* who was a caliphal appointee, and so an agent of government; but the actual control of the Law, its codification and subsequent modification, was in the hands of a body of jurisprudents known collectively as "the learned" or *'ulama*.

The *'ulama* were at first unofficial and unorganized students of the "traditions of the Prophet," but with the institution and spread of law schools (*madrasahs*), each supported

---

[52] See M. Khadduri, *The Islamic Law of Nations* (Baltimore: Johns Hopkins University Press, 1966), pp. 10-22, and his *War and Peace in Islam* (Baltimore: Johns Hopkins University Press, 1955).

[53] A. S. Tritton, *The Caliphs and Their Non-Muslim Subjects* (London: Oxford University Press, 1955); F. E. Peters, *Allah's Commonwealth* (New York: Simon and Schuster, 1973), pp. 49-51, 84-86, 449-452; *Hodgson, *Venture*, I, 305-308, 447-448.

[54] See Chapter IV below.

by a permanent and inalienable endowment (*waqf*), the *ʿulama* acquired a remarkable power and cohesiveness. The jurisprudents had their differences, of course, on both detail and theory, which in time resolved themselves into four major schools (*madhahib*) of legal interpretaton in Sunni Islam. But in the end they agreed to differ, and, more importantly, to accept each other's orthodoxy.[55]

It is tempting to see in the *ʿulama* the rabbis of Islam. In a sense the comparison is just. Both groups constituted a relatively well-defined class that enjoyed the power and prestige of a religious elite, and both received a standardized education in jurisprudence in an institutionalized setting. Neither were legislators in the strict sense, but both rabbis and *ʿulama* were at the same time the conservative guardians and the cautiously innovative exegetes of a long and complex legal tradition.

But there were important differences. The rabbis were assigned a political role among their fellow Jews, first by the Romans and Sasanians and then by their Muslim masters. The Jews were granted a degree of community autonomy in the *millet* system under which they lived in the Roman and Sasanian empires as well as the Dar al-Islam, and the rabbis served, by delegation and with the acceptance of their coreligionists, as the administrators of that restricted autonomy. They not only maintained a legal tradition; they also administered it, as judges and surrogates of a higher judicial authority, that of the Patriarch, Exilarch, or the *geonim*.

The *ʿulama*, on the other hand, were only one element among the classes and elites contesting for power in the Dar al-Islam. Before Ottoman times they neither possessed nor delegated any political authority, and they eschewed the administration of the *shariʿah*, a task that fell to the government-appointed and supported *qadi*. Their power lay elsewhere, in the prestige they enjoyed as the custodians of the

---

[55] On the evolution of the legal schools, see *J. Schacht, *An Introduction to Islamic Law* (London: Oxford University Press, 1964), pp. 57-75.

obviously Islamic component in what was professedly an Islamic society; in their independence of the state, which they could castigate or applaud as circumstances dictated; and in the network of marriages by which they could forge ties with other powerful classes like the large landowners and the wholesale merchants.[56] Unlike their episcopal counterparts, the *ulama* did not hold the keys of the kingdom in their hands; they could neither bind nor loose nor force a Caliph to his knees or out of the Church. But power they possessed, a genuine political power. Like their Jesuit contemporaries in Europe, they educated an Islamic intelligentsia in their school system: after the eleventh century higher education across the face of Islam was uniquely an *ulama*-inspired and directed education in *madrasahs* where they shaped Islamic consciences and indeed Islam itself through the instrument of the *shari'ah*.

[56] *Hodgson, *Venture*, II, 108-125; and for case studies of the influence of the *ulama* class, see R. Bulliet, *The Patricians of Nishapur* (Cambridge: Harvard University Press, 1972), and N. Keddie, ed., *Scholars, Saints and Sufis* (Los Angeles and Berkeley: University of California Press pb., 1978).

CHAPTER IV

The Law

THE tradition of a society governed by law is a very old one in the Near East, and where societies were governed by sovereigns whose powers were intimately bound up with divine descent, designation, or approbation, the distinction between secular and religious law is not easily or even profitably made. The Israelites were no exception in this regard, and even the oldest parts of the Bible contain legal codes not very dissimilar from those we find among the Babylonians and Canaanites.[1] Then, with the return from the Exile, there is silence. The text of the Torah was complete, and there would be no more absolute Scriptural ordinances (*mitzvot*). What we have in place of the direct written testimony of the earlier period is circumstantial evidence for continued legal activity among the Jews: the presence of a class of scribes (*soferim*) devoted to the study of Scripture, and part of whose activity must surely have been legal in nature; and the existence from Maccabean times onward of the Pharisees, whose chief preoccupation was the Mosaic Law. But for all this we know of no legal enactments (*halakot*) that can be unhesitatingly attributed to either the scribes or the Pharisees.[2]

In attempting to understand the Jewish legal tradition between the Exile and the beginnings of the Talmud, there are two other directions in which one might turn, to Philo and to whatever legal evidence can be elicited from the Dead Sea

[1] See T. J. Meek, *Hebrew Origins* (New York: Harper Torchbook, 1960), pp. 49-81; and cf. *L. Ginzberg, *On Jewish Law and Lore* (New York: Atheneum pb., 1970), pp. 153-158.

[2] So J. Neussner, *The Rabbinic Traditions about the Pharisees before 70*, 3 vols. (Leiden: E. J. Brill, 1971), but compare Z. Falk, *Introduction to Jewish Law of the Second Commonwealth*, 2 parts (Leiden: E. J. Brill, 1972, 1978).

Scrolls. Philo, the Hellenized Jewish intellectual of Alexandria, was not much interested in the *halakot* as such, and yet he was engaged in commenting, from his own Hellenized philosophical point of view, on the legal books of the Bible, and so it is possible to understand something at least of his view of the positive precepts of the Law—those concerning the Sabbath, for example. Philo, it has been maintained, followed Palestinian practice, or, with equal emphasis, was chiefly influenced by Greco-Egyptian legal custom. The truth may lie somewhere in between the two theses, though what "Palestinian practice" was in Philo's day is not easy to discern.[3]

The Dead Sea Scrolls have provided a new and unexpected glimpse into the evolution of Jewish Law.[4] Though the community was admittedly sectarian, we must recall that there was probably no truly "normative" Judaism in the centuries just before and after the beginning of the Christian era, and that the Qumran Covenanters, and so their view of *halaka*, may fruitfully be compared with other contemporary Jewish views of the Law and its derived positive prescriptions.

Two facts emerge at once: the Qumran community, like most other Jewish groups, derived its laws from an exegesis (*midrash*) of Scripture, and at the same time it had no recourse to a theory of an oral law like that (later?) proposed by the rabbis. Indeed, the Essenes at Qumran did not hesitate to write down and publicly promulgate in the form of lists or orders their exegetically derived *halakot*.[5] When it came to exegesis, they did, however, draw an interesting distinction. All law was contained in Scripture, including the Prophets, but although some precepts flow from a plain understanding of the text, other "hidden" precepts can be derived only by the special understanding possessed by the "Sons of Zadok."[6]

---

[3] So S. Belkin, *Philo and the Oral Law* (Cambridge: Harvard University Press, 1940).

[4] See especially L. Schiffman, *The Halakhah at Qumran* (Leiden: E. J. Brill, 1975).

[5] Summary in Schiffman, *Halakhah at Qumran*, pp. 75-76.

[6] Ibid., pp. 22-32.

The "hidden precepts" of the Essenes are not the legal siblings of the rabbis' oral law, since this latter included *halakot* not explicitly derived from the written Torah, an alien notion at Qumran. The Scrolls' "hidden precepts" stand rather closer to a Gnostic understanding of Scripture that distinguished, in all its manifestations, between a "plain" and a "hidden" sense of Revelation, the latter the privileged terrain of the adepts of the community.[7] The question of the oral law apart, the community at Qumran shows little that is surprising or anomalous in the evolution of Jewish Law.

Post-Exilic Judaism is absolutely consistent in deriving its positive law directly from Scripture, narrowly from the Torah and somewhat more widely, on occasion, from the Prophets as well. Essenes, Pharisees and Hellenizers, rabbis and Karaites all turned to God's revealed Word for instruction on the good to be done and the evil to be avoided. There were differences, of course, on how literally or broadly the scrutiny (*midrash*) of Scripture should be conducted, but none on the fact that Scripture was the fount and origin of the Law. Where the fundamental disagreement arose was on the question of whether there was any other source from which religious law might be derived. The Sadducees, Essenes, and Karaites denied that there was such; the Pharisees, followed by the rabbis and the main body of medieval Judaism, affirmed the existence of a "tradition from the Fathers" that was an equally authoritative matrix of *halakot*.

The genesis and evolution of this "tradition from the Fathers" is overgrown, like much else in the study of revelational religions, with claims of absolute antiquity: "from the Fathers" meant at base from Moses and so from God. All the historian can do is to note that the claim for such was first advanced by the Pharisees, as both Josephus and the Gospels bear witness, and that the claim was denied explicitly by the Sadducees and implicitly by the Essenes. It has long been assumed that the Pharisees' "tradition from the Fathers" was in fact the "Unwritten Torah" frequently al-

[7] See Chapter V below.

luded to in the Talmud,[8] and Birger Gerhardsson in his *Memory and Manuscript* attempted to sketch the mechanics of the presumed oral tradition that lay behind both.[9]

Gerhardsson's rather traditional thesis has recently been subjected to severe criticism, and Jacob Neusner has found no evidence from before 70 C.E. of claims that there was an oral tradition that preserved the actual words of Mosaic precepts not included in the written Torah.[10] Nor is there any sign before that same date of a professional class of reciters or memorizers who, like the *tannaim* and *amoraim* of the rabbinic era, were a necessary condition of such an oral tradition.[11]

If we conclude with Neusner that the notion of an "oral Torah" that claimed to reproduce the exact words of halakic prescriptions given to Moses was the creation of the rabbis who reconstituted the foundations of Jewish life in the dark years after 70 C.E., it does not follow, of course, that the content of those legal traditions has no claim to antiquity, though how ancient it might be we cannot guess. Where one is on somewhat firmer ground is in tracing the redaction of those traditions from oral to written form as the Mishna.

It is probably incorrect to think of the Mishna as a written book in the modern sense, at least in the beginning, since no one of the sages who commented upon it ever refers to a written document. It is perhaps more accurate to suppose that from the time of Rabbi Akiba (ca. 135 C.E.) onward there were in circulation written *halakot*, and that when these had been collected and arranged, they were committed to memory by a professional reciter, a *tanna*; and that once the

[8] So the Babylonian *gemara* to the Mishnaic tractate *Erubin* translated by Neusner, *Rabbinic Traditions*, III, 143, and the classic text from *Pirke Abot* cited in *C. K. Barrett, *The New Testament Background* (New York: Harper Torchbook, 1961), pp. 139-142.

[9] Uppsala, C.W.K. Gleerup, 1961.

[10] *Rabbinic Traditions*, III, 143-179 on the entire question of the oral tradition.

[11] Ibid., pp. 152-153.

whole had been memorized and recited, it was regarded as "published," that is, it possessed a canonical authority.[12] Subsequent additions were made down to the time of Rabbi Judah (ca. 170-217 C.E.), called "The Prince," who made a new and, as it turned out, definitive edition of the Mishna.[13]

There is some evidence of what did and did not go into Rabbi Judah's Mishna and why. *Halakot* cited by Judah's successors from one or other of his predecessors but not included in his Mishna are known generically as *baraita* or "additional material,"[14] and there is, moreover, a rather formal collection of such material in the Tosefta or Supplement.[15] Its author is anonymous and his purpose unclear, but the arrangement of the legal material in it and its manner of dealing with the *halakot* already supposes the existence of the Mishna.[16] And when we compare the considerably more diffuse *baraita* with the Mishna, we can observe what Judah, and probably Akiba before him, had done: compress, abbreviate, and refine a great body of legal argument and discussion.

As we possess it, Judah's Mishna is divided into six "orders" (*sedarim*) that are devoted to the most minute details of the laws governing: 1. agricultural produce and the shares of it owed to the priests and Levites ("Seeds"); 2. the prescribed holy days ("Festivals"); 3. women ("Women"); 4. property,

[12] Lieberman, *Hellenism in Jewish Palestine*, pp. 89-99: "The Publication of the Mishnah." On the derivation of *tanna/tannaim*, see *H. L. Strack, *Introduction to the Talmud and Midrash* (New York: Jewish Publication Society pb., 1959), p. 4. The generations of the *tannaim* from the disciples of Hillel and Shammai down to the younger contemporaries of Rabbi Judah are listed ibid., pp. 109-119.

[13] A. Guttman, *Rabbinic Judaism in the Making* (Detroit: Wayne State University Press, 1970), pp. 237-255; cf. *Strack, *Introduction*, pp. 20-25 and *Ginzberg, *On Jewish Law and Lore*, pp. 159-164; English translation by H. Danby, *The Mishnah* (London: Oxford University Press, 1933).

[14] *Strack, *Introduction*, pp. 4-5.

[15] There are examples of the *Tosefta* in English in W. Oesterly and G. Box's translation of the tractates *Sanhedrin* (London: SPCK, 1919), *Berakoth* (London: SPCK, 1921), and *Sukhah* (London: SPCK, 1925).

[16] *Strack, *Introduction*, pp. 75-76.

damages, penalties ("Damages"); 5. Temple paraphernalia ("Holy Things"); and 6. ritual purity and impurity ("Purities").[17] To the secular eye, the Mishna is an extraordinarily detailed casebook compiled by lawyers for their own use and instruction. It deals chiefly with ceremonial practice, much of it already irrelevant to Jewish life in the new Diaspora, and has little to say on matters of ethics, theology, and devotion, with which Jews of that and later ages also concerned themselves. It surely did not appear so to its editors, who preserved its contents as a testament to a tradition that they regarded, in the best Pharisaic manner, as the heart and essence of Judaism. The Covenant was the Law, and the Mishna was the pledge of fidelity to both by a new generation of Jews.

As has already been remarked, the Hebrew Mishna received two separate sets of Aramaic commentary (*gemara*) in the generations following Rabbi Judah, one at the hands of the newly emergent schools in Babylonia, and another in the Palestinian academies.[18] The sages who labored over the *gemara* were known, in contradistinction to the earlier *tannaim*, as "speakers" (*amoraim*), and their number stretches from the successors of Rabbi Judah in the early third century to the last distinguished members of the declining academies at the close of the fifth century.[19] The body of *halakot*, whether

[17] Ibid., pp. 29-64, has provided a detailed analysis of the sixty-three tractates into which the six orders are divided. The principle of arrangement is not entirely clear, despite the fact that a great deal of exegetical energy and ingenuity has been expended on defining and defending the sequence of the orders and their tractates; cf. Danby, *The Mishnah*, pp. xxiii-xxvii.

[18] The Soncino Press of London and Jerusalem has embarked upon a new English translation of the entire Babylonian Talmud under the general editorship of Rabbi I. Epstein. The Mishna with *gemara* and the English translation are printed on facing pages. The text page offers a collective medieval commentary known as the Tosafot (see *Strack, *Introduction*, p. 151, and *Ginzberg, *On Jewish Law and Lore*, pp. 172-174) in the left margin, and Rashi's commentary (see below) in the right in the now classical manner of editions of the Talmud, but neither is included in the facing English translation.

[19] For their identity, *Strack, *Introduction*, pp. 119-133.

derived by the exegesis of Scripture or recourse to the oral tradition, was now complete, and the function of the *amoraim* was essentially to explicate, reconcile, and expound the inner logic of the *halakot* enunciated by their tannaitic predecessors.

The Mishna with its respective *gemarot* took final form as the two Talmuds, the Babylonian and the Palestinian, of which the former was to gain a preeminent position of authority. Though neither was intended to be nor in fact became the final word on Jewish Law, the respect given to both Talmuds derived from the fact that they were the products of a scholarly and legal consensus at a time when the academy (*yeshiba*) and the religious court (*bet din*) guided the fortunes of Judaism without peer or rival. But no matter how great its authority, neither Talmud was a legal code; it was rather a shorthand transcription of discussions concerning legal questions that occupied lawyers from the second to the fifth century of the Christian era.

The disengagement of the *halakot*, positive legal precepts with binding authority, from the surrounding mass of discussion, debate, and speculation occurred during the Islamic period of Jewish history and continued among scholars who lived in the rapidly expanding Jewish community outside the Abode of Islam, and at a time when the former paramount authority of the Near Eastern academies was flowing to new centers and new scholars.[20] Only two examples need be cited here. The *Mishneh Torah* of Moses Maimonides, which was written in Cairo and completed in 1190 C.E., though it was not the first such, is a genuine code produced by a scholar who belonged to a larger intellectual tradition than that of the Talmud. Maimonides was a philosopher and theologian of the first order who was schooled in both Greek rationalism and the by then sophisticated legal traditions of Islam, and his *Mishneh Torah* reflects both those strains in its intro-

[20] On the codification of Jewish Law, see *Ginzberg, *On Jewish Law and Lore*, pp. 164-184.

ductory discourse on the modes of knowledge and the foundations of Judaism, its logical arrangement of the *halakot*, and its exclusion of what Maimonides judged to be irrelevant or nonlegal material.

Maimonides' view of the Law was to a large degree determined by his political theory, much of which derived from the Muslim philosopher al-Farabi (d. 950), and through him from Plato.[21] For Maimonides no less than for Farabi, the prophet was both philosopher and lawgiver. By his surpassing intelligence, he had attained to—or been granted (there are important nuances here)—eternal truths, and by the power of his imaginative faculty he converted them into law. Law, then, revealed Law, had the twofold aspect of regulating human life and society, just as human law did, and embodying the same truths that the philosopher struggled to achieve.

The Torah, in Maimonides' view, had this same double purpose: to order society and to bring men to an understanding of the highest truths; in sum, an ethical and a religious purpose.[22] To concentrate exclusively on the first, as many of the Talmudic scholars did, was simply to enter the grounds of the royal palace without going inside.[23] To understand the second and more profound intent of the Torah, one must penetrate deeper into the mysteries of revelation through the use of allegorical exegesis, and this is in fact one of the purposes of the *Guide of the Perplexed*. Elsewhere Maimonides is far more direct, and presents in dogmatic form the articles of faith necessary for salvation, and so formulated the nearest thing Judaism had to a formal creed.[24]

Maimonides provides some guidance on the ethical intent

---

[21] On this connection, see S. Pines, *Moses Maimonides: The Guide of the Perplexed* (Chicago: Chicago University Press, 1963), pp. xc-xcii.

[22] Ibid., III, 27-28 = Pines, pp. 510-514. For Maimonides' own view of the ethical intent of the *mitzvot*, see *Guide* III, 35 which is a résumé of much of the material in his *Mishneh Torah*.

[23] *Guide* III, 51 = Pines, pp. 618-619. The rabbis in the parable are better off than the theologians, who are rapidly striding off in the wrong direction.

[24] See Chapter VIII below.

of the Torah as well, guidance that must have sounded alien indeed in a *bet ha-midrash*. In a remarkable passage in the *Guide* (III, 32), he compares God's indirect yet purposeful working through natural causes with His similar activity among men. Moses was given the Law to modify pagan custom for the better, and so provide a bridge from idolatry to a belief in the unique God. Maimonides can support his contention with considerable documentation, since he had available what passed in his day for an authentic description of pre-Abrahamic Aramaic paganism.[25] The Law appears, then— and most clearly in its cultic and sacrificial aspects—to be a transitional and ameliorative instrument rather than final and perfect, at least when viewed from a historical perspective.

This was not a widely shared view, but even among the traditionalists the Talmud was not looked upon as a legal system that had been frozen in permanent stasis. A generation before Maimonides a French scholar, Rabbi Solomon ben Isaac (d. 1105), now generally known as Rashi, had written an immensely learned and exhaustive commentary on the Talmud that cast new light on its meaning and interpretation, and other scholars continued to render legal responsa to Jewish communities all over the European continent and the Islamic empire. Maimonides had ignored much of this new legal material in his somewhat idealized version of the Law, but other, later attempts at codification were more responsive to the changing circumstances of Jewish life. One such code eventually gained a position of almost absolute authority, the *Shulkhan Aruk* or *Set Table* of Joseph Caro (d. 1575). But no authority was absolute in the face of the Torah and the Talmud, and the *Shulkhan Aruk* underwent its own revisions, though chiefly in the form of deferential glosses and commentaries.[26]

---

[25] See Pines, *Guide*, pp. cxxiii-cxxiv.

[26] The easiest access to the *Shulkhan* in English is through one of its latter-day descendents, the *Kitzur Shulkhan Aruk* of Rabbi Solomon Ganzfried, which has been translated into English as the *Code of Jewish Law* (New York: Hebrew Publishing Company, 1961).

To return to the first century, the Gospels present Jesus in a world in which the Pharisees' preoccupation with the *halakot* is very much in the foreground. Jesus was "observant" in some sense—he kept the Sabbath, for example, and participated in the Passover liturgy—but clearly did not share the Pharisees' views on how close that observance should be: whether one may violate the letter of the Sabbath rest to perform an act of compassion, for instance, or whether ritual purity was a higher value than winning souls. These are debatable questions, surely, but on other occasions Jesus appears to suggest that it was rather his own messianic presence that rendered the ceremonial *halakot* moot, a theme that was richly developed by Paul.[27]

Not all of Jesus' followers construed the advent of the messianic age as abrogating either the *mitzvot* or the *halakot*—witness James and the Judeo-Christians in Jerusalem—but Paul for one did, and argued fiercely, if occasionally with some personal ambivalence, that the establishment of a New Covenant meant that the Mosaic Law as a general concept and its specific precepts were no longer binding on the Christian who had found his manumission from sin not in observance but in redemption.[28] Jesus' death, Paul declared, bought freedom from sin and from its necessary corollary, the Law. But in the selfsame letters Paul laid down his own Christian *halakot* for the regulation of a Christian life, and the "elders" and "overseers" of the early Christian community showed the same dual concern for faith and morals. Faith there must be, but faith alone would not suffice. The Christian, no less than the Pharisee, had to hold himself apart from the practices of the pagan world that surrounded him, and precepts were set forth to regulate his conduct.[29]

[27] On the rabbinic debate over the question of whether the coming of the Messiah abrogated ceremonial law, see J. Klausner, *From Jesus to Paul* (Boston: Beacon Press pb., 1961), p. 321 and n. 13.

[28] Ibid., pp. 496-507; see Chapter II above.

[29] *J. G. Davies, *A History of the Christian Church* (Garden City: Doubleday Anchor pb., 1967), pp. 90, 146. How the Mosaic *mitzvot* could be

So much can be gathered from the preaching and catechetical teaching of the early Christian Fathers and from the anonymous "Apostolic Constitutions" of the period from 150-400 C.E. But there were, in addition, the disciplinary canons enacted by the provincial and ecumenical synods of the fourth and fifth centuries.[30] This legal material continued to accumulate with each new council, but not until Emperor Justinian (527-565 C.E.) offered his own codification of Roman law in his Corpus Juris did the Church attempt to put its own juridical house in order. The Antiochene lawyer John, later the Patriarch of Constantinople (565-577 C.E.), drew up his Collection of Ecclesiastical Canons, the antecedent of all later codes of canon law, which arranged the conciliar enactments by subject matter rather than chronologically by council. As a further innovation, he introduced into his collection certain patristic regulations, canons drawn up by Saint Basil, for example. Somewhat later John brought together those civil laws of Justinian that pertained to religious matters.

Justinian's translation of religious questions into civil law was in no way extraordinary. The process had begun as early as Constantine, who legislated on the Sunday rest, celibacy, and divorce. Far from being a usurpation of the Church's judicial prerogatives, Justinian's legislative work recognized in an open and official way the parity of civil and canon law in a Christian Roman Empire: whatever the ecclesiastical canons forbid, the civil statutes also forbid. The Church was accepted as a legislative partner of the state, just as earlier bishops had been granted the right to hear civil appeals. Indeed, by the time of Justinian the Christian bishop had become a major administrative official, and was frequently used as a check upon the unscrupulousness of secular functionaries at all levels of provincial administration. The bishop had the power to force officials to perform their duties, and he had

---

allegorized to serve this end is illustrated in the *Letter of Barnabas*; see Chapter V below.

[30] See H. Hess, *Canons of the Council of Sardica A.D. 343: A Landmark in the Early Development of Canon Law* (London: Oxford University Press, 1958).

to be rendered an account of public funds. He reported to the emperor on local conditions, and in his own community the bishop was an ex officio member of the election board and one of the group of four notables whose task it was to supervise baths, granaries, aqueducts, and bridges.[31]

To pass from Justinian to Muhammad, who was born only a few years after the death of that emperor, is to move from the province of a millennial tradition of Roman law codes and all the apparatus of a sophisticated legal scholasticism to the shadowy domains of unwritten tribal custom and of a society in slow and uncertain transition from the nomadic to the sedentary life. The Qur'an, particularly in its later *surahs*, is filled with prescriptive enactments, as Muhammad struggled to reform, in the light of a new Islamic consciousness, the customary practices (*sunnah*) of his fellow Arabs.[32] To the rabbinic scholar, Muhammad's enactments might appear to be *taqqanot*, the creation of new institutions to improve the conditions of social, economic, and religious life.[33] But they were, in the eyes of the Prophet and his fellow Muslims, genuine *mitzvot*, absolute Scriptural injunctions.

However the historian might view it, the Qur'an presented itself as a divine revelation with a direct and explicit connection to those earlier and authentic revelations given to the Jews and the Christians, the Tawrah and Injil as Muhammad called them, and like those earlier Scriptures—Muhammad may have been uncertain about the contents of the Gospels—the Qur'an was intended to spell out what *islam*, "submission to the will of God," signified in terms of concrete human acts. Some small part of the Qur'anic injunctions is devoted to what might broadly be called ceremonial or liturgical acts: prayer, fasting, and the like. But where

[31] J. M. Hussey, ed., *The Cambridge Medieval History* (Cambridge: Cambridge University Press, 1967), IV/2, pp. 10-12, 125-129.

[32] On the Arab customary law background of Muhammad's enactments (*ahkam*), see N. J. Coulson, *A History of Islamic Law* (Edinburgh: Edinburgh University Press, 1971), pp. 9-20.

[33] See Chapter II above.

specific acts are prescribed or forbidden, most of them have to do with questions of personal status such as the treatment of heirs, women, slaves, and orphans; with the reformation of morals, criminal procedures, and the observance of binding contracts.[34] Muhammad could address these issues as they arose in his small community of believers. We may suppose that there were at least some other prescriptions rendered by him that are not recorded in the Qur'an and, what is virtually certain, that Muhammad acted as sole judge and arbitrator for the Muslims.

There is implicit in all that Muhammad did and preached the notion that there is such a thing as an Islamic "way" (*shari'ah*), which resembled the Jewish and the Christian "way" in that it came from God and which stood in sharp opposition to both the religious paganism and degenerate tribal custom of the contemporary Arabs. But the Islamic "way" was no more explicit and formal than the random precepts of the Qur'an that defined it, and at Muhammad's death in 632 C.E., God's revelation was ended and the Qur'an had become forever a closed Book. At that very moment, however, the Muslim community, which was endowed with only the most rudimentary religious and secular institutions, was poised at the beginning of an immense military and political expansion that would carry it within a short space of time from Spain to the Indus.

We possess only the vaguest idea of how the Muslims conducted their legal affairs in the first century after the death of the Prophet. The Caliph was recognized as the chief judge (*qadi*) of the community, as Muhammad had been, and he delegated this judicial power to others in the provinces of the new Islamic empire. But how the *qadis* rendered their judgments to other Muslims—Muslim justice applied only to Muslims; Jews and Christians continued under their own juridical traditions—we can only surmise, though it was

[34] *J. Schacht, *Introduction to Muslim Law* (London: Oxford University Press, 1964), pp. 10-14.

probably on the basis of local custom, caliphal instruction, their own understanding of the Qur'an and perhaps an embryonic sense of an Islamic "tradition."[35]

There were those who found such pragmatic and even secular arrangements in God's own community unsettling, and out of that dissatisfaction, which was reenforced by political, financial, and tribal disenchantment with the current dynasty of Muslim rulers, there arose in certain traditionist circles the first debates over what it meant to be a Muslim and pursue an Islamic "way" in all its ethical and legal implications. The results are sketchy, but we can observe that to validate their conclusions those early pioneers in Muslim jurisprudence (fiqh) appealed not only to the Qur'an, as might be expected in a revealed religion, but increasingly to "the practice (sunnah) of the Prophet." This latter was by no means the only or even the chief method used to fashion the norms of Muslim conduct at that point; legal scholars could still resort, in certain cases, to local custom or the exercise of their own legal discretion.[36]

One jurist (faqih) would not have it so. Shafi'i, whose important Essay has been translated into English,[37] argued for the absolute priority in Islam of the "custom of the Prophet" over that of Muhammad's contemporaries and followers, no matter how well-intentioned or pious. Further, he maintained, with great consequence, that the Prophet's sunnah was authentically contained in the great body of reports (hadith) transmitted by those who had lived and worked with him.[38] And what of the Qur'an, God's own Word? Shafi'i had already faced the issue: the Qur'an never contradicts the traditions, but the traditions from the Prophet explain the Qur'an;

[35] *Schacht, Introduction, pp. 15-22.

[36] Ibid., pp. 33-48.

[37] M. Khadduri, Islamic Jurisprudence, Shafi'i's Risala (Baltimore: Johns Hopkins University Press, 1961).

[38] J. Schacht, The Origins of Muhammadan Jurisprudence (London: Oxford University Press, 1953), pp. 11-18, 77-80; cf. *Schacht, Introduction, pp. 47-48, and *Hodgson, Venture, I, 326-329.

no *sunnah* ever contradicts the Qur'an; it specifies its meaning.[39]

Shafi'i had not only canonized the position of tradition in Islam; he had specified and attempted to defend the medium of its transmission, to wit, the body of oral reports or *hadith* that were already circulating in pious and legal circles in his own day. Shafi'i knew perfectly well that many of those *hadith* contradicted others reported by the very same authority, and that others were simply contrary to reason or common sense. There were various ways of reconciling some traditions and rationalizing others,[40] but the method that eventually came to be favored by those who accepted Shafi'i's premise, as all came eventually to do, was to scrutinize the *isnad* or chain of transmitters of the tradition in question.

All *isnads* went back to the testimony of the generation of Muhammad's contemporaries, who were later canonized as the Companions of the Prophet. Were they and the others in the chain reliable reporters? The question sounds like a historiographical one, and to some extent it was: were X and Y in the same place at the same time, to enable them to pass on the story? But when the Muslim spoke of reliability, he meant in fact moral probity, a quality that was eventually granted to the entire first generation of Muslims. The Companions of the Prophet may have enjoyed an ex post facto infallibility in the eyes of later generations of Muslim lawyers (*fuqaha*), but they were in fact and in theory mere eyewitness reporters of the words and deeds of the Prophet: there was no Pentecost and no laying on of hands at this critical point in the Islamic tradition. Nor was there any parallel to the Unwritten Torah; Muhammad was simply and not unreasonably understood by Shafi'i and succeeding generations as the best interpreter of the Qur'an, and the conclusion flowed easily that the Prophet's interpretation of the Qur'an was best displayed in his own words and acts.

[39] Schacht, *Origins*, pp. 15-16.
[40] Ibid., pp. 40-57.

The historical problem is that not everyone accepted or acted upon or even knew about that premise before Shafi'i, and many of the oldest *hadith* concerning the Prophet have what were, by later standards, extremely untidy *isnads*. The fact that the later *isnads* are far more complete than the earlier ones has raised a great deal of modern skepticism on the historicity of most of the *hadith*, many of which are, in addition, tendentious and reflect issues and controversies that arose long after the Prophet.[41]

The Muslims were aware of at least some of these problems and long ago collected, examined, and attempted to verify the vast body of traditions that purportedly came down from the Prophet.[42] And since it was a question of normative halakic *hadith* and not the haggadic or historical variety, it was chiefly the lawyers who were engaged in this critical enterprise, and it is their judgment that is reflected in the selection and arrangement of "sound" *hadith* in the great canonical collections of the late ninth century.[43]

The early legal theorists in Islam had grounded the case for their own view of the law on a consensus of scholars in that "school." Shafi'i was uneasy with the notion of consensus (*ijma*) and preferred, if there was no explicit *hadith* on a given subject, to appeal to the consensus of the entire Muslim community, its acceptance of a practice such as circumcision or of an institution such as the caliphate, for instance.

[41] I. Goldziher, *Muslim Studies* (1898; revised translation London: Allen and Unwin, 1967), II, 17-254; cf. Schacht, *Origins*, pp. 163-175, and *Introduction*, p. 34; *Gibb, *Mohammedanism*, pp. 49-59.

[42] F. E. Peters, *Allah's Commonwealth* (New York: Simon and Schuster, 1973), pp. 242-243.

[43] See A. Guillaume, *The Traditions of Islam* (London: Oxford University Press, 1924) and J. Robson, *An Introduction to the Science of Tradition* (London: Royal Asiatic Society of Great Britain and Ireland, 1953). To read traditions as such is not, perhaps, a very useful exercise, since they were collected and arranged primarily to serve other, largely legal purposes, but there is a representative selection of them in English in Arthur Jeffrey's *Reader on Islam* (The Hague: Mouton, 1962), pp. 79-252, and one can get some idea of the range of subjects covered by the extant *hadith* from A. J. Wensinck, *A Handbook of Early Muhammadan Tradition* (1927; reprint Leiden: E. J. Brill, 1971).

And to bolster his own wavering confidence in the legal applicability of consensus, Shafi'i not unnaturally cited a *hadith* to the effect that the *ummah* would never agree in error.[44]

Since the *fuqaha* of Islam were essentially rabbis and not bishops speaking comfortably ex cathedra, they had early begun to employ various forms of legal reasoning that have been the staples of lawyers always and everywhere. In Islamic Law, this use of legal reasoning is called *ijtihad* or "personal effort," and its most common formal manifestation is "analogy" (*qiyas*).[45] "Analogy" was acceptable to Shafi'i, as it was to most subsequent jurists, but only if it was used to erect "hedges for the Law," to use the Talmudic phrase,[46] and not to extend exceptions into general rules; that it start from the literal and not the allegorical understanding of the text; and that, finally, it be regarded as the fourth and weakest of the "roots of the Law" after the Qur'an, the custom of the Prophet, and the consensus of the *ummah*.

In the traditional Islamic view, then, the Qur'an was Scripture, whereas the *sunnah* of the Prophet and, by extension, the consensus of the *ummah* that was presumably reflected in the same *sunnah*, was tradition, neither in the sense of customary law nor in the charismatic sense understood in the Christian *paradosis*, but somewhat in the manner of the Mishna. The Mishna possesses some very imperfect *isnads*, few of which go back before Hillel and none before the Maccabees. For the earlier period one must always be content with "Moses received the Torah—always glossed to include the Unwritten Torah—from Sinai and handed it on to Joshua, Joshua to the Elders, the Elders to the Prophets and the Prophets handed it on to the men of the Great Assembly."[47] Eusebius is rather more detailed in drawing up in his *Eccle-*

---

[44] Schacht, *Origins*, pp. 88-97, esp. p. 91.

[45] On *qiyas* and its parallels in Jewish and Roman law, see ibid., pp. 99-100.

[46] See *S. Sandmel, *Judaism and Christian Beginnings* (London: Oxford University Press pb., 1978), p. 110.

[47] *Pirke Abot*, Chapter I = Danby, *The Mishnah*, pp. 446-447; cf. J. Goldin, *The Living Talmud* (New York: Mentor pb., 1957), pp. 43-46.

siastical History the lines of the Apostolic succession in the various Sees of the Great Church, but bishops were not much given to reciting *isnads* of their predecessors back to the "Companions of Jesus" before pronouncing on faith and morals. Episcopal consecration sealed what was an internalized tradition; Islamic tradition, on the other hand, was reported, often copied down by the recipient, and certified by the tradent in the manner of a contract.[48]

The early evolution of Islamic Law took place in widely scattered centers across the Dar al-Islam, and not even Shafi'i's attempts at imposing a kind of order on its development eradicated or even inhibited the continued growth of different schools of legal interpretation, each of them recognized as orthodox and legitimate by the others. Thus the Shafi'ite, Malikite, Hanafite, and Hanbalite schools founded by and named after early masters of Islamic jurisprudence flourished and continued to flourish among Muslims.[49] They differ on specific points of theory and practice,[50] but their differences are not very substantial, nor do their practices much differ from the positive precepts of Shi'ite law, though this latter has a considerably divergent view of what lawyers call "the roots of jurisprudence."[51] The four major Sunni schools recognized, with varying degrees of enthusiasm, the Qur'an, the *sunnah* of the Prophet (as expressed in the *hadith*), the consensus of the community, and a measure of personal interpretation (*ijtihad*) as the basis of the *shari'ah*; the Shi'ites, on the other hand, relied heavily upon the infallible teachings of the Imams and rejected the consensus of the community out of hand.

[48] See the important distinctions between *hadith* reports and the Jewish and Christian understanding of tradition underlined by *Hodgson, *Venture*, I, 63-66.

[49] For their geographical distribution, see *Schacht, *Introduction*, pp. 65-67.

[50] See Coulson, *Islamic Law*, pp. 21-73.

[51] A. Fyzee, "Shi'i Legal Theories" in M. Khadduri and H. J. Liebesny, eds., *Law in the Middle East* (Washington, D. C.: Middle East Institute, 1955), I, 113-122.

After Shafi'i and as a result of the debate over the validity of independent reasoning, the freedom granted to earlier jurists to elicit legal conclusions from even the most traditional material was severely circumscribed, and by about 900 C.E. a new consensus was developing, that the "gate of *ijtihad*" had closed.[52] The phrase has an ominous ring, but it should be understood in a not very different sense from the closure of the Talmud, as a herald for the advent of scholasticism, when scholars had to couch their legal speculations in the form of commentary and explication on an established body of masters, in this case the developed doctrine of the canonical schools.

The analogy with the Talmud should not be pressed too closely. In a sense the *shari'ah* or Islamic Law was fundamentally in place by the beginning of the tenth century, just as the Mishna was complete in the third, and the two Talmuds in the sixth. But all these latter were formal texts, whereas the *shari'ah* continued to exist, even after the tenth century, in the form of a somewhat inchoate, if consensually agreed upon, mass of propositions whose exact formulation had only as much authority as the jurisprudent from whose pen it came.[53]

A more serious consequence of the closing of "the gate of *ijtihad*" was to confirm the tendency in Islamic Law—a tendency already present in talmudic speculation—to create a body of idealized law whose legitimate sources were so carefully and artificially defined that it became all but impervious to local custom and the changing circumstances of life under Islam. But even here Islamic jurisprudence, no less than Jewish legal practice, had at hand sophisticated resources. Though the *qadi* in his court had to judge cases on the letter of the *shari'ah*, the individual Muslim could resort to more informal types of arbitration, or could appeal away from the *qadi*'s court to the jurisdiction known as *mazalim*. The *mazalim* was

---

[52] *Schacht, *Introduction*, pp. 69-75.
[53] For a representative list of such works, see ibid., pp. 261-269.

a type of court of complaints that had its justification in the discretionary powers of the ruler and that could address grievances or inequities ignored by the *shari'ah*. Again, individual cases could be submitted to legal specialists known as *muftis* who, like their Jewish counterparts, could render a *fatwa* or *responsum*. The *muftis* could neither judge nor legislate, and their *fatwas* had no binding force in the *qadis'* courts.[54] But the appeal of the *fatwa* literature is that it reflects on how actual and specific cases were addressed by Muslim lawyers, and so supplies a corrective to the idealizing qualities of many *shari'ah* treatises.

Nowhere does the discrepancy between theory and practice in Islamic law appear more clearly than in the question of taxation. Taxation, which fell under secular jurisdiction in the Christian Roman Empire and was imposed upon Jewish communities from without, was part of the preserve of religious law in Islam. Muslim jurists drew up neat categories distinguishing between the tithe (*zakat*) paid by Muslims and the tax, whether land-tax (*kharaj*) or poll-tax (*jizya*), uniformly imposed upon non-Muslims in the Dar al-Islam. But an inspection from historical sources of the arrangements in force in various parts of the Islamic empire shows great differences between one locality and another, and an immense gap between canonical theory and the actual practices dictated by political considerations, financial need, and local custom.[55]

The clash of the ideal and the real against the background of the *shari'ah* has led some scholars to look upon the *shari'ah* as an impressive but unrealizable ideal that most Muslims ignored in practice.[56] This judgment may, however, be as

[54] Ibid., pp. 73-75.

[55] F. Løkkegard, *Islamic Taxation in the Classical Period* (Copenhagen: Branner and Korch, 1950); and D. C. Dennett, *Conversion and Poll Tax in Early Islam* (Cambridge: Harvard University Press, 1950), both reprinted in *Islamic Taxation: Two Studies* (New York: Arno Press, 1973).

[56] So S. Hurgronje, *Selected Works* (Leiden: E. J. Brill, 1957), pp. 260, 290.

idealized as it claims the *shari'ah* to have been, and a closer inspection of at least some areas of legal practice has revealed a somewhat more complex reality.[57] Commercial law in particular was a marvelously intricate exercise in enlarging the *shari'ah* categories dealing with commerce to permit the inclusion of a large body of customary law.[58] The *shari'ah* denied, for example, the validity of written documents in cases at law, but permitted their extensive and obviously indispensable use in dealing with commercial contracts.[59] And it was here too, in commercial law, that the lavish use of "devices" (*hiyal*), the legal fictions familiar from Roman and Jewish law, enabled the Muslim merchant to bring his customary practice in line with the letter of the *shari'ah*.[60]

The needs of the state were less easily satisfied than those of the merchant by the resources of Islamic law. There had been no Jewish state since the dissolution of the Hasmonean monarchy early in the first century C.E., and so the Jews of the Talmudic period had no need of either a secular law code or a constitutional theory. There were, however, Christian states—the Byzantine Empire was the first—and an Islamic empire that eventually dissolved into Islamic states. Where they differed was in that the Christian states had an antecedent tradition of Roman law, and the later Roman emperors, both before and after they became Christian, had among their principal powers that of legislating. Thus civil and canon law could and did exist side by side, each influencing the other, but possessing separate and autonomous jurisdictions nonetheless.

[57] *Schacht, *Introduction*, pp. 76–85.

[58] See A. Udovitch, *Partnership and Profit in Medieval Islam* (Princeton: Princeton University Press, 1970).

[59] J. Wakin, *The Function of Documents in Islamic Law* (Albany: SUNY Press, 1972); cf. Udovitch, *Partnership*, pp. 9–10.

[60] *Schacht, *Introduction*, pp. 78–82; Udovitch, *Partnership*, pp. 11–12. An entire tractate of the mishnaic order *Sabbath* is given over to the legal fiction of *erubin*, whereby one can extend the permissible limits of the domain within which Sabbath activity may be carried on: Danby, *The Mishnah*, pp. 121–136.

Islam had no such tradition: the Caliph was the chief judge of Islam, but he was never a legislator.[61] The Caliph, it was understood, did possess certain discretionary powers, if not to legislate then at least to insure the general social and political circumstances under which the idealized Muslim life envisioned by the *shari'ah* might unfold. These generalized powers were later called "policy" (*siyasah*), and though there was no lack of theory on the subject, *siyasah* had no real claim to autonomy, and there was no vehicle for either its expression or its promulgation until the later Middle Ages, when both the Mamluk rulers of Egypt and the Ottoman sultans began to legislate in a relatively open fashion.[62]

The merchant and the prince were not the only Muslims who had problems with the Islamic law. One notable Muslim thought that the *shari'ah* had altogether too much to do with the market place and the palace, and too little with religion. Ghazali (d. 1111) was a theologian who did not have a great deal of respect for the value of theology (*kalam*), and he was an antagonist of philosophy who borrowed a great deal from the philosophers.[63] Early on in Jewish *kalam*, as we have seen, an organic relationship began to develop between theology and the Law. The same did not occur in Islam; those who took up *kalam* showed only a peripheral interest in the *shari'ah*.[64] The Law belonged to the "traditioned" sci-

---

[61] See Chapter III above and Peters, *Allah's Commonwealth*, pp. 471-473 on the powers of Caliph and emperor, and compare the interesting study by S. D. Goitein, *Studies in Islamic History and Institutions* (Leiden: E. J. Brill, 1968), pp. 149-167: "A Turning-Point in the History of the Muslim State."

[62] See E.I.J. Rosenthal, *Political Thought in Medieval Islam* (Cambridge: Cambridge University Press, 1962), pp. 21-112; *Schacht, *Introduction*, pp. 54-55. The first constitution promulgated in any Islamic state was the Turkish Constitution of 1876, which was based on a secular Belgian model of 1831. Attempts at fashioning a constitution on purely Islamic or Jewish lines have so far come to naught in both Pakistan and Israel.

[63] See Chapter VIII below.

[64] See the two interesting contributions by J. Schacht, "Theology and Law in Islam" (pp. 3-24), and F. Rahman, "Functional Interdependence of Law and Theology" (pp. 89-98), in G. von Grunebaum, *Theology and Law in Islam* (Wiesbaden: Harrassowitz, 1971).

ences, whereas *kalam* was numbered among the "rational" sciences, and the early but influential theologian Ash'ari (d. 935) warned that the two domains should never be confounded.[65] They rarely were, in fact. Theologians found some kind of acceptance within the legal schools—all save the Hanbali, which resisted *kalam* to the end—but had little visible effect on the *shari'ah* itself, and little to say in its defense or justification.

Ghazali had no interest in either project, though he was both a theologian (*mutakallim*) and a lawyer (*faqih*). His most influential work, *The Revivification of the Sciences of Religion*, had quite another end in mind. It is divided into four quarters that have as their subject: 1. the liturgical acts of the Muslim; 2. his life in society; 3. the interior dispositions of the soul; and 4. "the qualities of salvation."[66] The entire work is an extraordinary attempt at interiorizing Muslim life. It is about "the science of the hereafter," one part of which has to do with "the sciences of revelation," which is only a question of knowledge, and which Ghazali here ignores. Its other part is "the sciences of religion," which deal with both knowledge and action, with external acts and internal dispositions. Ghazali proposed to integrate the two, which he considered had been unnecessarily disassociated by the jurisprudents.

Religion is primarily concerned with the next world, and the *shari'ah* with man's actions in this life. The two are con-

---

[65] On the "traditioned" and "rational" sciences, see Peters, *Allah's Commonwealth*, pp. 212-215, and the careful distinctions drawn between the two by Ibn Khaldun (d. 1406): F. Rosenthal, *Ibn Khaldun: The Muqaddimah*, 3 vols. (rev. ed. Princeton: Princeton University Press, 1967), II, 436-439, and in the one-volume abridgment of Rosenthal's translation by N. Dawood (Princeton: Princeton University Press pb., 1969), pp. 343-344.

[66] Only very limited parts of this massive work are available in English translation. The intent and structure of the entire work are explained in the "Introduction" to Book 1 of the First Quarter, and this book has been translated by N. A. Faris, *Al-Ghazzali: The Book of Knowledge* (1962, reprinted Lahore: Sh. Muhammad Ashraf, 1970); cf. Peters, *Allah's Commonwealth*, pp. 706-712.

nected, of course, through the agency of the Islamic state, which administers justice and guarantees the appropriate political conditions for the pursuit of a Muslim life. Thus the *fuqaha* have concerned themselves with externals and have paid no attention to the "science of the heart," which is directed immediately to the future life, and so is the heart and soul of religion. In this spirit Ghazali first takes up the liturgical Pillars of Islam and shows the spirit and intent with which they should be performed. The Second Quarter, on "The Usages of Life," sets out the etiquette (*adab*) of the true Muslim life, how the Muslim should conduct himself in public and private, at table, on the road, at work. The Third Quarter is a rare attempt in medieval Islam at constructing an ethical theory in a Muslim context.[67] The Fourth Quarter unfolds entirely within the heart. Here at the climax of the work is Ghazali's final response to the Law: it is the ascetical life and the mystical knowledge of the Sufi that is the true "science of the heart" and the surest road to salvation.

[67] For some other examples, all of which lean heavily, as Ghazali did, on Greek ethical theory, see D. M. Donaldson, *Studies in Muslim Ethics* (London: SPCK, 1953); Peters, *Allah's Commonwealth*, pp. 535-539 (Miskawayh d. 1030); M. M. Sharif, ed., *A History of Muslim Philosophy*, 2 vols. (Wiesbaden: Harrassowitz, 1966), I, 565ff. (Nasir al-Din Tusi, d. 1274), and II, 883ff. (al-Dawwani, d. 1501).

CHAPTER V

Scripture and Tradition

BEFORE there was Talmud and *hadith*, there was Torah and Qur'an, and those who affirmed that these were indeed sacred Scripture were committed to an understanding of what was meant and what was intended by the words of God. There is no getting at the beginning of the process; we are in possession only of sophisticated finished works of commentary upon Scripture. But the existence of a class of professional scribes or bookmen (*soferim*) in the Jewish community after the Exile suggests that already the task of expounding the Jewish Scriptures for learned and laity alike was well under way. The work itself and some of the works that embody it are called *midrash*, and *midrash* is the single most characteristic act of post-Exilic Judaism.[1] The root from which the word derives means simply to "study" or "expound," but when it was connected with Scripture, it took on for many Jews the quality of a liturgical act.

From the available evidence we can conclude that in the decades following the return from Exile two processes were going on: in their own schools (*bet ha-midrash*), the *soferim* were extracting, comparing, and combining legal precepts (*halakot*) derived from Scripture, a work that came to term in the Mishna; and in more general religious contexts, perhaps the forerunners of the later synagogues, these same and other Scriptural texts were adduced and expanded, in the manner of a homily (*haggada*), for purposes of moral formation, edification, and piety.

We have already spoken of the halakic *midrash* in the pages

[1] See *S. Sandmel, *Judaism and Christian Beginnings* (London: Oxford University Press pb., 1978), pp. 121-126.

devoted to the Law; the present discussion will confine itself to the narrower sense in which *midrash* is, as a matter of fact, generally understood, that is, haggadic *midrash*. Even though the two genres are distinguished here and elsewhere as a matter of course, there is no essential conflict between halakic and haggadic *midrash*. They differ widely in style, but their fundamental agreement rests upon what Leo Baeck has called Jewish "monobiblism," the presence of a single, authoritative Scripture accepted by all exegetes. Whether it is explicitly referred to or not, the Bible underlies all Jewish *midrash*. There are, moreover, *halakot* in the Midrashim and the haggadic method was often applied, as we shall see, to halakic material.

A further distinction must be drawn. Haggadic *midrash*, hereafter simply *midrash*, is a method that appears in many different contexts. Translations of the Bible are a prime locus for the exercise of the midrashic method, for example. The language of post-Exilic Judaism was changing from Hebrew to Aramaic in the immediate pre-Christian centuries. Since large numbers of the laity could no longer understand Scripture in its original form, it was translated into the common Aramaic tongue of Palestine, just as it was turned into Greek at Alexandria for the Greek-speaking Jews living there and elsewhere in the Diaspora. The Alexandrian Greek translation, the Septuagint, whose origins are surrounded by stories calculated to guarantee its authenticity,[2] was a relatively straightforward and literal exercise, but the Aramaic translations, called *targums*, were often paraphrastic and approached commentaries in their haggadic manner.[3] Their principal use was for oral liturgical recitation in the synagogue service.[4]

The *targums* are obviously midrashic but not yet Mid-

[2] *C. K. Barrett, *The New Testament Background* (New York: Harper Torchbook, 1961), pp. 208-215.

[3] J. Bowker, *The Targums and Rabbinic Literature* (Cambridge: Cambridge University Press, 1969).

[4] See Chapter VI below.

rashim in the formal, literary sense. The earliest preserved examples of these latter are the sectarian commentaries (*pesharim*) from Qumran[5] and the works of the rabbis, both *tannaim* and *amoraim*, of the talmudic era. These latter fall into two general categories.[6] The first or expositional Midrash is a commentary proper that puts the midrashic method at the service of halakic concerns. It treats the Scripture in the order of its verses, each verse expounded by an appropriate tale or parable. The purely homiletic Midrashim differ in two ways. First, they treat Scripture according to its liturgical divisions, that is, the Torah pericopes read daily in the synagogue over a cycle of three years or the "section" (*pesiqta*) reserved for Sabbaths and special festivals. Second, the homiletic exegete began each of the divisions of his work with the citation of a verse drawn from the "Writings" to which he added one or more explanations from different sources. The last of these was designed to lead into the homily proper, which generally confined its attention to one significant verse of the original pericope.

The earliest rabbinic Midrashim, as has been remarked, had as their object the extraction of halakic material from Scripture by an application of the *midrash* method. Such are Sifra or The Book on Leviticus, the Sifre Zuta on Numbers and the Mekilta on the legal material (chaps. 12 to 23:19), and that alone, in Exodus.[7] Examples of purely expository Midrashim are the Bereshit Rabba on Genesis and the Midrash on Lamentations.[8] Among the oldest homiletic Midrashim are the Pesiqta of Rab Kahana, the Tanchuma and the

---

[5] See G. Vermes, *The Dead Sea Scrolls: Qumran in Perspective* (London: Collins, 1977), pp. 66-83.

[6] *H. L. Strack, *Introduction to the Talmud and Midrash* (New York: Jewish Publication Society pb., 1959), pp. 204-205.

[7] Ibid., pp. 206-209.

[8] Ibid., pp. 217-219. On the early Judeo-Christian *midrash* on Genesis, see J. Daniélou, *Theology of Jewish Christianity* (Chicago: Regnery, 1964), pp. 107-115.

Pesiqta Rabbati.[9] Few if any of these Midrashim are available in English in their published form, but a great deal of the material contained in them has been incorporated into L. Ginzberg's *Legends of the Jews*.[10]

The development of *midrash* is not unlike the history of logic. There is a kind of logic in almost all forms of human thought, but it was only after arriving at a certain degree of self-consciousness about the process that the "rules" governing such thought were first formulated. Aristotle did not invent logic; he simply abstracted and formalized an operation many could perform but few could describe. The *soferim* too must have been practicing *midrash* without formalizing the process, though their growing self-consciousness is already reflected in the encomium of the *sofer* and his work in the second-century B.C.E. *Wisdom of Jesus ben Sirah* (39, 1-8). Tradition, however, grants to Jesus' contemporary Hillel the glory of being the Aristotle of Jewish *midrash*.[11] Some of Hillel's rules for elucidating the meaning of a text were by then commonplace in the Greek and Roman rhetorical and philosophical schools—so commonplace, perhaps, that there was no need to "borrow" them in any formal sense of that word.[12]

If we turn from the methods of Jewish exegesis to trying to understand its motives and intent, we are confronted with a far more complex problem.[13] Vermes and others have dis-

---

[9] See *Strack, *Introduction*, pp. 210-232 for a complete list of homiletic Midrashim and cf. G. F. Moore, *Judaism in the First Centuries of the Christian Era* (New York: Schocken pb., 1971), I, 161-173.

[10] 7 vols. (1909; 10th ed., Philadelphia: Jewish Publishing Society of America, 1954). There are some brief selections from the Midrashim in *Barrett, *Background*, pp. 145-151.

[11] *Strack, *Introduction*, pp. 93-94. On the career of Hillel, see *Sandmel, *Beginnings*, pp. 237-240.

[12] H. A. Fischel, *Rabbinic Literature and Greco-Roman Philosophy: A Study of the Epicurea and Rhetorica in Early Midrashic Writings* (Leiden: E. J. Brill, 1973) and compare S. Lieberman, *Hellenism in Jewish Palestine* (New York: Hebrew Union College, 1950), pp. 47-68.

[13] See G. Vermes, *Scripture and Tradition in Judaism: Haggadic Studies*, 2nd ed. (Leiden: E. J. Brill, 1973) and his contribution, "Biblical Midrash: Early Old Testament Exegesis," in *P. R. Ackroyd and C. F. Evans, *The Cam-

tinguished between "pure" exegesis, which attempted to understand the meaning of a text, and "applied" exegesis, which had as its intent the eliciting of a scriptural answer to what was essentially a nonscriptural question. The first type of *midrash* arises out of the obscurities, lacunae, and self-contradictions of Scripture itself, or the impossibility of accepting what the plain sense (*peshat*) says. There are words in the Bible whose meaning was obscure at best. Stories sometimes lacked important details, and biblical *mitzvot* do not always spell out the terms of their applicability.[14] Further, the Bible is a composite book, and its various enactments were not always harmonized by the original editors; the task fell to the exegetes. Finally, some of the accounts in the Bible— instances of polygamy and incest, for example—had to be explained and mitigated for a generation that found them somewhat less than edifying.[15]

It was a Pharisee, it should be noted, who codified the rules of exegesis, probably, as Vermes has argued, because the Pharisees could not claim the priestly authority of the Sadducees and their scribes in the interpretation of Scripture, and so if they wished to depart from the literal sense (*peshat*), as the Sadducees refused to do, they had to justify their *mid-*

---

bridge History of the Bible (Cambridge: Cambridge University Press, 1970), I, 199-231.

[14] Vermes, "Biblical Midrash," pp. 205-207, cites the classic instance of the biblical regulation of divorce (Deuteronomy 24:1), where the grounds are simply described as a man's finding "some indecency" in his wife, and so left the door open for a great deal of midrashic debate on precisely what constituted "indecency."

[15] A reverse example is the use of images whose biblical prohibition is absolute (Exodus 20:4-5; Deuteronomy 5:8-9), and was still understood as such at the time of Josephus. By the beginning of the second century C.E., however, attitudes were changing, and soon both secular and religious buildings of the Jews in Palestine and the Diaspora were being adorned with frescoes and mosaics of men and animals. The exegesis of the biblical passages on the subject was adapted accordingly, and the rabbis explained that the prohibition was against the worship of images and not their use for decorative purposes: Vermes, "Biblical Midrash," pp. 217-218.

101

rash carefully on technical grounds.[16] But the Pharisees were not the only ones to "apply" the Scripture to their own point of view. The community at Qumran did the same,[17] and so too did the followers of Jesus. Pharisaic *midrash*, and the rabbinic *midrash* that grew out of it, had as its chief aim the extraction of a deeper understanding (and a wider application) of the legal and ethical principles inherent in Scripture. The Essenes and Christians had other interests: to read in the Scriptures the foreshadowing of future events, the future that was now present or still to come in the Messianic Age or the End Time.[18]

The exegetical technique of both the Essenes and the Christians involves a kind of allegorizing in that it takes as its premise the principle that although Scripture is talking about one thing (the present), it is really referring to something else (the future). But the method of allegory found its broadest extension in Philo of Alexandria (ca. 20 B.C.E.–45 C.E.R.) whose understanding of "the other" was the whole body of contemporary Greek philosophy.[19] Philo understood well enough the value of the *peshat*, and could also compose moral *midrash* in the best Palestinian style.[20] But his chief contribution to scriptural exegesis was his application of the peculiar Greek sense of *allegoria* (other-referent) and *hyponoia* (under-thought) to the Bible. The Greeks, particularly the Stoics, allegorized Homer and the poets for much the same reason that Jewish exegetes "interpreted" Patriarchal polygamy and incest: the stories were morally offensive and yet occurred in a context of divine inspiration.[21] Philo did not

---

[16] "Biblical Midrash," p. 221.

[17] Texts in G. Vermes, *Dead Sea Scrolls in English* (Harmondsworth: Penguin pb., 1975), pp. 214-249; cf. F. F. Bruce, *Biblical Exegesis in the Qumran Texts* (London: Tyndale Press, 1960).

[18] On this type of "historical" or eschatological exegesis, see *L. Ginzberg, *On Jewish Law and Lore* (New York: Atheneum pb., 1970), pp. 127-138 and H. A. Wolfson, *The Philosophy of the Church Fathers*, 3rd ed. (Cambridge: Harvard University Press, 1970), pp. 26-29.

[19] See Chapter VIII below.

[20] See the texts cited in *Barrett, *Background*, pp. 173-175.

[21] On the poets as theologians, see Chapter VIII below.

allegorize on quite the same moral grounds, but rather because of his conviction that Scripture and philosophy were speaking of the same truths, though in different forms of discourse. The Scriptures themselves invited allegorization, somewhat in the way the poets did, by presenting things in a manner that made the literal interpretation offensive or absurd.[22]

With the opening pages of the Gospels we find ourselves not in Alexandria but in the Palestinian world of historical and eschatological *midrash*. The Scriptures, that is, the Bible, are scrutinized for their foreshadowing of Jesus as the Messiah.[23] None of this is particularly novel in the context of Jewish *midrash*—in Luke 4:16-30 Jesus is shown doing much the same thing in a Galilean synagogue service—and it was obviously a persuasive way of arguing Jesus' claims on a Jewish audience.[24] The early Jewish Christians went a step further; one of their number, Symmachus, prepared a new Greek translation of the Bible. It no longer survives, but from Eusebius' remarks about it, it was almost certainly a *targum* that argued as well as translated.[25] A very early example of Christian exegesis that comes directly out of a context of Jewish *midrash*, perhaps by a converted Jew, is the Letter of Barnabas, which allegorizes the Bible in a quite remarkable fashion.[26]

In the course of time the Christians lost their audience of Jews or Jewish converts to whom Barnabas addressed his

---

[22] See Philo's own explanation of his method cited in *Barrett, *Background*, pp. 180-182; for a more general treatment of his exegetical method, see H. A. Wolfson, *Philo*, 2 vols., 2nd ed. (Cambridge: Harvard University Press, 1947), I, 1-150.

[23] See A. T. Hanson, *Jesus Christ in the Old Testament* (London: SPCK, 1965) and C. H. Dodd, *According to the Scriptures* (London: Nisbet, 1952).

[24] See M. McNamara, *Targum and Testament* (Shannon: Irish University Press, 1972; Edinburgh: Oliver and Boyd, 1956).

[25] H.-J. Schoeps, *Jewish Christianity* (Philadelphia: Fortress Press, 1967), p. 15; Daniélou, *Theology of Jewish Christianity*, pp. 88ff.

[26] Translated in M. Staniforth, *Early Christian Writings: The Apostolic Fathers* (Harmondsworth: Penguin pb., 1968), pp. 193-220; cf. Daniélou, *Theology of Jewish Christianity*, pp. 97-107.

Letter and as a result turned away from the methods of rabbinic *midrash* to the *allegoria* of Philo. The Christian Fathers knew Philo's allegorical method very well, as Wolfson has demonstrated in his *Philosophy of the Church Fathers*.[27] Whether or not they read Philo himself, they received ample instruction on allegorical interpretation from those who had: the two Alexandrian Christians of the early third century, Clement and Origen.[28] All of these scholars—Philo, Clement, and Origen and their Greek and Latin successors—tried their hand at formalizing *allegoria* by subdividing it in one way or another. There was general agreement that there existed both a literal and a "spiritual" sense of Scripture. A common division of the latter was into a moral sense not very different from rabbinic haggadic *midrash* and a Philonian *allegoria* that penetrated into the deeper, that is, philosophical truths embodied in the Sacred Book. Occasionally too there was added the older eschatological sense under the title of anagogy.

Though the Christian Fathers paid lip service to the literal sense of Scripture, they did not expend a great deal of exegetical energy on explaining it. Not unnaturally perhaps, in the case of the Jewish Bible whose *mitzvot* they had quite explicitly rejected. One who did take it seriously and who, as a Christian, was led to conclude that the Jewish Bible was not Scripture at all, was Marcion.[29] Where Barnabas managed to embrace the Jewish Bible by allegorizing it almost beyond recognition, Marcion simply rejected it. Marcion was rejected by the Church in turn—he was excommunicated at Rome in 144 C.E.—and most of the Christian Fathers followed the example of the Gospels themselves and offered a typological interpretation of what they called "The Old Tes-

[27] Pp. 43-72.

[28] On the exegetical work of these two, see the contributions of R. Hanson (pp. 412-453) and M. F. Wiles (pp. 454-489) to *Ackroyd and Evans, eds., *Cambridge History of the Bible*, I.

[29] See R. M. Grant, *Gnosticism and Early Christianity* (New York: Harper Torchbook, 1966), pp. 121-128.

tament,"[30] or followed where Philo had led, to the conversion of a "Mosaic philosophy" into a Platonic one.

One exception should be noted. Though Judeo-Christianity passed out of the Great Church as a heretical movement, it left as its legacy traces of an attitude toward Scripture that played an important part of the Christian exegetical tradition. That legacy appears most clearly at Antioch and in the work of the Syrian exegete Theodore of Mopsuestia (d. 428), who wrote a treatise entitled *On Allegory and History* that was directed against Origen, and whose own scriptural commentaries on both the Bible and the New Testament show a marked preference for a historical over an allegorical and philosophical approach to the sacred writings.[31]

Theodore's work carries us deep into Christian theology and the christological disputes of the fifth century.[32] Those debates were fought out of an arsenal of scriptural exegesis deeply impregnated with philosophical discourse. Scripture, whether biblical or evangelical, was simply the starting point; the steering mechanism was exegesis. And behind exegesis stood another reality, that of tradition.

Judaism, Christianity, and Islam each possessed a Scripture that was, by universal consent, a closed Book. But God's silence was a relative thing, and His providential direction of the community could be detected and "read" in other ways. Early within the development of Christianity, for example, one is aware of a subtle balance operating between appeals to Scripture and tradition. It was not a novel enterprise. By Jesus' time the notion of an oral tradition separate from but obviously connected to the written Scriptures was already

[30] See J. Daniélou, *From Shadows to Reality: Studies in the Biblical Typology of the Fathers* (London: Burns and Oates, 1960).

[31] See M. F. Wiles in *Ackroyd and Evans, eds., *Cambridge History of the Bible*, I, 489-509; and R. A. Greer, *Theodore of Mopsuestia: Exegete and Theologian* (London: Faith Press, 1961).

[32] See, for example, A. Grillmeier, *Christ in Christian Tradition* (London: Sheed and Ward, 1965), pp. 338-362 for Theodore's role in the debate.

familiar, if not universally accepted, in Jewish circles.[33] Jesus and the Pharisees debated the authority of the oral tradition more than once, and though he does not appear to have denied the premise, Jesus substituted *his* authority for that of the "tradition of the Fathers." Thus Jesus was proposing himself as the source of a new tradition (*paradosis*) handed on to his followers and confirmed by the Holy Spirit on the day of Pentecost.

The view that there was a tradition distinct from the Scriptures may have begun with the early Christian understanding of Scripture as synonymous with the Bible—serious exegetical attention did not begin to be paid to the Gospels until the end of the second century—whereas the "tradition" was constituted of the teachings and redemptive death of Jesus, both of which Jesus himself had placed in their true "scriptural" context. Thus, even when parts of Jesus' teachings and actions had been committed to writing in the Gospels and so began to constitute a new, specifically Christian Scripture, the distinction between Scripture in the biblical sense and tradition in the Christian sense continued to be felt in the Christian community.

If the Christian *paradosis* came from Jesus, its witnesses and transmitters were the Apostles. The written Gospels go back to them and so does that other, unwritten part of the tradition that in the second century came to be called "the rule of faith" or "the rule of truth," and that, in the words of Irenaeus, was "received from the Apostles and guarded in the Church by the succession of presbyters." Here the Apostolic tradition, which included the correct interpretation of Scripture as well as certain prescribed forms of behavior, is explicitly tied to the bishops' being the direct spiritual descendants of the Apostles, a notion that was already formalized about 175 C.E., and is possessed by the entire Church.[34]

---

[33] B. Gerhardsson, *Memory and Manuscript* (Hund: C.W.K. Gleerup, 1961), pp. 71-192.

[34] This crucial development has been traced by J.N.D. Kelly, *Early Christian Doctrines*, 4th ed. (London: Black, 1968), chapter I; and G. L. Prestige,

The bishops spoke, then, with the authority of the "Apostolic tradition" behind them. At times their voices were single, that of an Ignatius, an Irenaeus, a Basil, or a Chrysostom, but there was also a broad stream of consensual tradition that manifested itself by the bishops sitting in synods or, from the fourth century, in the ecumenical councils of the Great Church. They might refer to Scripture, but Scripture was not their justification.[35] And though their common pronouncements were cast in the form of dogma—"It has been decided"—the voice was that of the Apostolic tradition and so of Jesus himself. Once expressed, it suffered no appeal.

The "teachings of the Fathers" was an important ingredient in the formulation of Christian doctrine and of canon law,[36] but its influence is no less visible in the interpretation of Scripture.[37] In all three religious communities, the Jewish, Christian, and Muslim, tradition controlled the interpretation of Scripture by its definition of the canon of sacred writings, by its choice of proof-texts, and by its authoritative understanding of the meaning of those texts. Attacks upon tradition and its guardians were made by appealing back to a literalist reading of Scripture and an assertion of its absolute priority, as was done by the Sadducees and Karaites in Judaism and, somewhat differently, by the Hanbalis and Zahiris in Islam and the Protestant reformers of Christianity; or by recourse to an alternate Gnostic form of tradition, one more akin to a private revelation, which permitted one a more allegorical and spiritual reading of the Sacred Book and so freed one from the Law of the traditionalists: so the Jewish

---

Fathers and Heretics (London: SPCK pb., 1963), chapter I. The sources illustrating the growth of the concept are collected in *H. Bettenson, *Documents of the Christian Church* (London: Oxford pb., 1970), pp. 95-103.

[35] Y. Congar, *Tradition and Traditions* (New York: Macmillan, 1966), pp. 50-64.

[36] See Chapter IV above.

[37] Congar, *Tradition*, pp. 64-85; H. Turner, *The Pattern of Christian Truth* (London: SPCK, 1954), pp. 258-306.

kabbalists, Christian Gnostics, and the Islamic Shi'ah and Batini groups.[38]

Since the Qur'an was not a historically conditioned revelation but rather reflects an eternal heavenly archetype composed of the self-same Arabic words, the Muslim approach to its exegesis was initially quite different from that pursued by the Jews and Christians.[39] The Qur'an did not easily suffer either translation or paraphrase—note that Mohammed Pickthall calls his translation, which is actually quite literal, "The *Meaning* of the Glorious Koran." On the Christian premise, Jesus was his own revelation. He could teach its significance with authority and pass on that teaching to his disciples in a formal and imperative fashion. Muhammad, on the other hand, was the conduit of God's revelation, much as Moses was, and during his own lifetime there was no question that he and only he was the authoritative interpreter of that revelation for the Muslim community, and his verbal explanations of the Qur'an formed part of that later collected body of *hadith* of which note has already been taken.

We may posit, then, a body of oral tradition in early Islam, some of it historical narrative, which was later incorporated into the *Lives* of the Prophet; some of it halakic, the discrete pieces later shaped into the Islamic Law; and some, finally, exegetical in character. These over-neat categories were by no means observed by Muslim authors themselves. Since they, like us, were using Qur'anic texts to illuminate the life of Muhammad and vice versa, long exegetical passages occur in early biographies of the Prophet, whereas professed works of exegesis (*tafsir*) devoted considerable attention to describing the historical circumstances surrounding the revelation of individual *surahs* or even verses of the Qur'an.

According to one tradition, there was an early prohibition against interpreting the Qur'an. This does not seem to have

[38] See Chapter VII below.

[39] On Arabic as a sacred language, see J. Wansbrough, *Qur'anic Studies* (London: Oxford University Press, 1977), pp. 99-106.

been the case, however,[40] and the earliest identifiable types of Qur'anic exegesis were very similar to the familiar forms of Jewish haggadic *midrash*, and showed some of the same motives: to fill in gaps in Qur'anic narratives, and the construction of a genuine Islamic piety.[41] Most of the narratives in question were biblical, and according to the Muslim tradition itself, details for their haggadic elaboration were supplied by Muslims with a particular knowledge of the Jewish tradition, both biblical and midrashic.[42]

The fashioning of an Islamic piety through homiletic means is not the same as the derivation of a body of legal enactments, *ahkam*, the Hebrew *halakot*, out of Muslim Scripture. As we have seen, a case has recently been made that the latter activity did not begin until the late eighth or early ninth century, and so perhaps well after the "custom of the Prophet" had been firmly established as the primary ground for the derivation of *ahkam*. On this paradoxical view, it was the text of the Qur'an that was elevated to the same status as the *sunnah* of the Prophet, and not vice versa.[43] Once this occurred, and only then, according to Wansbrough, did the lawyers turn to what may be called halakic exegesis of Scripture, supplying a historical context for the *surahs* by working out a chronology and the various "occasions of revelation," and so eliciting binding rules of conduct from the sacred text.[44]

[40] See H. Birkeland, *Old Muslim Opposition against Interpretation of the Qur'an* (Oslo: I Kommisjon Hos J. Dybwad, 1955); and N. Abbott, *Studies in Arabic Literary Papyri*, I: *Qur'anic Commentary and Tradition* (Chicago: Chicago University Press, 1967).

[41] See Wansbrough, *Qur'anic Studies*, pp. 122-149 and esp. 145-148, where Wansbrough underlines the role of the public and popular Friday sermon (*khutbah*) in the evolution of this basic form of Muslim exegesis.

[42] Some of the Jewish parallels to the narrative *surahs* 2 and 3 can be found in I. Katsch, *Judaism in Islam* (New York: New York University Press, 1954).

[43] Wansbrough, *Qur'anic Studies*, pp. 174-176.

[44] *Qur'anic Studies*, pp. 177-201. Here again the issue of "abrogation," Qur'an of Qur'an, *sunnah* of Qur'an and Qur'an of *sunnah*, is crucial: Wansbrough, pp. 192-201; J. Burton, *The Collection of the Qur'an* (Cambridge: Cambridge University Press, 1977), 46-104.

A common form of Muslim commentary on the Qur'an is the explication of the text itself, a procedure that presumes the existence of an authoritative canonical text.[45] The language of the Qur'an was, of course, Arabic, a "clear Arabic speech," in the Scripture's own words (Qur'an 16:103; 26:195). If Qur'anic Arabic was "clear" to Muhammad's audience at Mecca and Medina, as it surely must have been, it is not so to modern scholars, and has provoked considerable controversy on whether it was a local dialect, perhaps that of the Quraysh of Mecca, or a kind of ecumenical art-speech common to Bedouin oral bards.[46] Nor was it entirely "clear" to a later generation of Muslims, many of whom did not have Arabic as their native tongue, and who turned in a somewhat unexpected direction for help in explicating the text—to the works of the otherwise reprehensible pre-Islamic poets. This turning promoted a parallel activity in the collecting and editing of that poetry.[47]

Many of these developments in Islamic exegesis are traditionally attributed to Ibn al-'Abbas (d. 687), but like many other such attributions in early Islamic history, its object may have been to confer antiquity on something that occurred a century or more later. What we know for a certainty is that most of what was done in the earliest Islamic exegesis was caught up and assimilated into the *Collection of Explanations for the Exegesis of the Qur'an*, simply called *The Exegesis (al-Tafsir)*, of al-Tabari (d. 923), which from that day to this has held pride of place in Muslim exegesis. It proceeds majestically through the Qur'an *surah* by *surah*, combining legal, historical, and philological comment of great density, and it supports each judgment by a chain of authorities going back

---

[45] See Chapter II above, and for this so-called "masoretic commentary," Wansbrough, *Qur'anic Studies*, pp. 202-227.

[46] See C. Rabin, *Ancient West Arabian* (London: Taylor's Foreign Press, 1951), and Wansbrough, *Qur'anic Studies*, pp. 85-93 for a review of the question.

[47] Wansbrough, *Qur'anic Studies*, pp. 94-98, 216-219, and F. E. Peters, *Allah's Commonwealth* (New York: Simon and Schuster, 1973), pp. 221-229.

to Muhammad's own contemporaries, the famous Companions of the Prophet.

Since he occasionally addressed himself to the question, it appears from Tabari's commentary that in his day there was already understood to be another distinction in exegetical approach that cut across the categories just discussed: that between *tafsir*, "plain" exegesis, and *ta'wil*, which is often understood as allegorical exegesis. The distinction may go back to the Qur'an itself (3:7), which seems to suggest that there are two kinds of verses in Scripture, those whose meaning is clear and those others that require some kind of explanation (*ta'wil*).[48] That explanation may originally have been no more than the application of personal reasoning (*ijtihad*) or research (*nazar*) to the text, as opposed to the acceptance on authority of the plain meaning—a distinction current, and debated, in legal circles.[49] On that understanding, the difference between *tafsir* and *ta'wil* was not between exoteric and esoteric passages but rather between clear and ambiguous ones. Where *ta'wil* took on its allegorical association was its use in Vermes' category of "applied exegesis," that is, the use of exegetical principles to elicit from Scripture dogmatic and mystical understandings of which both Muhammad and the Qur'an were totally innocent.[50]

Dogmatic commentary, though more often accomplished by philology than by resort to allegorical exegesis, is on broad display in Islam's two other great monuments of *tafsir*, *The Unveiler of the Realities of the Secrets of Revelation* by Zamakhshari (d. 1144) and *The Lights of Revelation and the Secrets of Interpretation* of Baydawi (d. 1286). Neither these commentaries, Tabari's earlier work, or that of later exegetes has been readily available in English. Now, however, there is H. Gätje's

[48] On the various understandings of this difficult text, see Wansbrough, *Qur'anic Studies*, pp. 148-151.

[49] See Chapter IV above.

[50] See Wansbrough, *Qur'anic Studies*, pp. 245-246, and for the mystics' exegesis, Chapter VII below.

The Qur'an and Its Exegesis,[51] with generous selections from all the classical commentaries; and for an insight into modern exegetical trends, J. Baljon, *Modern Muslim Koran Interpretation*[52] and J. Jansen, *The Interpretation of the Koran in Modern Egypt.*[53]

Most of the commentators and commentaries discussed to this point operated within a tradition that regarded the body of *hadith* as the primary exegetical instrument for understanding the Qur'an, particularly on legal matters, much in the way the Talmud served that end vis-à-vis the Torah in Judaism. But the tradition did not go unchallenged. In both religious contexts there were challenges from "spiritualists" who claimed a deeper understanding of the Book, and hence a freedom from the body of positive prescriptions that the sages had exegetically extracted from it by resort to "tradition." The Essenes and Christians confronted the Pharisees with just such a special understanding in their day, as later the kabbalists did the rabbis.[54] In Islam, Sufi and Shi'ite alike could counterpose the spiritual tradition passed on by their *pirs* and *imams* to the *'ulamas'* tradition-derived *halakot.*[55]

But the challenge could be mounted in another way. Josephus' brief remarks about the Sadducees characterize them as a group that rejected any law not explicitly contained in the Torah.[56] This was a direct denial of the Pharisees' "tradition of the Fathers": the Torah alone was revelation, and it should be interpreted in a direct, literal fashion; all else is at best speculation and at worst innovation. We hear this charge once again in Judaism, there urged by a group called the Karaites against Babylonian rabbis of the eighth century.[57]

[51] Berkeley and Los Angeles: California University Press, 1976.
[52] Leiden: E. J. Brill, 1961.
[53] Leiden: E. J. Brill, 1974.
[54] See Chapter VII below.
[55] See Chapter VII below.
[56] *Sandmel, *Beginnings,* pp. 156-158; and *Moore, *Judaism,* I, 57-61.
[57] There may be a connection; see Gerhardsson, *Memory and Manuscript,* pp. 172-173, 284-287; and N. Wieder, *The Judean Scrolls and Karaism* (London: East and West Library, 1962), pp. 53-62.

The Karaites were literally "readers" who confined their reading to Scripture and attempted to live according to its precepts (*mitzvot*) and those alone.[58] We do not know how the Karaites managed this in a society already remote from the mores and manner of life of the Patriarchal Age. Literalism brought freedom from the *halakot*, it is true, but many of these latter were not the "burden" sometimes suggested by Christian sources but effectively brought the Biblical *mitzvot* into line with local custom and evolving circumstances, much as the *hadith* did in Islam. The Karaites' attraction was the threat they posed to the power of the rabbinate. But it is doubtful whether the Torah could indeed serve in its literal sense as a normative code for an eighth-century Jewish community, and the version of a Torah society put forward by the Karaite leader Anan ben David may have foundered on its own literalism.

A later generation of Karaites under Benjamin al-Nihawandi and Daniel al-Qumisi took a different path; they granted to each Jew the privilege of being his own rabbi, to construct his own Talmud out of a commonly held Torah. It was, once again, an attractive possibility, and Karaism spread far beyond its Babylonian place of origin to Jewish communities all over the Dar al-Islam and beyond.[59] The intellectual leadership turned away from the *mitzvot* to what at first seems like an unexpected direction, to philosophical speculation and the allegorical interpretation of Scripture. They may have been following an Islamic lead. As the early Muslim theologians known as Mu'tazilites had shown, Scripture could be controlled as effectively by rational enquiry as by an appeal to tradition.

In Islam we find distinct parallels to the Karaite position in the Kharijites, whose sense of Islamic community has al-

[58] S. Baron, *A Social and Religious History of the Jews*, V, 209-235; L. Nemoy, *Karaite Anthology* (New Haven: Yale University Press, 1952).

[59] See Z. Ankori, *Karaites in Byzantium* (New York: Columbia University Press, 1959).

ready been discussed.[60] The Kharijites attempted to establish a Muslim community and a Muslim way of life based on the Qur'an without benefit of "interpreting" the plain meaning of the text, and again like the early Karaites, took a severe view of associating with those who did not share their views.[61] The Kharijites were putting forward these views late in the seventh century, well before the imposing body of *hadith* and its derived prescriptions were in place, and so it is likely that they were reacting to what they construed as worldly and non-Islamic behavior rather than to an oppressive tradition.

Tradition was and is a powerful force in Islam. Though the evidence is not plentiful, it can hardly be doubted that the tribal life of the pre-Islamic Arabs, and that of their seventh-century brethren in the somewhat more urban milieus of Mecca and Medina, were governed by *sunnah*, custom either decreed or instituted by an individual that later became the common practice of the tribe.[62] There are instances of the Prophet himself regarding his own acts as setting a precedent for the *ummah*,[63] but the firmest evidence for the existence of the idea that the "custom of the Prophet" was somehow normative in Islam is its inclusion in the oath sworn by the third Caliph 'Uthman at his accession in 644 c.e.[64]

Shafi'i neither invented nor popularized *hadith* as a form of popular piety; he was discussing the priority of certain legal principles. The broader reach of *hadith* may be observed in the "traditionists" (*ahl al-hadith*), a large and amorphous category of Muslims who, like the Kharijites, longed for a Qur'an-oriented society, now supplemented by that idealized version of the earlier generation of Muslims that found its

[60] See Chapter III above.

[61] W. M. Watt, *The Formative Period of Islamic Thought* (Chicago: Aldine, 1973), pp. 21-25.

[62] See M. Bravman, *The Spiritual Background of Early Islam* (Leiden: E. J. Brill, 1972), pp. 123-176, esp. p. 164.

[63] A. Guillaume, *Life of Muhammad* (London: Oxford pb., 1967), p. 387.

[64] *Schacht, *Introduction*, pp. 17-18; Bravman, *Spiritual Background*, pp. 123-139.

definitive portrait in the *hadith*.[65] As for the Qur'an, they venerated it next to God himself, and inclined toward a reverentially strict interpretation of its text.

Opposition to the *ahl al-hadith* came from the *ahl al-kalam*, "partisans of dialectic,"[66] and particularly from the group known as the Mu'tazilites. It is not known whether these latter rejected *hadith* or, as seems more likely, took a more hypercritical view of it than was common in most Muslim circles.[67] What is certain is that they preferred to rely upon the Qur'an, which they did not hesitate to interpret in a metaphorical fashion in order to avoid the gross anthropomorphisms of the simple-minded pietists.[68] But their dispute with the *ahl al-hadith* went deeper than this. The latter's veneration for the *ipsissima verba* of the Qur'an and the Mu'tazilite insistence on using dialectical methods of analysis came to term in the profound debate on whether the Qur'an was created, as the Mu'tazilites held, or whether it was eternal, coeval and coequal with God.[69]

For the Mu'tazilites, an uncreated Qur'an was a theological affront to a unique God as well as a manacle that chained human reason and conscience to a text, however revered that latter might be. In *hadithi* eyes the uncreated Qur'an was a mysterious embodiment of the sacred, an almost sacramental link between a transcendent God and His earthly creation. In a verbal struggle in which all the weapons belonged to the dialecticians, it is difficult to piece together the nuances of the traditionist position, but out of the *ahl al-hadith* came two Islamic "schools," those of Ahmad ibn Hanbal (d. 855) and Dawud ibn Khalaf (d. 884), from which a coherent position can be derived. Both insisted on the evident (*zahir*; Dawud's

---

[65] *M. G. Hodgson, *The Venture of Islam* (Chicago: University of Chicago Press pb., 1974), I, 386-389.

[66] See Chapter VIII below.

[67] Compare Schacht, *Origins*, pp. 40-41 and 128.

[68] Watt, *Formative Period*, pp. 247-248; *Hodgson, *Venture*, I, 391-392.

[69] H. Wolfson, *The Philosophy of the Kalam* (Cambridge: Harvard University Press, 1976), pp. 235-303, and *Hodgson, *Venture*, I, 388-392.

followers were called Zahiris) sense of both the Qur'an and the *hadith*—on pious, conservative grounds, to be sure, but almost as surely as a reaction to Mu'tazilite exegesis based on analogy (*qiyas*) and systematic investigation (*nazar*).[70]

As we shall see in our discussion of theology, exegesis lay at the heart of the debate over the conflicting claims of faith and reason in the domain of revealed religion. The rationalizing theologians wrested some of the rights of exegesis away from the lawyers because they were more skillful in allegorical exegesis. Traditionists were tied by their own legal premises to the literal interpretation of Scripture, a connection that committed them in non-halakic passages to certain gross anthropomorphisms that the dialecticians could devour with arguments. More, the theologians permitted themselves a far wider exegetical range, and could apply both learning and imagination to the text of Scripture, whereas the traditionists were largely limited to rhetoric and philology. The attractiveness of theological *tafsir* is demonstrated by the position won by the Mu'tazilite Zamakhshari's Qur'anic commentary among all segments of the Islamic community, and by the fact that Philo's discredited allegorical exegesis found a new audience once Jewish theologians under Islam rediscovered philosophy.[71]

The philosophers made bolder claims. For the theologian, rational discourse, whether in exegesis or elsewhere, was complementary to and defensive of the higher truths of revelation,[72] but the philosopher, the Muslim Avicenna or the Jewish Maimonides, regarded philosophy's claim as the higher one: Scripture figured truth for the unphilosophical masses; philosophy uttered its very name. There can be no conflict, however. Where Scripture appears to conflict with the con-

---

[70] *Schacht, *Introduction*, pp. 63-64; I. Goldziher, *The Zahiris, Their Doctrine and Their History* (1884; revised translation, Leiden: E. J. Brill, 1971).

[71] On the revival of the Jewish allegorical exegesis under Islam, see *Ginzberg, *On Jewish Law and Lore*, pp. 138-147.

[72] On philosophy as the handmaiden of Scripture, see H. A. Wolfson, *Church Fathers*, pp. 97-101.

clusions of demonstrative reasoning, it is a clear sign that the literal meaning of Scripture must be interpreted allegorically, not by the lawyer or the theologian, whose powers of reasoning are undermined by faulty premises, but by the philosopher, who alone possesses demonstrative knowledge.[73]

[73] These are the arguments advanced by Averroes (d. 1198) in his *Decisive Treatise*, translated by G. Hourani, *Averroes on the Harmony of Religion and Philosophy* (London: Luzac and Co., 1961); see pp. 22-28, 50-51.

CHAPTER VI

The Liturgy

MOST religious communities have commended or mandated various external forms of worship to their adherents, and central to all of them is prayer. The address of words to God, accompanied by appropriate postures and gestures, is best fulfilled, of course, by using God's own words, that is, by using Scripture as a source of liturgical or public prayer.

In Judaism there is an obvious distinction to be made between the liturgical practices connected with the temple cult, which was centralized in Jerusalem in 621 B.C.E. when King Josiah ordered the destruction of all local cult shrines, and the kinds of public devotion that developed after the destruction of the Temple. Temple services had been restored in Judea by Ezra and Nehemiah after the return from exile in Babylonia. The code in Deuteronomy may be the clearest expression of that restoration, but modern scholarship suspects that the editing of many of the earlier books of the Bible may have occurred at the same time in order to validate the liturgical practices of post-Exilic Judaism.[1]

Those practices were twofold. First were the animal sacrifices offered in the Temple built by Solomon and restored by Herod the Great. These were conducted by regular courses of priests (*kohanim*) chosen out of a priestly clan—the Sadducees are not necessarily identical with this class, but they were almost certainly connected with them in some way—with a hereditary High Priest, assisted by the lower order of Levites. There were as well at least three pilgrimage festivals connected with the temple cult, that of "Booths" (Sukkot),

---

[1] See *S. Sandmel, *Judaism and Christian Beginnings* (London: Oxford University Press pb., 1978), pp. 20-25; and A. Idelsohn, *Jewish Liturgy and Its Development* (New York: Schocken pb., 1975), chapter 3.

of "Passover" (Pesach), and of "Weeks" (Shabuot).[2] These three festivals probably had agricultural as well as pilgrimage associations. Such was certainly the case in the celebration of the New Year (Rosh ha-shana), which originally fell on the Spring equinox but was later shifted to the first day of the lunar month Tishre. Apart from beginning the calendrical lunar year, Rosh ha-shana also opened a penitential period that came to its climax on the tenth day of Tishre in the "Day of Atonement" (Yom kippur), when a great atonement liturgy was conducted in the Temple.[3]

All of these feasts, with the possible exception of Rosh ha-shana, were intimately linked with the Jerusalem Temple in post-Exilic times, and with the destruction of that institution and its cult in 70 C.E., they had to be transferred to either the home or the synagogue. The origins of this latter institution (*bet ha-knesset*) are still the subject of debate. Some argue that it arose during the Babylonian Exile, when Jews were cut off from the Jerusalem cult center, while others see it as a Pharisee-inspired institution with a totally different intent. Whatever the case, the synagogue had evolved, perhaps even before the destruction of the Temple, from a simple House of Assembly (*bet ha-knesset*) into a genuine House of Prayer (*bet ha-tefilla*). It became the focus of Jewish liturgical life after 70 C.E., and by the fourth century had developed not only a fixed liturgy but a distinctive architectural form.[4]

---

[2] All are described in *Sandmel, *Beginnings*, pp. 24, 213-218.

[3] Ibid., pp. 213-227. Services for both the pilgrimage festivals and the holy days are described in Idelsohn, *Jewish Liturgy*, pp. 188-256, and there is a selection of liturgical texts drawn from rabbinic sources in *C. K. Barrett, *The New Testament Background* (New York: Harper Torchbook, 1961), pp. 153-162.

[4] E. L. Sukenik, *Ancient Synagogues in Palestine and Greece* (London: Oxford University Press, 1934) described the architectural evolution of the synagogue as it was understood in his day, but his sketch has been rendered in part obsolete by many new finds and a very different picture will be found in M. Avi-Yonah's article "Synagogues" in volume IV (1978) of the *Encyclopedia of Archaeological Excavations in the Holy Land*; cf. B. de Breffny, *The Synagogue* (New York: Macmillan, 1978).

The public synagogue service took place on the Sabbath, a weekly day of rejoicing and restraint from work, and on other holy days of celebration, atonement, or recollection. It began with recitations from the Scriptures, first with serial passages from the Torah distributed across either a three-year cycle current in Palestine from the second to the fifth century C.E., or a single-year cycle that was in use in Babylonia at about the same time and that eventually came to prevail in most Jewish communities.[5] The recitation of the weekly Torah passage (a *seder* in the Palestinian cycle; a *parasha* in the Babylonian), which was accompanied verse by verse by the Aramaic translation (*targum*), was followed by the *haftara*, an appropriately chosen passage of about ten verses drawn from the Prophets and again accompanied by a *targum*. After the chanting of a psalm, the preacher began the homiletic part of the liturgy. He first cited an "opening verse" (*petiha*) of his own selection from the Prophets or the "Writings," and then proceeded to weave together *seder*, *haftara*, and the various *petihot* into a coherent exegetical and ethical whole.

We can reconstruct this ceremony because early preserved homiletic commentaries on Scripture follow this format and presumably reflect synagogue practice. Private prayer, normally three times daily, and the domestic liturgy of Judaism,[6] which has no real parallel in either Christianity or Islam, have left far fewer traces of their evolution. Even though they are largely composed of scriptural passages, and some, like the *Shema'* and the benedictions of the *Amida*, were already being recited in some form during the Tannaitic period and perhaps even earlier, the formalization of the Jewish liturgy—even allowing for regional and sectarian differences—

---

[5] The various divisions of the Jewish Scriptures for liturgical purposes have been studied by J. Mann, *The Bible as Read and Preached in the Old Synagogue*, 2 vols. (New York: Hebrew Union College, 1940, 1966), and the liturgical prayers are described in *Sandmel, *Beginnings*, pp. 147-173 and Idelsohn, *Jewish Liturgy*, pp. 73-121.

[6] See Idelsohn, *Jewish Liturgy*, pp. 151-157, 173-187.

was the work of medieval scholars in Europe and the Dar al-Islam.[7]

The Gospels portray Jesus participating in a synagogue service in Galilee and celebrating the Passover in a private house in Jerusalem with his disciples. After his death these same disciples continued to participate in the Temple liturgy in Jerusalem. Paul, who was constrained by the disciples to make an appearance at the Temple to dispel the impression that he, like the "Hellenists," had no regard for the official cult, preached his message of the risen Jesus in synagogues of the Diaspora. As the Christians developed their own particular liturgy it is natural to think that they behaved like the Jews they were and built upon Jewish liturgical practices familiar to all of them.[8] Such appears to have been the case, in fact, and Dom Gregory Dix has demonstrated that the earliest Christians had a prayer meeting (*synaxis*) constructed on the model of a synagogue and a separate eucharistic celebration that may have had associations with Passover.[9] Eventually the two became fused in the eucharistic liturgy, whose original parts are still fairly evident. The first is the "mass of the catechumens," that is, those under instruction (*catechesis*) for baptism, and here the synagogue antecedents are obvious: scriptural readings, a homily, and common prayer.[10] The catechumens were then dismissed and the mass of the faithful began with a procession bringing in the offerings. There followed the Eucharist proper and finally the communion whereby the faithful shared in the consecrated bread and wine.[11]

[7] Ibid., pp. 89-110 (*Shema' and Amida*); 56-70 (evolution).

[8] See W. Oesterly, *The Jewish Background of the Christian Liturgy* (London: Oxford University Press, 1925); C. A. Dugmore, *The Influence of the Synagogue upon the Divine Office* (1944; reprint London: Faith Press, 1965).

[9] *The Shape of the Liturgy* (London: Dacre Press, 1945).

[10] J. A. Lamb in *P. R. Ackroyd and C. F. Evans, eds., *The Cambridge History of the Bible* (Cambridge: Cambridge University Press, 1970), I, 563-586: "The Place of the Bible in the Liturgy."

[11] *Dix, *The Shape of the Liturgy*; and B. Steuart, *The Development of Christian Worship* (London: Longmans, 1953).

If historians of religion found the mass of the catechumens comfortingly familiar, there were others who thought they detected something similar between the rituals of communion and baptism, on the one hand, and the rites of Greco-Roman paganism, and particularly those of the so-called "mystery religions," on the other.[12] A relatively moderate argument for that influence was made by Samuel Angus in his *The Mystery Religions and Christianity*.[13] It may have been the last such. Subsequent investigation of the question has been far more careful to distinguish between the original form of the Greek mysteries—those of Eleusis, for example—which were agrarian and cyclical in nature and were both localized and restricted, and the later cosmopolitan mysteries, which promised a more universal form of salvation all over the Roman Mediterranean.[14]

All our evidence for these latter universalist mysteries derives from the second and third century C.E., and a close analysis of the Gospels and the Letters of Paul from the point of view of the terminology of the mystery religions shows that in fact neither was indebted to or even much aware of the pagan mysteries.[15] When Paul, for example, spoke of "mystery"—never "mysteries"—he always meant it in the Septuagint sense of the divine plan of redemption; it had none of the cultic significance it inevitably bore for pagan authors.

As Christianity moved out of its original Jewish environment into the Hellenic world, there was doubtless an interpenetration of spirit and vocabulary between the pagan mysteries, which were at their apogee in the third century, and

[12] Described by F. Cumont, *Oriental Religions in Roman Paganism* (1911; New York: Dover pb., 1956), and more recently by J. Ferguson, *The Religions of the Roman Empire* (Ithaca: Cornell University Press, 1970).

[13] New York: C. Scribner's Sons, 1928.

[14] H. Rahner, "The Christian Mystery and the Pagan Mysteries" in J. Campbell, ed., *Pagan and Christian Mysteries* (New York: Harper Torchbook, 1963), pp. 146-210.

[15] A. D. Nock, "Hellenistic Mysteries and Christian Sacraments" in Z. Stewart, ed., *Essays on Religion in the Ancient World* (London: Oxford University Press, 1972), I, 791-820 and his briefer "The Vocabulary of the New Testament" in *Essays*, I, 341-347.

the Christian sacramental system. Christian writers drew sharp distinctions between their own Christian sacramentalism and the pagan mysteries of which they were increasingly aware, but at the same time they did not hesitate to expropriate the popular terminology of their rivals. A burgeoning Christianity was, however, an even more potent rival to the mysteries, and it is equally probable that the broadening and spiritualizing of those mysteries in their final period owed a great deal to the success of the Christian opposition.

From the beginning, the celebration of the Christian "thanksgiving" (*eucharistia*) ritual took place on Sunday, the Lord's Day, as a commemoration of his Resurrection. Thus Jesus' Last Supper, a Passover *seder*, ran together with the reenactment of a messianic event, with its own biblical typology, to constitute a new Christian action. This was the new sacrifice of the New Covenant in which Jesus is both priest and sacrifice. The bread and wine are transformed, by God's appointment, into Jesus' flesh and blood.[16] The ceremony was conducted by the "elders" (*presbyteroi*) of the community, and all those who had been admitted to the community by baptism, another very early sacramental rite, participated in it.[17]

The Eucharist and other sacramental and nonsacramental forms of Christian liturgy became more elaborate and more standardized with the passage of time.[18] At first they were conducted, like some contemporary synagogue services, in

[16] J.N.D. Kelly, *Early Christian Doctrines*, 4th ed. (London: Black, 1968), pp. 193-198. Some early Christian prayers and orders are preserved, such as the Didache of the late first or early second century, which has been translated in M. Staniforth, *Early Christian Writers: The Apostolic Fathers* (Harmondsworth: Penguin, 1968), pp. 227-235, and H. Musurillo, *The Fathers of the Primitive Church* (New York: Mentor Omega pb., 1966), pp. 57-62.

[17] *H. G. Davies, *The Early Christian Church* (Garden City: Doubleday Anchor, 1967), pp. 75-85; H. Chadwick, *The Early Church* (Harmondsworth: Penguin, 1967), pp. 261-271. The early sources are in *H. Bettenson, *Documents of the Christian Church* (London: Oxford University Press pb., 1970), pp. 104-107.

[18] Their evolution is traced by *Davies, *Christian Church*, pp. 136-145, 196-207, 264-279, 346-365.

private homes, which also served as a *bet ha-knesset*, in Greek *ekklesia*, for the community. With the end of the persecutions, Christians constructed a special prayer hall that took over a common type of Roman building, the basilica, and modified it for Christian liturgical purposes.[19]

The exact form of the Christian liturgy varied from place to place, as can be observed from the texts translated by F. E. Brightman in his *Liturgies Eastern and Western*.[20] Most of the available material for the reconstruction of the early Christian eucharistic liturgy, like the Didache of the late first or early second century and the Apostolic Constitution of about 380 C.E., refer to a type of service in use in the urban centers of Syria to about 400 C.E. Another different form was current in Egypt about the same time. Both of these were in Greek, but the Eucharist was early celebrated in Christian Aramaic—the dialect called Syriac—at Edessa, and it is still in use in eastern churches today under the rubric of "the liturgy of Mari and Addai." In Rome and the African provinces of the empire, services were in Latin, and again, the form of the Roman "mass," as the eucharistic liturgy was called, differed in details from contemporary Eastern versions of the same service.[21]

What followed in the East testifies, as certainly as the evolution of the hierarchical structure,[22] to the growing centralization of the Great Church and the consequent standardization of its practices. A "liturgy of Saint James," which may have had its beginnings in Jerusalem, and a parallel service attributed to Saint Mark began to drive out all the local liturgies in the patriarchal sees of Antioch and Alexandria,

[19] See R. Krautheimer, *Early Christian and Byzantine Architecture* (London: Penguin, 1965), pp. 1-44.

[20] 1896; reprint London: Oxford University Press, 1956; S. Salaville, *Eastern Liturgies* (London: Sands and Co., 1938); A. King, *The Rites of Eastern Christendom* (Rome: Catholic Book Agency, 1947-1948).

[21] J. A. Jungmann, *The Mass of the Roman Rite* (Westminster, Md.: Christian Classics, 1959).

[22] See Chapter III above.

respectively. And with the growth in political power and prestige of Constantinople, its liturgical practice, the so-called "Saint Basil," not only dominated in the churches of Anatolia but, as nationalism and separatism grew in Syria and Egypt, gained an official cachet as the liturgy of the Eastern Orthodox Church.[23]

Within these types there were, of course, all manner of variations, but certain elements remained constant.[24] The division into two parts has already been mentioned. The first, the Synaxis, was preceded by the "little entrance" of the celebrants into the sanctuary area, and was composed of readings from the Bible, Paul, and the Gospels, interspersed with psalms and concluded by the dismissal of the catechumens. At this point began the Eucharist proper. After the "great entrance" there were various prayers of greeting and commemoration, the recitation of a creed (*symbolon*), and the kiss of peace. The diptychs were read, lists of the living and the dead in communion with a particular church, and a number of offertory prayers recited. The priestly celebrant then began the most sacred part of the liturgy, the Anaphora, which he initiated by exhorting the faithful to lift up their minds to God. A hymn to the angels followed, then a remembrance (*anamnesis*) of Jesus' passion, and an invocation (*epiklesis*) directed to the Holy Spirit to descend upon the bread and wine that had been placed upon the altar. There was a final blessing, and the Anaphora ended with the Lord's Prayer. What remained was the breaking of the bread, now transformed into the Body of Christ, and the sharing of the wine/Blood with the faithful.

A certain evolution can be traced in these rites that have just been sketched in their fully developed form. The earliest

[23] J. H. Srawley, *The Early History of the Liturgy* (1913; reprint Cambridge: Cambridge University Press, 1947); L. Duchesne, *Christian Worship: Its Origins and Evolution* (London: SPCK, 1956); T. S. Garrett, *Christian Worship* (London: Oxford University Press, 1961). The "Saint Basil" has been translated under the title of *The Orthodox Liturgy* (London: SPCK, 1939).

[24] See A. Baumstark, *Comparative Liturgy* (London: Newman Press, 1958).

examples, the liturgy embedded in the Apostolic Constitution, for example, were more obviously oriented toward prayer than toward ceremonial. With the liturgies of James and Mark a new dramatic element appears. The altar has become a stage for the sacrifice of the Christ; the audience for the drama is cosmic: angels, priests, people. Finally, with the liturgy attributed to Saint Basil, the ecstatic quality becomes subdued and the imagery and expression more restrained. The language is precise, almost juridical, rejecting the more abstract terminology derived from Greek philosophy that was beginning to make inroads into the theological discourse of the period.[25]

Jewish sacrificial cult ended with the destruction of the Temple, and thereafter its place was taken by services that offered prayers of praise and expiation rather than live sacrifices for those same ends. But Judaism was far more than the offering of prayers or even a certain type of ethical behavior. What Moses had been given on Sinai, the written Law of the Torah and the oral tradition finally embodied in the Talmud, were not simply the terms of a covenant to be observed by every Jew but the stuff of a special liturgical vocation. The *bet ha-midrash*, where the Talmud was studied with such loving care, was as much a place of worship as the synagogal *bet ha-tefilla*, and the study of Torah and Talmud was a moral imperative as efficacious as prayer.[26]

Islam never knew liturgical sacrifice. Muhammad was either unaware of or completely disinterested in the earlier Jewish temple cult, and the Qur'an's one possible reference to the Eucharist suggests that it was thought of as some kind of meal sent down from heaven to sustain the believers.[27] Islamic liturgy was, then, akin to that of rabbinic Judaism, one of prayers (*salat*). The practice began with Muhammad, and

---

[25] See Chapter VIII below.

[26] See the passages cited in C. G. Montefiore and H. Loewe, *A Rabbinic Anthology* (New York: Schocken pb., 1974), pp. 137ff.

[27] G. Parrinder, *Jesus in the Qur'an* (London: Oxford pb., 1977), pp. 85-89.

even then the substance of the liturgical prayer was the Qur'an itself. The very word Qur'an means "recitation," which is suggestive of liturgical intent, and Muhammad was well aware that the Books of the Jews and Christians, to which the Qur'an was akin, were used for liturgical purposes.[28] Prayer, in any event, preceded by a ritual ablution and accompanied by appropriate gestures and prostrations, is the heart of the Islamic liturgy and the chief duty of every Muslim. Though the practice is still somewhat fluid in the Qur'an, prayer soon became standardized at five times a day, when the faithful are summoned by a "caller" (mu'adhdhin; English, muezzin). At first, the prayers were said facing Jerusalem, but later the direction of prayer, the qiblah, was changed to the Ka'bah at Mecca.[29]

The daily prayers of the Muslim might be said in private in any dignified setting, but the noon prayer on Friday had a special liturgical significance in that it was a prescribed congregational prayer. Friday came to be called "the day of assembly"—a fact that Goitein has argued went back to a pre-Islamic market day in Medina[30]—and the place of congregation, "the assembly" (jami'). This was the mosque, though the English word goes back to another name and another function of the same place: masjid, a place of prostration or worship.

The first mosque in Islam was Muhammad's own house in Medina, and its successors in the Islamic diaspora served much the same purpose as the original building: a simple structure used indifferently for political assembly and liturgy. There were few architectural requirements: a place for ablution in an open court and a tower or minaret from which the muezzin might summon the faithful to prayer; within, a

---

[28] *W. M. Watt, *Bell's Introduction to the Qur'an* (Chicago: Aldine, 1970), pp. 137-138.

[29] H.A.R. Gibb, *Mohammedanism* (London: Oxford University Press pb., 1970), pp. 42-43; S. D. Goitein, *Studies in Islamic History and Institutions* (Leiden: E. J. Brill, 1968), pp. 73-89.

[30] *Studies*, pp. 111-125.

niche (*mihrab*) to note the *qiblah* and a raised throne (*minbar*), which originally served as a kind of political rostrum but which developed, with the progressive restriction of the mosque to liturgical functions, into a pulpit for the Friday sermon.[31]

Daily prayer is one of the "Pillars of Islam," obligations incumbent upon all Muslims. Another is the *hajj*, the pilgrimage to the holy places of Mecca and its environs, which every Muslim must make during his lifetime if circumstances permit. The *hajj* and the cult surrounding the Kaʿbah or House of God at Mecca existed before Muhammad and before Islam, and in accepting them as a genuine form of Muslim religious sentiment, Muhammad preserved within the *hajj* a treasure-trove of early Semitic cult practice barely concealed beneath its Muslim veneer.[32]

Daily prayer and pilgrimage by no means exhaust the liturgical and ritualistic side of Islam. The Muslims, like the Christians, possess a liturgical calendar that marks the occurrence of certain days of festival (*ʿid*) across the lunar year.[33] Two of them are observed by all Muslims. The "sacrificial feast" (*ʿid al-adha*) was and remains connected with the animal sacrifice that was an original, pre-Islamic part of the *hajj* ritual, but in the course of time it extended itself to all Muslims, whether on pilgrimage or not. A second festival, "breaking of the fast" (*ʿid al-fitr*), is celebrated on the first day of the month following the penitential season of Ramadan. Both require community prayer, whether they fall upon Friday or not. Another nearly universal festival is that of the

[31] O. Grabar, *The Formation of Islamic Art* (New Haven: Yale University Press, 1973), pp. 104-138.

[32] The complex ritual of the pilgrimage is outlined in the article "Hadjdj" in the revised edition of the *Encyclopaedia of Islam*, and there is an extraordinary nineteenth-century eyewitness account by Richard Burton in his *Personal Narrative of a Pilgrimage to Al Madinah and Mecca*, 1893; reprint 2 vols. (New York: Dover pb., 1964). It includes (II, 281-293) the translation of a short Muslim treatise on the legal and ritual requirements of the pilgrimage.

[33] Cf. A. A. McArthur, *The Evolution of the Christian Year* (London: SCM Press, 1953).

birthday of the Prophet (*mawlid al-nabi*), although it has been opposed at various times and places by Muslim purists who objected to such veneration being given to a mortal, or who were scandalized by some of the more extravagant Sufi manifestations that accompanied the celebration.[34]

The birthday of the Prophet is not the only *mawlid* celebrated in Islam. The veneration of great men after their death is an ancient practice based on the belief that they continued to possess, in some degree, the political or religious power they had in life. The tombs of Abraham and Sarah and other Jewish Patriarchs are still venerated at Hebron, and it is likely that at least some of the Muslim shrines commemorating biblical figures go back to a pre-Islamic and pre-Christian Jewish tradition, though we have no idea what rites might have been celebrated there.[35]

For Christians, the first posthumous heroes were the martyrs who died for their faith in the Roman persecutions. W. C. Frend in his *Martyrdom and Persecution in the Early Church*[36] has argued that here too there were Jewish antecedents. By the third century c.e. there were, in any event, memorial buildings over martyrs' graves outside the cities of the empire, and the date of their martyrdom was being celebrated in both liturgical and literary form.[37] In the new religious climate established by the conversion of Constantine, what were simply tombs were expanded into magnificent churches where the feast day of the saint could be celebrated before large crowds with liturgical pomp. It was Constantine too who converted Palestine into a Christian Holy Land by con-

[34] A lively portrait of the celebration of religious festivals in late traditional Muslim society is given by E. L. Lane, *An Account of the Manners and Customs of the Modern Egyptians*, 1836 (reprint New York: Dover pb., 1973), chaps. 24-26; see also G. E. von Grunebaum, *Muhammadan Festivals* (New York: Schuman, 1951).

[35] Many of them are described in T. Canaan, *Mohammedan Saints and Sanctuaries in Palestine* (London: Luzac, 1927).

[36] New York: New York University Press, 1967, pp. 22-57.

[37] H. Delehaye, *The Legends of the Saints* (New York: Fordham University Press, 1962).

structing notable churches over the sites associated with Jesus' life and death.[38]

The cult of saints, living or dead, was not an entirely natural development in Islam, which placed an almost infinite gulf between a transcendent Allah and His creation here below. It occurred nonetheless, and with some speed.[39] Note has already been taken of the opposition to the *mawlid al-nabi*. Muhammad, who never claimed to be anything other than mortal, and stoutly refused to produce supernatural signs to verify his claims as a prophet, was soon after his death credited with marvelous powers,[40] and those gifts and graces (*karamat*) bestowed by Allah upon His Prophet were quickly extended to Allah's "friends" (*wali*; pl. *awliya*), male and female, who thus became the objects of a special cult, even during their lifetimes, and whose tombs and shrines are centers of local and even pan-Islamic veneration.[41]

Islam possesses one prototypical martyr, Husayn, the son of the fourth Caliph ʿAli and Muhammad's grandson. He and his companions were slaughtered in a political uprising at the town of Karbela in Iraq on the tenth day of the month Muharram in 680 C.E. Both the day and the place have taken on extraordinary significance for Muslims, particularly the Shiʿites. Not only has Karbela become a richly endowed shrine and pilgrimage city, but the celebration of Muharram has

---

[38] *Davies, *Christian Church*, pp. 356-362; Krautheimer, *Early Christian Architecture*, pp. 27-44; on Christian pilgrimages to Palestine, see J. Wilkinson, *Jerusalem Pilgrims before the Crusades* (Warminster: Aris and Phillips, 1977).

[39] I. Goldziher, *Muslim Studies* (1898), revised translation by S. M. Stern (London: Allen and Unwin, 1967), II, 255-262.

[40] A. Schimmel, *Mystical Dimensions of Islam* (Chapel Hill: North Carolina University Press pb., 1975), pp. 213-227.

[41] Goldziher, *Muslim Studies*, II, 262-279; Schimmel, *Mystical Dimensions*, pp. 119-213; and on North Africa, where the cult of Muslim saints, locally called *marabouts*, is particularly strong, see E. Westermarck, *Ritual and Belief in Morocco*, 2 vols. (London: Macmillan, 1926); E. Gellner, *Saints of the Atlas* (London: Wiedenfeld and Nicolson, 1969); and C. Geertz, *Islam Observed* (Chicago: Chicago University Press pb., 1971).

generated a rich liturgical and dramatic reenactment (*ta'ziya*) of the martyrdom of Husayn.[42]

Christianity early institutionalized the veneration of its holy men. The martyrs were the first to be so honored, as we have seen, but the same practices were soon extended to the "confessor," those holy men and women whose lifelong pursuit of virtue proclaimed their sanctity as eloquently as the blood of the martyrs did theirs. There appears to have been little opposition to the liturgical rites that grew up around the tombs of the Christian saints, nor is there any reason to think there should have been in a community whose founder had already sanctified flesh by appropriating it to his own Godhead.

Judaism and Islam produced their own ranks of both martyrs and confessors whom they honor but to whom they are reluctant to extend the veneration due only to God. Jews and Muslims share the biblical jealousy of adoration, and the Christian theologians' willingness to distinguish, carefully in theory but somewhat less so in liturgical practice, between the adoration paid only to God and the veneration legitimately granted the saints has not convinced them otherwise. The doctrine of the Incarnation was truly a "scandal to the Jews," as Paul had foreseen, and was equally predictably so to the Muslims; and the liturgical veneration of the saints, which flows as naturally as the sacramental system itself from that doctrine, was simply a lesser form of the same scandal.

Jewish liturgy is symbolic and historical. It remembers events; it commemorates promises received and weeps for disappointed hopes; like the Bible, it is both a record and a celebration. Christian liturgy is cosmic and yet professedly literal. "This is my body" seeks at the same time to draw God down from heaven and exalt matter to a supernatural

[42] G. von Grunebaum, *Muhammad Festivals*, pp. 85ff.; Lewis Pelly, *The Miracle Plays of Hasan and Husain*, 2 vols. (London: W. H. Allen, 1879); and the collected papers in P. Chelkowski, ed., *Ta'zieh: Ritual and Drama* (New York: New York University Press, 1979).

plane in a manner alien to Muslim and Jew alike. Both of these latter knew how to be literal—all prayer is literal—but do not endeavor either to ground God or to sanctify matter. God will intervene in history when and where He wills; but He will not dwell among us.

CHAPTER VII

Asceticism and Mysticism

ASCETICISM, the adoption of a way of life primarily characterized by some form of self-denial, and mysticism, the direct experience of God, are both primitive and widespread forms of religious life. From Moses to Ezekiel there were Jews who moved from the human to the supernatural dimension of experience, and though asceticism was never central to Jewish life—we exclude here forms of self-denial prescribed by law on moral grounds, abstention from certain food, for example—there were always on the fringes of the Jewish community groups such as the Rechabites and Nazirites, who chose what can fairly be described as an ascetical path to holiness.

Post-Exilic Judaism had, as we have seen, a marked fondness for visionary recitals of the apocalyptic kind, but these are examples of a popular literary genre rather than individual experiences of the presence of God. Philo, however, gives in one of his works a circumstantial description of a group of Jewish ascetics who lived in monastic communities and devoted themselves to the study of Scripture. We know little of what to make of this story, since we have no other evidence of Philo's "Therapeutae," but early Christian authors such as Eusebius, who were well acquainted with Philo's work, cited the account with obviously enthusiastic approval.[1]

In Judea in Jesus' lifetime we have the ascetical example of both the Qumran community and John the Baptist. Qumran asceticism was motivated, like somewhat similar practices in

---

[1] *Ecclesiastical History* 2, 17 = G. A. Williamson, *Eusebius: The History of the Church* (Baltimore: Penguin pb., 1965), pp. 89-93.

the early Christian community, by eschatological considerations, a disengaged state of readiness—the military overtones are everywhere apparent in the Qumran literature—for the messianic Return. John the Baptist, on the other hand, appears closer to the Nazirite ideal, and so too does James, "the brother of the Lord" who assumed the leadership of the Christian community in Jerusalem at Jesus' death and whose character and practices are described at some length by Eusebius.[2] Jesus' own attitude toward the pleasures or even the needs of the flesh appears to be more one of indifference than asceticism. And Paul, who was scarcely indifferent to anything, was more concerned with fashioning a new moral ideal for all Christians in the light of an imminent End Time. He does note in passing, however, the existence of groups of Christian ascetics-celibates, but it is likely that they too were operating on an eschatological premise.

When and where an eschatological unworldliness yielded to a fully realized ascetical life as a more perfect path to holiness open to all Christians cannot be determined. The classical prototype of such a life was Antony, an Alexandrian who died in 356 C.E., and though he was surely not the first to choose withdrawal from the world (*anachoresis*) as a way of life, his well-publicized career in the desert of eastern Egypt provided the model and incentive for future generations.[3]

Antony lived alone but soon his eremitical existence inspired entire communities (*koinobia*) of ascetics, and to Antony's original practice of poverty and celibacy was added, in this cenobitical setting, a new feature: the denial of the will by submission to a monastic superior. Both eremitical and cenobitical forms of Christian monasticism spread rapidly over Egypt, Palestine, Syria, and Mesopotamia and eventually to the Western churches.[4]

[2] *Ecclesiastical History* 2, 23 = Williamson, pp. 99-103.

[3] *J. G. Davies, *The Early Christian Church* (Garden City: Doubleday Anchor, 1967), pp. 244-248; H. Chadwick, *The Early Church* (Harmondsworth: Penguin, 1967), pp. 174-183.

[4] There are selections from the lives and sayings of the early Christian

One who had considerable experience of monasticism in most of its Near Eastern varieties was Basil, the wealthy nobleman who was himself a monk and later the bishop of Caesarea in Cappadocia. He had visited monastic communities in Egypt, Palestine, and Syria about 358 C.E. and his own earlier experience of the disorganized and even anarchical monastic tradition in his native Cappadocia led him to draw up a set of rules for the governance of the monastic life. These are extant in a longer and a shorter version,[5] and they set out in great detail not only the ideals but the practices of the monk's life from standards of admission to the monastery to the manner of dress there.

For Basil, community life was far preferable to the eremitical because of its greater social good. It was, in fact, Basil who set monasticism the social goals—with their economic and intellectual consequences—that are so evident in monastic life in the West, where Benedict took over much of Basil's thinking for his own Rule at Monte Cassino.[6] Basil believed in work, physical and intellectual, and the life of the monk was to be one of work and prayer. Daily morning and evening prayers were not uncommon in some of the larger Christian churches, but Basil set a standard of monastic prayer eight times a day, beginning at dawn and proceeding at about three-hour intervals through the day and the night as well, since the monks were obliged to rise at midnight and just before dawn to pray once again.

Basil put the monastery under the firm control of the superior (*hegoumenos*) or abbot, but the Great Church went fur-

---

ascetics in Helen Waddell, *The Desert Fathers* (Ann Arbor: Univ. of Michigan Press pb., 1957). The history of the Egyptian and Palestinian forms of monasticism is sketched by D. J. Chitty, *The Desert a City* (Crestwood, N.Y.: St. Vladimir's Seminary Press pb., 1977), and the Syrian form, which may have had very different indigenous roots, by A. Vööbus, *History of Asceticism in the Syrian Orient*, 2 vols. (Louvain: CSCO, 1958).

[5] Translated by W.K.L. Clarke, *The Ascetic Works of Saint Basil* (London: SPCK, 1925).

[6] *H. Bettenson, *Documents of the Christian Church* (London: Oxford pb., 1970), pp. 164-181.

ther in its own enactments. Monastic communities, it turned out, could be as troublesome to Church order as individual monks, and the theological disputes of the fifth and sixth centuries were often accompanied by monastic riots. The Council of Chalcedon reacted in 451 C.E. by placing monastic communities under the jurisdiction of the bishops, and succeeding councils attempted, not always successfully, to strengthen the grip of the hierarchy on the "athletes of God." And when in the sixth century the imperial government began to intervene more directly in affairs of canon law, the emperor too took up the cause of monastic regulation and reform.

Basil thought to guide monastic spirituality by regulating its discipline. The Eastern monks never quite accepted the premise of the *sacra regula* to the extent their Western counterparts did. Their spiritual paths led in other directions, to the theologians whose chief concern was mysticism rather than asceticism. Even before Antony withdrew to the desert, theologians such as Origen (d. 254), again following Philo and before him Plato and Aristotle, were fashioning a new ideal for the ascetic, that of the contemplative life. Whereas the earliest Christian ascetics stressed a simple scriptural meditation, imitation of Christ, and the training of the will, such fourth-century masters of the spiritual life as Evagrius of Pontus in the East and John Cassian in the West changed their regard from the will to the intellect and its illumination: at the upper end of the ascetic's "spiritual ladder," whose lower rungs still consisted of pragmatic asceticism, stood the new ideal of unity with God, *theoria* or *theologia*, as it was called in the new Hellenic-inspired vocabulary.[7]

One of Evagrius' most prominent disciples was John Climacus (d. 605), a monk of Sinai whose *Ladder of Divine Ascent*[8] stands a world apart from Basil's community-oriented and

[7] *Davies, *Christian Church*, pp. 321-326; M. Smith, *Studies in Early Mysticism in the Near and Middle East* (1931; reprint Amsterdam: Philo Press, 1973), chapters 4-5.

[8] Translated by L. Moore (London: Faber and Faber, 1959).

highly regulated version of the monastic ideal. John's monk strives, in the best Evagrian tradition, for that tranquillity (*hesychia*) of body and mind which invites the divine grace to fill the soul with light from on high. Neither tranquillity nor divine illumination were novel ideas in the fifth century, but they were becoming the centerpieces of monasticism in the East—in the writings of Symeon (d. 1022), the so-called "New Theologian," for example. They erupted into controversy on Mount Athos, a veritable society of monasteries in northern Greece, where by the fourteenth century the achievement of *hesychia* was conditioned by an elaborate set of physical exercises that had less to do with traditional Christian ascetisicm than with a type of Byzantine yoga: contemplation of the navel, regulated breathing and the repetitious intoning of the "Jesus-prayer" formula. The climax of this regimen was an infusion of the divine light, the same seen by Jesus' disciples on Mount Tabor (Mark 9:2-8; Matthew 17:1-8), and a union with the divine essence—in short, a kind of deification.[9]

The evolution of Islamic spirituality reflects almost exactly the Christian experience. Muhammad had no marked ascetic leanings, and certainly did not encourage monasticism, whose Christian form he knew. But early in Islam some Muslims were already expressing their disdain for the worldliness of certain of their coreligionists by a mild form of *anachoresis*. Some of them adopted a simple woolen (*suf*) cloak, perhaps in imitation of the Christian monks, and so came to be called Sufis.[10]

Ascetical pursuits, which tended to be somewhat more occasional and less wilderness-oriented than they were in Christianity, soon took on mystical aspirations, with a

---

[9] See V. Lossky, *The Mystical Theology of the Eastern Church* (London: J. Clarke, 1957); *Orthodox Spirituality, by a Monk of the Eastern Church*, rev. ed. (London, SPCK pb., 1978); cf. J. Hussey, ed., *The Cambridge Medieval History* (Cambridge: Cambridge University Press, 1967), IV/2, pp. 197-204.

[10] F. E. Peters, *Allah's Commonwealth* (New York: Simon and Schuster, 1973), pp. 413-438; Smith, *Studies in Early Mysticism*, chapters 7-8.

yearning for union with a God whom most Muslims regarded as absolutely transcendent. Later Sufi theoreticians formalized this path to the Absolute into a series of "stations," which were akin to the Christians' *via purgativa*, followed by the "states" through which God's grace guided the Sufi toward union with Himself.[11] But this simple distinction between "stations" and "states" is perhaps the least complex thing that can be said about Sufism in Islam, and one need look at only three fairly representative modern presentations of Sufism to understand some of that complexity, if not Sufism itself: A. J. Arberry's straightforward *Sufism*;[12] A. Schimmel's more sophisticated and nuanced *Mystical Dimensions of Islam*;[13] and the opaque and anti-Western polemic of Idries Shah's *The Way of the Sufi*.[14]

The polar opposition of Arberry and Shah springs from the nature of Sufism itself. Arberry and Peters[15] regard it as a spiritual discipline whose meaning can be read in the lives of Sufis and theoretical treatises by masters such as Junayd (d. 910).[16] Such is true in part. Shah and Schuon[17] look upon Sufism as a gnosis (*hikmah*) whose occult context is understood only by adepts and whose external expression is characterized by parable and parabola. Such is also true in part. Theologians categorize and simplify; mystics mystify from either prudence or despair. Schimmel has been almost unique in understanding and combining the two perspectives.

Sufism, like all forms of mysticism, has as its acknowledged object an immediate experience of God, an experience that is usually expressed in terms of union or identity. It is,

[11] F. E. Peters, *Allah's Commonwealth*, pp. 559-563.

[12] New York: Harper Torchbook, 1970.

[13] Chapel Hill: North Carolina University Press, 1975.

[14] New York: Dutton pb., 1970, especially Part One: "The Study of Sufism in the West." Schimmel's judgment on Shah's works (*Mystical Dimensions*, p. 9 n. 5) is succinct: "should be avoided by serious students."

[15] *Allah's Commonwealth*, pp. 545-569.

[16] His works are available in English: A. H. Abdel-Kader, *The Life, Personality and Writings of al-Junayd* (London: Luzac and Co., 1962).

[17] *Understanding Islam* (London: Allen and Unwin pb., 1963).

by common consent, a transient state. For some it has been a unique and almost random event, but it is clear that in Islam many pious souls aspired to this state and took well-defined and even scholastic steps to attain it. Sufism was a "way" (*tariqah*) that for most passed across the terrain of asceticism and spiritual exercises in the company of an accomplished master (*murshid, pir*). At first that elder may have simply been a skilled and experienced director of souls, but eventually that ideal was replaced, as it was in Christianity, by the notion of a charismatic guide, a "spiritual father" who possessed the gift of divine grace (*barakah*).

It was the *murshid* who introduced the novice into two of the most common practices of Sufism, the "recollection" (*dhikr*) and the "hearing" (*sama'*). *Dhikr* has its spiritual, internal sense of recollecting God's blessings, but its more visible form in Sufism is the repetition of set formulae, notably the Muslim profession of faith or of the ninety-nine names of Allah. The repetition was rhythmical and often accompanied, as was the "Jesus-prayer" used to the same end in Christianity, by controlled breathing.[18] The ecstatic state of annihilation (*fana*) which was for the Sufi a natural antecedent of union with the Divine, was often accompanied by an elaborate ritual of singing and dancing within which the *dhikr* might be commingled. This *sama'*, as it was called, though highly characteristic of certain Sufi associations such as the whirling dervishes, was not everywhere approved or accepted. Why some more sober Muslims might be scandalized becomes apparent in Edward Lane's account of *dhikrs* of the more extravagant type that he witnessed in Cairo in 1825.[19]

The attraction of charismatic holy men is universal, and in Islam it brought to the feet of Sufi masters crowds of disciples. The *barakah* passed from master to novice, and so was established an ongoing chain (*silsilah*) of spiritually authenti-

[18] Schimmel, *Mystical Dimensions*, pp. 167-178.
[19] E. W. Lane, *An Account of the Manners and Customs of the Modern Egyptians* (1836; reprint New York: Dover pb., 1973), chapter 24; on the *sama'*, see Schimmel, *Mystical Dimensions*, pp. 178-186.

cated adepts whose external regime might be common knowledge but whose share in the mysteries of the divine union was at base ineffable. The mystic's gnosis was understood as a special knowledge (*ma'rifah*) of the "higher realities," and though it might be communicated obliquely in the poetry of a Jalal al-Din Rumi[20] or an Ibn al-'Arabi,[21] or through Zen-like tales such as those of Nasruddin retold by Idries Shah in *The Sufis*,[22] the central "reality" could not and should not be revealed to the uninitiated.

Spiritual attraction and spiritual authority came together to form the Sufi orders, also called "ways" (*tariqat*).[23] These orders, which were generally neither monastic nor enclosed, and so quite different from the Christian religious orders, had an immense popular appeal in Islam, not least because they were a social and spiritual reaction to the increasingly clerical and legal character of what had come to be official Islam, which was dominated by a rabbinate with powerful economic, social, and political connections.[24]

Whereas the Sufi orders represent the popular side of mysticism in Islam, its more elitist and esoteric aspects are associated with that peculiar strain of religion, myth, and philosophy known as Gnosticism. If a religion is a complex of attitudes toward God, man, and the world, then Gnosticism was indeed a religion, as Hans Jonas called it.[25] But it was a

[20] A. J. Arberry, *The Ruba'iyat of Jalaluddin Rumi* (London: E. Walker, 1959); *Tales from the Mathnawi* (London: Allen and Unwin, 1961) and *More Tales from the Mathnawi* (London: Allen and Unwin, 1963); cf. his *Mystical Poems of Rumi* (Chicago: University of Chicago Press, 1968).

[21] R. A. Nicholson, *The Tarjuman al-ashwaq: A Collection of Mystical Odes by Muhyiu'ddin ibn al-'Arabi* (London: Royal Asiatic Society, 1911); cf. H. Corbin, *Creative Imagination in the Sufism of Ibn 'Arabi* (Princeton: Princeton University Press, 1969).

[22] Garden City, N.Y.: Doubleday Anchor pb., 1971, pp. 63-110.

[23] These are described by J. S. Trimingham, *The Sufi Orders in Islam* (London: Oxford University Press pb., 1973); Schimmel, *Mystical Dimensions*, pp. 228-258.

[24] *M. G. Hodgson, *The Venture of Islam* (Chicago: Chicago University Press pb., 1974), II, 201-254.

[25] *The Gnostic Religion* (Boston: Beacon Press pb., 1963).

most peculiar form of religion, since it appears to have had no independent existence but rather to have survived as a parasitic ideology deep within the bodies of the more formal and institutionalized religions of Judaism, Christianity, and Islam. Gnostics there indeed were, and gnosis; but Gnosticism is our construct.[26]

Rapidly defined, gnosis is a wisdom necessary for salvation. Unlike the wisdom of the philosophers, gnosis is grounded in revelation and transmitted through restricted channels from one initiate to another, chiefly through an esoteric understanding of religious texts already in the public domain. The content of the gnosis is in some ways familiar. There is a single transcendent and unknowable God who, together with His successive emanations, generally called Aeons, constitutes the spiritual universe—for Gnostics, the *pleroma* or the "Fullness." But unlike the later forms of Platonic thought to which it is obviously akin, Gnosticism views the material cosmos, the "Emptiness" (*kenoma*), not as a mere diminution of God's creative emanation but as the product of a totally different metaphysics and ethic: the *kenoma* was created and is ruled by an autonomous principle of evil.

The heart of the gnosis was a cosmic drama in which one of the spiritual beings of the *pleroma* fell from grace, and by its fall broadcast fragments of the divine essence into the darkling world below, sparks of the Divine Light that were thereafter immersed as soul in the bodies of men. At some point a Redeemeer ventured down into the *kenoma* to reveal to those who would hear the message of salvation; whence they had come and whither they were intended to return.

There are almost infinite varieties on these basic themes, but its earliest known version appears in a Christian context, in the texts translated in the first volume of W. Foerster's

[26] On the historical problem posed by Gnosticism, see R. McL. Wilson, *The Gnostic Problem* (London: Mowbray, 1958) and the proceedings of the symposium edited by U. Bianchi and entitled *The Origins of Gnosticism* (Leiden: E. J. Brill, 1967).

Gnosis: A Selection of Gnostic Texts.[27] Most of them are cited
as heretical aberrations from Christians orthodoxy, but there
are proto-Gnostic ideas in orthodox Christianity as well, in
certain passages of the Gospels and Paul, and in Clement and
Origen's understanding of what the Christian "tradition" was
and how it was transmitted, for example.[28] Grant and others
are by no means convinced, however, that Gnosticism was
in fact a Christian phenomenon, despite the lack of evidence
for it from the pre-Christian era. Apocalyptic Judaism, Iranian religion, and later Greek philosophy have all been regarded as equally likely points of departure for the Gnostic
world view.

The origins of Gnosticism need not concern us here. Its
rejection of the world and history were in the end of little
interest to religions committed to the historical process and
God's direct intervention in His creation. What was more
attractive, however, was its seizure of the commonplace Greek
idea of a literal and allegorical sense of Scripture, and its endowment of the latter with a salvational value. Gnosticism
created a dual community of believers in its host bodies: ex-
oterics who were condemned to the limited horizons of the
literal truths of revelation, and esoterics who could penetrate
surface banalities to the "realities" that lay beneath.

As has been remarked, there are some who have professed
to see the beginning of Gnosticism in the apocalyptic and
wisdom literature of post-Exilic Judaism. Some of the evidence is fossilized, like the testimony of the Mandaeans, a
Gnostic sect still in existence in southern Iraq, who show
signs of being still another, in this case Gnostic, growth out
of the divergent strains of first century Judaism.[29] A more
direct approach is the scrutiny of such biblical Apocrypha as

[27] 2 vols. (London: Oxford University Press, 1972).
[28] R. C. Grant, *Gnosticism and Early Christianity* (New York: Harper
Torchbook, 1966); cf. F. E. Peters, *The Harvest of Hellenism* (New York:
Clarion pb., 1970), pp. 648-662.
[29] Foerster, *Gnosis*, II, 141-143, with a selection of texts, pp. 148-317.

the Book of Enoch.[30] Some of the Apocrypha are so carefully concealed within false names and fictive contexts that we have little idea of the actual individuals or circles who were meditating those ideas of a Heavenly Wisdom that descended to earth either as a messianic figure or through the mechanics of a visionary revelation whereby the subject is carried to the highest heavens where the mysteries of creation are revealed.[31]

At Qumran we have such a context. The community there may not have been a Gnostic association, but its preserved literature, which includes several of the Apocrypha, shows that they entertained apocalyptic expectations, and that such expectations deeply colored their reading of the canonical Scriptures and the Apocrypha.[32] And they were, moreover, the likely bearers of that apocalyptic tradition into the nascent Christian community.[33] Qumran, Christianity, and Gnosticism come together in another interesting context. The Christian sources attribute the origins of Gnosticism to Simon Magus, the Samaritan wonder-worker who was a contemporary of Peter.[34] Simon's own teacher was Dositheus, who was connected with John the Baptist, and who may have been an Essene.[35]

If this path, however ill-defined, leads from apocalyptic Judaism to Christian Gnosticism, the connection between the mystical element implicit in apocalypticism and the Pharisaic and rabbinic strain in Judaism is almost totally invisible. There

---

[30] Selections are included in *C. K. Barrett, *The New Testament Background* (New York: Harper Torchbook, 1961), pp. 227-255.

[31] On the parallel experience credited to Muhammed by the Islamic tradition, see G. Widengren, *Muhammed, the Apostle of God, and His Ascension* (Uppsala: Lundequistska bokhandeln, 1955).

[32] See F. M. Cross, *The Ancient Library at Qumran* (New York: Anchor pb., 1961), pp. 77-78, 112-113, and H. H. Rowley, *Jewish Apocrypha and the Dead Sea Scrolls* (London: Athlone Press, 1957).

[33] Cross, *Library at Qumran*, pp. 198-206.

[34] Texts in Foerster, *Gnosis*, I, 27-33.

[35] J. Daniélou, *The Dead Sea Scrolls and Primitive Christianity* (New York: Menton Omega pb., 1958), pp. 94-96.

143

is reason to think that the Pharisees—Josephus is the best example—deliberately underplayed this side of Judaism, particularly for the benefit of the Romans. And yet we have Yohanan ben Zakkai (d. ca. 80 C.E.), a crucial figure in the passage from Pharisaic to rabbinic Judaism, engaged in a matter-of-fact discussion of common mystical and apocalyptic themes.[36]

On somewhat closer inspection these and similar themes appear on occasion elsewhere in the Talmud, and from them and other, anonymous works written during the same period between 200-500 C.E., Gershom Scholem has fashioned a preliminary portrait of early rabbinic mysticism.[37] The Talmud was, of course, a public text whose study was generally commended. But as the Talmud itself points out,[38] meditation on the mysteries implicit in two of the most common ground-texts of Jewish mystical speculation, the opening chapter of Genesis and that of Ezekiel, where God's throne chariot is described, was not recommended for the body of Jewish believers.

Since so much of this early speculation is anonymous, it is extremely difficult to date. But Scholem for one is convinced that two such anonymous works, the *Measure of the Body* (*Shi'ur Qomah*) and the *Book of Creation* (*Sefer Yetzirah*),[39] go back to talmudic times. The first is a mystic's meditation on the "body of God," its shape and dimensions, and is a typical Gnostic exercise of turning literalism in upon itself to reveal deeper realities. The second is more philosophical in nature,

[36] See the passages translated by J. Neusner in his *Life of Yohanan ben Zakkai* (Leiden: E. J. Brill, 1970), pp. 134-142.

[37] *Major Trends in Jewish Mysticism* (New York: Schocken pb., 1954), pp. 40-79; *Jewish Gnosticism, Merkabah Mysticism and Talmudic Tradition* (New York: Schocken, 1960); and *Kabbalah* (Utica: Meridien pb., 1974); cf. *L. Ginzberg, *On Jewish Law and Lore* (New York: Atheneum pb., 1970), pp. 187-238.

[38] Translated by H. Danby, *The Mishnah* (London: Oxford University Press, 1933), pp. 212-213.

[39] Translated into English by K. Stenring, *The Book of Formation* (New York: Ktav, 1970).

and shows clearly the working of Greek ideas on Jewish mystical speculation about the origins and form of the universe.[40] The occult meaning of names and numbers are explored; the hierarchy of divine emanations (*sefirot*) is laid out in detail.

The development of this esoteric and mystical form of Judaism, which evolved simultaneously, if far less publicly, with the halakic work of the rabbis, eventually came to be called kabbala (*qabbala*), literally "that which is handed down." The Mishna too had once been "handed down," but the distinction is the same as that which can be seen between Greek philosophy and the occult sciences; between Christian theology and Gnosticism; between the teachings of the Islamic lawyers and those of the Sufis: one kind of knowledge is public, literal, and discursive; the other is esoteric, allegorical, and mystical. It is the difference between theology and theosophy; between law and allegory; between intellect and intuition.

The kabbalistic tradition has had a long and distinguished history in Judaism, as described in the works of Scholem cited above. That it was deeply esoteric is manifest at every turn, and nowhere more clearly than in what became one of its classic texts, the *Zohar*, which was written—or better composed—by Moses of Leon in Spain between 1270 and 1300 C.E.[41] The bulk of the *Zohar* is given over to a kabbalistic Midrash on the Torah, divided, in the classic fashion of the rabbinic Midrashim, according to the liturgical recitation cycle of the Law. This arcane and convoluted understanding of the "reality" behind plain texts and the material world now appears hopelessly difficult, as it was probably intended to be from the outset. But deep within it lay the mystic's urge to approach God in a paradoxically more direct way, an urge too·powerful to remain concealed within the folds of esotericism. In Islam mysticism became popularized in the

---

[40] Scholem, *Kabbalah*, pp. 23-31.

[41] Selections have been translated by G. Scholem, *Zohar: The Book of Splendor* (New York: Schocken pb., 1963).

Sufi orders; in Christianity by such clerics as Ignatius of Loyola and Francis de Sales, who in the late sixteenth century brought the monks' spiritual exercises to the secular clergy and the laity alike;[42] and in Judaism by the Hasidic movement, which in the eighteenth century divested kabbalism of some of its more esoteric and inaccessible features to render it a kind of popular revelation.[43]

Note has already been taken of the Gnostic current in Islamic Sufism and its eventual wedding with a parallel strain in Shi'ism. Though this union was officially consummated in the creation of the Safavid state in the sixteenth century,[44] the liaison was being prepared much earlier. It is not certain when the affinities between Shi'ism and Sufism first developed, but they were already present when Shi'ism elaborated its theory of the Imam as a charismatic figure who possessed an authoritative spiritual knowledge and imparted it to adepts. The distance between the Shi'ite Imam and the Sufi saint, particularly the archetypical saint, the "pole" (*qutb*) around whom the saints of each generation revolved, was not great. From the twelfth century onward the distance grew even smaller with the evolution of what Schimmel has called "theosophical Sufism"[45] and others "Sophiology" and "Illuminationism." Wisdom (*hikmah*) was quite simply gnosis, and the convertability of the terms and their use as a heuristic device for reading the whole of Islamic sacred history are displayed in F. Schuon's *Understanding Islam*[46] and the introduction to Seyyid Hossein Nasr's *Science and Civilization in Islam.*[47]

[42] See K. E. Kirk, *The Vision of God: The Christian Doctrine of the Summum Bonum* (New York: Harper Torchbook, 1966), pp. 394-414.

[43] Scholem, *Major Trends*, pp. 325-350; see the texts collected and translated by Martin Buber in his *Tales of the Hasidim*, 2 vols. (New York: Schocken pb., 1947).

[44] See *Hodgson, *Venture*, III, 22-58, and M. Mazzaoui, *The Origins of the Safavids: Shi'ism, Sufism and the Ghulat* (Wiesbaden: F. Steiner, 1972).

[45] *Mystical Dimensions*, pp. 259-286.

[46] London: Penguin pb., 1963.

[47] New York: New American Library pb., 1970.

146

The chief agent of this turning of both philosophy and mysticism in the direction of theosophy was the philosopher Ibn Sina or Avicenna (d. 1038). His contribution to the development and refinement of Islamic philosophy in its then current blend of Plato and Aristotle was enormous, but there are hints throughout his work that Avicenna had, behind and beyond his public and scholastic treatments of philosophical themes, a more esoteric "oriental philosophy" whose contents could only be hinted at.[48] The obliqueness of Avicenna's own allusions make its identification somewhat problematic, but a great many Muslims who came after him understood Avicenna's esoteric philosophy as some form of mysticism, and identified its author as a Sufi.

Whether or not he was a Sufi in any formal sense, Avicenna laid heavy emphasis upon some form of divine illumination (*ishraq*) as the means whereby the philosopher received the knowledge that was the object of his quest. Avicenna's "illumination," like that of Evagrius of Pontus, probably owed a great deal more to Neoplatonism than his many commentators and imitators were prepared to admit. It was, at any rate, an individual effort and an individual achievement, this pursuit of union with God, and there is nothing in Avicenna of the passage of a spiritual *barakah* from master to novice, no charismatic "chain" upon which to mount on high.

One of Avicenna's most influential interpreters read him somewhat differently, however. Suhrawardi (d. 1191), who took up and completed Avicenna's "visionary recitals,"[49] interpreted the philosopher's "oriental philosophy" as a genu-

---

[48] See Chapter VII below; and on the "oriental philosophy," H. Corbin, *Avicenna and the Visionary Recital* (New York: Pantheon, 1960), pp. 271-278, and S. H. Nasr, *Three Muslim Sages* (Cambridge: Harvard University Press, 1964), pp. 20-51, and *An Introduction to Islamic Cosmological Doctrines* (Cambridge: Harvard University Press, 1964), pp. 185-196.

[49] Avicenna's versions are translated in Corbin, *Visionary Recital*, pp. 123-271.

ine renaissance of Eastern, that is, Persian wisdom.[50] For those ancient sages the First Being was Xvarneh, "the light of glory" of Zoroastrianism, and that opened for Suhrawardi the opportunity of converting what had been for Avicenna and Ghazali an epistemological metaphor into a true metaphysic: existence and light are identical; the Necessary Being is Absolute Light.

Though the Sunni lawyer and theologian was probably a less congenial figure to him than the Shi'ite philosopher, Suhrawardi learned as much from Ghazali as he did from Avicenna. Ghazali (d. 1111) had already anticipated, as we shall see, a new task for that perennial handmaiden, philosophy, and Suhrawardi developed it with enthusiasm. Speculative knowledge, the wisdom that comes from research and investigation, was simply a preparation for the "wisdom that savors," the experimental knowledge of God. Philosophy thus received its justification and at the same time was assigned an appropriate place as a preparation for the final stages of the search for the Absolute. Suhrawardi likewise followed Ghazali in his elaboration of the rich possibilities of allegorical exegesis in the service of mysticism.[51]

Suhrawardi's work, with its assertion of Persia's place in the history of Wisdom, its attractive metaphysic of light, its developed theory of allegorical exegesis, and its valorization of experience over theoretical knowledge, provided a program for both the philosophers and mystics of Iran, and a convenient bridge upon which they might thereafter meet. That the meetings were frequent and rewarding is attested by the twin traditions of mystical poetry in Persian[52] and the

[50] On Suhrawardi, see Nasr, *Three Muslim Sages*, pp. 52-82, and Schimmel, *Mystical Dimensions*, pp. 259-263.

[51] On theosophical *ta'wil*, see Corbin, *Visionary Recital*, pp. 28-35, where the distinction is made between allegory as an artificial sign of generalities that can be expressed in other ways, and the genuine symbol (*mithal*), which is the unique expression of a higher "reality." Theosophic *ta'wil* operates in this latter universe of symbols midway between this sensible world and the higher, spiritual pleroma.

[52] Schimmel, *Mystical Dimensions*, pp. 287-328.

ill-charted but impressive course of theosophical and philosophical speculation during the reign of the Safavids in Iran.[53]

Annemarie Schimmel has taken up the distinction between
the Mysticism of Infinity and the Mysticism of Personality,
and argued that later Sufism is unmistakably in the former
category, which acknowledges God as the Ultimate and
Unique Reality whereas the world possesses only the "limited reality" of a distant emanation from the One Being.[54] In
this latter view all Reality is in fact One, a position that was
not very congenial to Muslim revelation, which stresses the
gulf between the Creator and His creation, and preached, in
its mystical mode, an approach to God through moral activity and not identity with Him. Union or identity (ittihad)
with God was already a troublesome Sufi concept for the
traditionists, but even more scandalous was the message
broadcast by the influential philosopher and poet Ibn ʿArabi
(d. 1204), that of the "unity of Being."[55]

Sufism took eagerly to Ibn ʿArabi's version of a pantheis-
tic universe and its supporting apparatus of Gnostic esoterics,
and such traditionists as Ibn Taymiyyah (d. 1328) was equally
quick to discover the dangers of the Sufi metaphysic and its
free-wheeling exegesis to what had by then been shaped into
a consensual version of Sunni Islam. But the Sufis were by

[53] See S. H. Nasr, "The School of Ispahan" and "Sadr al-Din Shirazi
(Mulla Sadra)" in M. M. Sharif, ed., A History of Muslim Philosophy (Wies-
baden: Harrasowitz, 1966), II, 904-960. On Suhrawardi's, and through him
Avicenna's, influence on Iranian Sufism, see in particular S. H. Nasr, Sufi
Essays (Albany: SUNY Press, 1973).

[54] Mystical Dimensions, p. 5. There is a somewhat similar distinction and
a similar judgment in R. C. Zaehner, Mysticism Sacred and Profane (New
York: Oxford University Press pb., 1961), pp. 153-174, and Hindu and Muslim Mysticism (New York: Schocken pb., 1969), pp. 162-188.

[55] See S. H. Nasr, Three Muslim Sages, pp. 83-124; Schimmel, Mystical
Dimensions, pp. 263-267; T. Burchkhardt, Introduction to Sufi Doctrines (Lahore: Sh. Muhammad Ashraf, 1959), and Corbin, Creative Imagination. Not
much of Ibn ʿArabi's immense body of work is accessible in English, but
some idea of his thinking and expression may be gotten from R. A. Nicholson's translation of the Tarjuman al-ashwaq (London: Royal Asiatic Society, 1911).

no means the only proponents of Gnosticism in the Dar al-Islam. There are Gnostic premises at the base of most of the occult sciences that flourished in the ancient and medieval world—alchemy for one—and the ease with which so many of them passed from one to the other of the very different religious climates of ancient Greco-Roman paganism, Near Eastern Islam, and both Eastern and Western Christianity and Judaism underscores both the appeal and adaptability of Gnosticism.[56] And in Islam Gnosticism demonstrated that it could adapt itself as readily to political as to scientific ends.

The Isma'ilis were a subdivision of the Shi'ite movement who, unlike the main body of the Shi'ah in the Middle Ages, had a political program for overthrowing the Sunni Caliph and replacing him with a revolutionary Mahdi-Imam.[57] They were not successful, but they had access to and put to effective use the entire Gnostic apparatus of cosmic history, in which the Shi'ite Imams became the Gnostic Aeons; a secret revelation of the "realities" that lay hidden in the concealed (*batin*) rather than the evident sense of Scripture; an imamic guide who possessed an infallible and authoritative *magisterium* (*ta'lim*); and an initiated elite that formed, in the Isma'ili case, the core of an elaborate political underground. At their headquarters in Cairo, a city that the Isma'ili Fatimids founded in 969 C.E., agents were instructed in the Isma'ili gnosis and program, and were sent forth with the "call" of the Mahdi-Imam to cells and cadres that had been set up in the caliphal lands in Iraq and Iran.

Sunni and Isma'ili Islam shared a common foundation of reliance on authority and tradition. For the Sunni, that tradition was embodied in the elaborate structure of Muslim

---

[56] E. J. Holmyard, *Alchemy* (Baltimore, Penguin pb., 1968), and for the Gnostic side of this science, T. Burckhardt, *Alchemy* (Baltimore: Penguin pb., 1971). The history of the occult sciences in Islam is traced by Peters, *Allah's Commonwealth*, pp. 350-373, and for the "practical" side of kabbala, which comes from the same roots, see Scholem, *Kabbalah*, pp. 182-189 and 337-343.

[57] Peters, *Allah's Commonwealth*, pp. 592-617.

Law which in turn rested upon *hadith* reports that went back to the Prophet's own words and deeds, and so constituted a second revelation with an authority equal to the Qur'an's own.[58] The Qur'an and the *"sunnah* of the Prophet" prescribed a certain order in the religious sphere, but that order was impossible to achieve without the establishment of a parallel political order that could guarantee the performance of religious duties by securing for each believer the security of his life and property, and was capable at the same time of maintaining the unity of the community in the face of civil disorders. From this was derived the political authority (*siyasah*) of the Caliph and his delegates.

For the Isma'ilis, the Imam was not a political corollary of a religious system but an integral part of the religious system itself. In a famous Shi'ite *hadith*, Muhammad, upon his return from his "ascension" to the highest heavens where the truths of creation were revealed to him, cast his mantle over his daughter Fatimah and his grandsons Hasan and Husayn and so signified the transmission of those same truths to his Fatimid-'Alid descendants. Thus it was the Imam and he alone who held, at least in theory—every Sufi and philosopher from the twelfth century onward claimed the same privilege—the key to *ta'wil*, the allegorical exegesis of Scripture that penetrated the surface meaning to the Truths beneath.

The intellectual defense of Sunnism against this claim was undertaken by al-Ghazali in a series of tracts that mounted a frontal attack on what he called "the Batinis." But the issue appears in all its complexity in a more personal statement, his *Deliverer from Error*, which describes his own investigation of the competing claims upon the faith of the Muslim.[59] Faith tied to simple acceptance on the authority of others was

[58] See Chapter IV above and J. Wansbrough, *Qur'anic Studies* (London: Oxford University Press, 1972), pp. 51-52, 174-177.

[59] Translated by W. M. Watt, *The Faith and Practice of Al-Ghazali* (London: Allen and Unwin, 1953), pp. 19-85; cf. Schimmel, *Mystical Dimensions*, pp. 92-97.

insufficient for Ghazali; it could be shaken by the conflicting claims put forward by different parties and sects within Islam and by the equally strong adherence to their own faith by the Christians and Jews. Unless he was prepared to lapse into an agnostic skepticism, as Ghazali was not, there had to be some other way for the seeker after truth. Four possibilities presented themselves: the way of speculative theology, *kalam*, which professed to support its religious beliefs with rational argument; the way of the philosophers, who laid claim to true scientific demonstration; the Isma'ili way, which promised religious certitude by reliance upon the teaching of an infallible Imam; and finally the way of the Sufis or mystics, who offered intuitive understanding and a certitude born of standing in the presence of God.[60]

The attraction of *ta'lim* was undeniable, and Ghazali could reply that if such were the answer, then it was far preferable to accept the infallible teaching of the Prophet than of some derivative Imam, whose teachings turned out to be some debased form of Greek philosophy in any event.[61] But neither can really cure the malady: it is part of the human condition to doubt and to disagree, and on the rational level the only solution to such is not to throw oneself on the authority of another but to work out an answer with patience and intelligence, an answer based equally on the Qur'an and the principles of right reason. The solution is, in short, Ghazali's own rigorous version of *kalam*.[62]

Finally Ghazali turns to mysticism. It was, as remarked earlier, a "way" (*tariqah*) that could be entered from its scholastic, intellectualized side or by approaching it through ex-

[60] On the way of the theologians and philosophers, see Chapter VIII below.

[61] Debased or not, such it does indeed appear to be in one of the few preserved documents that contains the Isma'ili gnosis, the tenth-century encyclopedia called *The Letters of the Brethren of Purity*; see Nasr, *Cosmological Doctrines*, pp. 25-106, and M. Fakhry, *A History of Islamic Philosophy* (New York: Columbia University Press, 1970), pp. 184-204.

[62] Watt, *Faith and Practice*, pp. 48-54.

perience. Ghazali, with deep intellectual commitments and training—"knowledge was easier for me than activity"—entered by the first path: he read the classical theoretical treatises and the lives of the Sufi saints. It was a mistake, as he soon learned. It is better to experience intoxication than to know how to define drunkenness.[63] Ghazali in fact began straightway to define it. The Sufi way begins with the *via purgativa* of asceticism and leads to an annihilation of self (*fana*). Higher states follow, visions of the angels and the spirits of the prophets. Finally, the desired experience of God is achieved by some, whether it be called "infusion," "connection," or "identity" (*ittihad*). There Ghazali breaks off and retreats. It is all wrong. The apprehension of God is an experience that is incommunicable, and one can learn more by associating with Sufis than by explanations of their activities.[64]

Ghazali's spiritual autobiography might appear to be a series of radical turnings, of entrances and hasty withdrawals. The withdrawals are more apparent than real, however. He accepted and never surrendered the case for an intellectually strengthened theology. He admitted the philosophers' claims to possess in the logical method an instrument for gaining certitude. He conceded that for most Muslims a simple acceptance on faith was an inevitable and not entirely unworthy course. And he argued strenuously yet prudently that there was a legitimate and important place in Islamic life for the experimental knowledge of God claimed by the mystics. All of these themes are woven together in his great Muslim summa, *The Revivification of the Sciences of Religion.*[65]

The *Revivification* had its desired effect. Muslim theology did become more rigorous by prudently expropriating the

[63] On the Sufi tradition of "breaking the ink-pots and tearing up the books," see Schimmel, *Mystical Dimensions*, pp. 17-19. Thomas à Kempis (d. 1471) and many others of the Western *devotio moderna* likewise preferred to "feel compunction rather than to define it."

[64] Watt, *Faith and Practice*, pp. 60-62.

[65] See Chapter IV above.

methodology of the philosophers, without accepting all their conclusions. Mystical union with God and the Sufi way that led to it won a degree of cautious acceptance. Ghazali's language on mysticism in the *Revivification* is a carefully moderated version of "sober intoxication." When speaking more personally he could and did go further. His *Niche for Lights* is a meditation on the famous "Light verse" in the Qur'an (24:35), which served for Muslim mystics the same provocative function as the opening chapter in Ezekiel and the Gospels' Transfiguration episode did for Jews and Christians.[66]

The doctors of Islam embraced the *Revivification*; the mystics meditated the *Niche for Lights* and found there all of the themes that were converging in the Sufi consensus: the identification of God's essence with a Light whose ontological radiance was creation and whose cognitive function was to illumine the intellects of the saints and prophets; the distinction between the "plain" (*zahir*) and "concealed" (*batin*) sense of Scripture, and the need of allegorical exegesis to elicit the latter;[67] the elitism that distinguished the mystic from all others in Islam and the esotericism that made revelation of the "realities" to the nonadepts a dangerous and highly inadvisable enterprise.[68] Suhrawardi and Ibn 'Arabi are already present in embryo in the *Niche for Lights*.

Ghazali made Islam safe for Sufism, but he did not disarm the Isma'ilis, whose ideological and military assault upon Baghdad continued for well over two centuries, though not always with the same methods. In the twelfth century, the Isma'ili apparatus in Iraq and Iran broke loose from Egyptian political control and pursued its own revolutionary course.

[66] Translation by W.H.T. Gairdner, *Al-Ghazzali's Mishkat al-Anwar: The Niche for Lights* (1915; reprint Lahore: Sh. Muhammad Ashraf, 1952).

[67] A long passage of the *Niche* is devoted to expounding the method of *ta'wil* (Gairdner, pp. 122-149), but Ghazali severely criticized those who, like the Isma'ilis, thought the *batin* abrogated the *zahir* sense and the legal enactments authorized by the latter (Gairdner, pp. 136-141).

[68] For Ghazali's rogues' gallery of the "unenlightened" and those who suffered from indirect lighting, see Gairdner, *Niche*, pp. 157-175.

It decentralized the insurrection by seizing isolated strong-points and took up the demoralizing weapon of assassination against Sunni political and religious figures.[69] Sunni opposition hardened against these so-called "Batinis," and the Isma'ilis were forced to play their final trump, the announcement of the End Time, the Spiritual Resurrection (*qiyamah*).

The Isma'ili *qiyamah* was not a variant of the Jewish or Christian apocalypse. It was the glorious termination of the cosmic cycle of history. The millennia-long series of Prophets and Imams, of public revelations and private understandings was at an end: the Age of Perfection had dawned. There is something faintly Pauline in the Isma'ili declaration of the end of Islam and the abrogation of the Islamic Law. But whereas Paul could substitute a New Covenant for the Old and hail the New Law of Jesus indwelling in the members of the *ekklesia*, the Isma'ili theology of the Resurrection did not give to its adherents a reenergized sense of mission, but represented an admission that Sunni Islam was beyond its reach. Paul might surrender the Jews, but for the Isma'ilis there was no gentile mission; Paradise was limited to the narrow confines of their mountain fortresses, where the Mongols found and destroyed them.

[69] M. Hodgson, *The Order of Assassins* (The Hague: Mouton, 1955) and "The Isma'ili State" in J. Boyle, ed., *The Cambridge History of Iran* (Cambridge: Cambridge University Press, 1968), V, 422-482.

CHAPTER VIII

Theology

THEOLOGY, discourse about God according to the principles of reason, was the invention of a people without benefit of revelation. It is unnecessary here to discuss the origins of Greek religion except to note that by the time they began to produce a literary record, the Greeks were already expressing at least some of their religious sentiments in the form of myth, complex narratives about a whole family of anthropomorphized gods and goddesses.

Myth is a special form of discourse that is divorced from time and only circumstantially connected with place. Like art, it presents itself rather than explaining or arguing. For all its aesthetic splendors, a later generation of Greeks grew unhappy with the mythological account of the gods. Both the mythical form of discourse and the value system inherent in the myths themselves were being challenged in an evolving Greek society by new ethical attitudes, and particularly by a different kind of human understanding that found its external and formal expression in the form of discourse called *logos*.[1]

Logos is essentially a mode of understanding that pursues causes and a mode of discourse that can give an account of that pursuit; that argues and demonstrates rather than simply narrates, and that is subject to verification by criteria external to itself. The categories of truth and falsehood, which are totally irrelevant to myth, are part of that verification apparatus. *Logos* is, in short, what we call science and what the Greeks more broadly termed philosophy.[2]

[1] See both *mythos* and *logos* in F. E. Peters, *Greek Philosophical Terms: A Historical Lexicon* (New York: New York University Press pb., 1967).

[2] Ibid., s.v. *dialektike, philosophia,* and cross-references.

156

By the generation of Socrates and Plato, *logos* was being applied in every corner of the known universe as well as to the domain of human activity, and in the next generation Aristotle both formalized the method of *logos* in a series of works on logic (the science of *logos*), and distinguished and organized the already vast body of knowledge that had been won by philosophy. Science (*episteme*), according to Aristotle, could be divided into that which has to do with making (*poiesis*); with action (*praxis*), such as ethics and politics; and finally with pure speculation (*theoria*). This latter is true science and philosophy, and can be divided in turn into the physical sciences, the mathematical sciences, and, like a crown upon the entire work, a science that deals with substances which stand apart from all matter, motion, and change—the first philosophy or, since such substances are divine, theology.[3]

It was not Plato and Aristotle who introduced God or the gods, once only the subject of myth and the object of ceremonial worship, to the scrutiny of *logos*; nor, once introduced, did the supernatural surrender its other domains in the minds and the hearts of the Greeks.[4] But God and reason were joined by Plato and Aristotle in a manner that was to have a profound influence on Western thinking about God, and that was both to stimulate and disturb those chosen guardians of the divine Self-portrait, the Jews, Christians, and Muslims.

Greek philosophy, or rather its branch called "*logos* about the divine" (*theologia*), did not begin by presuming the existence of God, though every Greek accepted the fact of that existence. Its task was rather to demonstrate the existence and nature of the divine. Few had any doubts it could be done, and the Greek theologians laid out with their usual

[3] Ibid., s.v. *episteme, theologia*, and cross-references.
[4] See, for example, E. R. Dodds, *The Greeks and the Irrational* (Berkeley and Los Angeles, University of California Press, pb., 1964), and M. Nilsson, *A History of Greek Religion* (New York: Norton pb., 1964), chapters 6-8, and *Greek Folk Religion* (New York: Harper Torchbook, 1961).

157

elegant ease the various arguments, later so familiar, from the design and order of the universe, the consensus of mankind, and the necessity of a first cause in the great chain of being as it descends and a final cause to which it returns.[5]

All of these arguments simply demonstrated, in a more or less rigorous form, what the Greeks, Romans, and others already knew. Where the new science departed more radically from commonly held opinions was in the portrait of that being or beings whom the Greeks called "the Immortals." The method of *logos* soon stripped from the divine two of its most obvious and universally recognized attributes, plurality and anthropomorphism. Theology, with its hierarchical view of reality, struck at the heart of ancient polytheism and denied as well that God could be anything but pure spirit, beyond flesh and bones, surely; beyond human affects such as love and hate; beyond thought, perhaps; and even, it was maintained, beyond being itself.

The theologians' vision of God as a single, transcendent, and spiritual cause was not yet monotheism. Although it removed the Supreme Being from direct contact with the material universe, it posited a great many intermediary beings below the remote transcendence of God, some of them intelligences without matter, and others who dwelled in the planets.[6] These too were divine, God's own eternal emanations, which descended by degrees to the intelligences shared by mankind.[7]

The theologians were not unmindful of the shambles they had made of popular religious attitudes and beliefs. Some professed not to care, but others such as the Stoics attempted to salvage the traditional myths by allegorizing them: Homer too was a theologian, but his manner of describing the nature

---

[5] Peters, *Lexicon*, s.v. *kinoun, telos, proödos*; and for the last argument and its history, A. O. Lovejoy, *The Great Chain of Being* (New York: Harper Torchbook, 1960).

[6] Peters, *Lexicon*, s.v. *daimones, ouranioi*.

[7] F. E. Peters, *The Harvest of Hellenism* (New York: Clarion pb., 1970), pp. 461-470.

of the gods was determined by the nature of his audience, whereas the speculative theologians could present the same truths in the unvarnished scientific language of philosophy. Even the mystery religions with their transparently primitive rituals could be explained in rationalistic terms for the newly sophisticated intelligentsia.[8]

The Greek thinkers' desire to save Homer and the poets was not born of a conviction that they somehow represented a divine revelation, but was maintained because Homer was well understood to carry the traditions of the entire Hellenic cultural past. Revelation in the Judeo-Islamic style was an alien notion to the Greeks. If the gods spoke to men, as they assuredly did in dreams and through oracles, it was to warn or counsel some fairly circumscribed act and not to profer either covenants or salvation. If there was to be salvation, it would be through man's use of his own intellectual faculties to discover what was the good life and the skillful and prudent use of his will to achieve it.

PHILO AND THE FATHERS

Theology was one of the manifestations of Hellenism that came to the Near East in the wake of Alexander the Great's conquests in the fourth century B.C.E. It took root in the schools of higher learning that grew up in newly founded cities like Alexandria and Antioch, and in more popular form spread among the Hellenic and Hellenized intelligentsia that was a byproduct of Greco-Roman urbanism in the area. Note has already been taken of the encounter of Hellenism and Judaism in both Palestine and the Diaspora. Martin Hengel, who has paid particular attention to the cultural consequences of that encounter in Palestine, has professed to see the infiltration of Greek ethical ideals in the third century in

[8] See E. Zeller, *Stoics, Epicureans and Sceptics* (1879; reprint New York: Russell and Russell, 1962), pp. 341-380; Peters, *Harvest of Hellenism*, pp. 446-461.

the biblical Qohelet—Ecclesiastes in the Septuagint—and in the second century in the *Wisdom of Jesus ben Sirah*.[9]

Whatever one finds in such works falls, like the works themselves, into the category of semipopular attitudes intended for a general, literate audience. For evidence of more formal philosophical and theological speculation among the Jews one must turn from Palestine to the Diaspora community in Egypt. The first Jew we know of to profess interest in Greek theology was a certain Aristobulus, who was from a high-priestly family and worked in Alexandria in the second century B.C.E.[10] The scattered fragments of his works, which were written in Greek, show a typical theologian at work, though for the first time on Jewish scriptural material. At once we are counseled against being trapped into a literal interpretation on the Torah, which in Aristobulus' own day had been translated into Greek. A literal approach to the text shows up nothing particularly unusual about the Torah, but an allegorical understanding reveals Moses as a true prophet who shared the same gift of wisdom as the philosophers, though Moses' account is, for all its metaphorical expression, superior to the Greek version of wisdom by reason of its obvious antiquity.

The themes touched upon by Aristobulus—the identity of Greek and Jewish wisdom, for example, which is revealed by the prudent application of allegorical exegesis—are not only taken up by his fellow Alexandrian Philo (d. after 39 C.E.), but are surrounded by such a considerable body of philosophical theory that it is possible to locate the later theologian rather precisely in the eclectic blend of Stoicism and Platonism current in the Roman world of his day.[11] Philo's allegorical exegesis is in the true Stoic manner, but some of

---

[9] *Judaism and Hellenism*, 2 vols. (London: SCM, 1974), I, 115-153.

[10] M. Hengel, *Judaism and Hellenism* (London: SCM Press, 1974), I, 163-169. For the intellectual climate in Alexandria at the time, see P. M. Frazer, *Ptolemaic Alexandria* (London: Oxford University Press, 1972), pp. 480-494.

[11] See J. Dillon, *The Middle Platonists* (London: Duckworth, 1977), pp. 139-183.

his refinements of Platonic and Stoic metaphysics are far more remarkable.[12] The God of the philosophers was too transcendent and too remote to have a direct hand in either the creation or the governance of the world, and so Philo had recourse to an intermediary, or rather a series of intermediaries. God was for Philo, as He had been for Aristotle, Self-thinking Thought, and His ideas are the spiritual archetypes of creation. The first external manifestation of these is the Logos, both Word and Idea, whom Philo personifies as "the second God." The Logos serves both the heavenly spiritual archetype of human intelligence and the instrument whereby all the other "ideas" (*logoi*) are disseminated in matter, and so not only bring the material universe into existence but govern it according to God's providential plan, as well.[13]

Greek theologians had for some time been experimenting with the notion of a Logos or Word as the first emanation of God and the instrument of creation, and their influence is perhaps visible in earlier Jewish authors' treatment of "Wisdom" as a personified entity somehow distinct from God and even as an agent in creation.[14] If Philo's language on the Logos is somewhat bold, it is certainly not to be construed as a retreat from monotheism. On the contrary, it was designed to protect the transcendence of God and at the same time establish a link between this now philosophically remote Creator and His distant and somewhat degenerate creation.[15]

Philo is the first we know of, Greek, Roman, or Jew, to advance the notion that the Platonic *eide*, those spiritual and

[12] The enthusiastic volumes devoted to Philo by H. A. Wolfson, *Philo* (Cambridge: Harvard University Press, 1947) should be compared with the treatment by H. Chadwick in *A. H. Armstrong et al., *The Cambridge History of Later Greek and Early Medieval Philosophy* (Cambridge: Cambridge University Press, 1967), pp. 137-157, and by John Dillon, cited above.

[13] Texts in *C. K. Barrett, *The New Testament Background* (New York: Harper Torchbook, 1961), pp. 183-186.

[14] Hengel, *Judaism and Hellenism*, I, 153-157, and the texts translated in *Barrett, *Background*, pp. 217-221.

[15] On this latter, *Armstrong et al., *Philosophy*, pp. 145-146.

161

eternal archetypes of reality, are actually the thoughts of God,[16] a remarkably fruitful idea for those Jewish, Christian, and Islamic theologians who could restrain themselves from following the Greeks even further down the same path and deny even thought to God. And though Philo's doctrine of Logos had no great future in Judaism, it had an immediate and obvious appeal to Christian thinkers.[17]

Earlier theologians had to take into account that poets and others had had their say on the subject of God, and had attempted to reconcile "poetical" and "speculative" theology by allegorical exegesis. Philo's task was somewhat different. He accepted the fact of a historical revelation to Moses on Sinai without hesitation or reserve, just as he accepted the truths contained in that revelation. He accepted as well the truth of philosophy, and saw no contradiction between the two, at least in principle. There were, in fact, differences—the Greeks generally believed, for example, in a universe that was created but eternal and in a providence that was general but did not descend to particulars—and where they existed, Philo came down firmly on the side of the scriptural witness. Some of the apparent differences between Scripture and philosophy could be resolved by the application of rationalizing exegesis to the former, but where Philo deemed reconciliation impossible, he followed Moses and not Plato.

Philo's language was Greek, and his version of Scripture was the Greek Septuagint translated in Alexandria in the mid-third century B.C.E.[18] By this simple act of translation, Scripture was clothed in Greek raiment with its own set of connotations, some of them already philosophical. But it was the theologian Philo who took the decisive step in converting scriptural notions into philosophical ones by his method of allegorical exegesis, and so open the Septuagint to discussion in a manner denied to the legal exegetes. What remained to

[16] See Peters, *Lexicon*, s.v. *eidos*; and H. A. Wolfson, *Religious Philosophy: A Group of Essays* (New York: Atheneum pb., 1965), pp. 27-37.

[17] See also Wolfson, *Religious Philosophy*, pp. 38-48.

[18] *Barrett, *Background*, pp. 208-216.

his successors in Judaism, Christianity, and Islam was to measure the new currency against the old, a necessary but necessarily impossible task.

The work of Philo was greeted with no visible enthusiasm in Palestinian circles. To the Pharisees and other non-Hellenized Jews it was probably inaccessible in any event, and the voice of the Palestinian "Hellenists" of the day, while it can be heard on political questions, is inaudible on religious matters. But it must have been read in the Diaspora—Paul for one appears to have been aware of it—and it found, as has been said, its most appreciative audience among the Hellenized converts to Christianity, first from among the Jews and then the Gentiles. The Logos of the opening of John's Gospel probably owes nothing to Philo, but it was obviously capable of Philonian interpretation, which was freely applied at Philo's own city of Alexandria less than two centuries later by the Christian Hellenists Clement (d. ca. 215) and Origen (d. ca. 254).

Theology did not come into Christianity through Philo alone. Already in Paul and the Gospel of John there are theological notions, that is, ideas expressed in the abstract conceptual terminology that is typical of theological rather than scriptural discourse, with its preference for the concrete on the one hand and the metaphorical and parabolic expression on the other. Paul and John were no doubt exposed to theological ideas that they accepted and used. There was already a plentiful supply of such in Jewish apocryphal literature, which portrayed the divine Wisdom and the Messiah as spiritual realities that existed from the moment of creation. Paul took up and combined both notions in his description of Jesus as the preexistent Logos.[19]

Neither Paul nor John argued theologically, however; they simply asserted by virtue of their own authority as "apostles." Logical demonstration and proof was the hallmark of

[19] W. D. Davies, *Paul and Rabbinic Judaism* (New York: Harper Torchbook, 1967), pp. 158-163; H. A. Wolfson, *The Philosophy of the Church Fathers*, 3rd ed. (Cambridge: Harvard University Press, 1970), pp. 155-167.

the philosophical method. Every Jewish and Christian thinker who came into contact with philosophy at this time was aware of it. Apostolic authority did not much appeal to Gentiles as an alternative to proof, and so there was substituted for it something the Gentiles could and did understand; public miracle was the scriptural equivalent of demonstrative proof.[20] But these same thinkers were equally aware of the attractive dangers of speculative theology, and although some, like Philo and Justin, thought "the wisdom of the Greeks" and "the wisdom of God" could be reconciled, Paul was the first but by no means the last to set the two at odds as natural antagonists.

One example of how a Christian became a theologian is provided by the career of Justin, who was born of Hellenized pagan parents in Samaria and was martyred for his Christianity about 165 C.E. His *Dialogue with Trypho*, probably the Rabbi Tarphon mentioned in the Mishna, gives some account of the spiritual odyssey that led Justin to Christianity. A need for religious satisfaction drove him first to philosophy; "conversion" to philosophy was not uncommon at this period—later Greek philosophy with its strong emphasis on ethical regimens and its noticeable interest in piety was assuming for many the role of a religion[21]—but after he had investigated the major schools he finally found spiritual peace in Christianity.[22] Conversion to Christianity did not mean, however, either the rejection of philosophy or its total acceptance. Christianity was the true "philosophy," and the anticipation of many of the tenets of Christianity—the immortality of the soul remained a perennial example in this type of literature—was a clear demonstration that Jesus, the eternal Logos, had been at work in the world from the be-

[20] The argument is already present in Philo and in the second-century Christian Justin; see Wolfson, *Church Fathers*, pp. 19-21.

[21] A. D. Nock, *Conversion* (London: Oxford University Press pb., 1961), pp. 164-192.

[22] The Dialogue has been translated by A. L. Williams, *Justin Martyr: The Dialogue with Trypho* (London: SPCK, 1931).

ginning. "In the beginning was the Word. . . ." The argument worked equally well against Judaism: not only Socrates but Abraham himself was a Christian before Christ.[23]

If Justin represents a modest accommodation of philosophical and theological discourse with Christian revelation, what appeared to be the first wholesale and radical attempts in that direction took place in Alexandria in the same second century, at the hands of such Gnostics as Basilides and Valentinus.[24] The Christian Fathers who took up its refutation were convinced that the seed of Gnostic error lay in Greek philosophy.[25] We cannot easily judge for ourselves, since most of the Christian Gnostic treatises that came to light at Nag Hammadi in Egypt in 1946 are "scriptural" rather than philosophic in form, that is, they are principally apocryphal Gospels, apocalypses, and wisdom literature.[26] Irenaeus and Hippolytus are certainly correct to the extent that the Alexandrian Gnostic writings are filled with Greek philosophical concepts and terminology. But there is as little genuine demonstration in them as there is in Paul, and Wolfson and Grant among others have argued that Christian Gnosticism is essentially a mythic system, a cosmic drama in which the chief actors have been clothed in the abstract costumes of Greek philosophy.[27]

Whatever the modern historian might say, the Fathers made their own judgment: Gnosticism was another example of the perversions of the Greeks, and its spread among the intelligentsia simply underlined the basic opposition between pagan and Christian wisdom. The firmest statement of that

[23] *Armstrong et al., Philosophy, pp. 160-166.

[24] On Gnosticism see Chapter VII above.

[25] Texts in W. Foerster, Gnosis, I, Patristic Evidence (London: Oxford University Press, 1972).

[26] See J. Doresse, The Secret Books of the Egyptian Gnostics (London: Hollis and Carter, 1960). A selection of Nag Hammadi texts are presented in translation in W. Foerster, Gnosis, II, Coptic and Mandaic Sources (London: Oxford University Press, 1974), pp. 1-118.

[27] Wolfson, Church Fathers, pp. 559-574; R. C. Grant, Gnosticism and Early Christianity (New York: Harper Torchbook, 1966), pp. 120-150.

opposition was expressed by a Latin Christian, Tertullian (d. ca. 240), who rhetorically exclaimed "What has Athens to do with Jerusalem? What agreement between the Academy and the Church?" Tertullian had witnessed the effects of Gnosticism, and had like others traced its errors to Greek philosophy. It served to confirm his conviction that faith and faith alone was sufficient for the Christian, since the entire truth had been revealed. More, Tertullian was willing not merely to accept but even to boast of the differences: the Christian believes in the paradoxes of Christianity precisely because they are absurd.[28]

Tertullian, who had considerably greater confidence in human reason when it manifested itself in the form of Roman law rather than Greek philosophy, may reflect a basic cultural difference between the Latin and Greek forms of Christianity. Clement of Alexandria, who lived about the same time, came from a totally different environment and showed none of Tertullian's disdain for philosophy, and uttered no apostrophes against "wretched Aristotle."[29] For Clement the works of human reason served the same purpose for the Gentiles as the Law did for the Jews: they were an "evangelical preparation," as the historian Eusebius later called it. Greek wisdom was true wisdom in that it was the product of an intelligence that men share with God, or of a special kind of natural revelation that the Logos gave to the Gentiles. Clement, who knew Philo's work exceedingly well, was aware of one of the latter's arguments to justify recourse to philosophy, to wit, that the Greek thinkers had read the

[28] Tertullian's clearest statement of his position on Greek philosophy is probably in his *Prescription of Heretics*, translated by T. H. Bindley (London: SPCK, 1914), with selections in H. Bettenson, *The Early Christian Fathers* (London: Oxford University Press pb., 1969), pp. 104-167; cf. Wolfson, *Church Fathers*, pp. 102-106, and for the celebrated "I believe because it is absurd" formula, E. Gilson, *History of Christian Philosophy in the Middle Ages* (London: Sheed and Ward, 1955), p. 45.

[29] On Clement, see *Armstrong et al., *Philosophy*, pp. 168-181 and Wolfson, *Church Fathers*, pp. 120-126.

Scriptures and expropriated many of its doctrines, and did not hesitate to invoke it for his own case.

Clement joined the issue directly, though not explicitly with Tertullian, on the question of "naked faith." Faith (*pistis*), if understood as an acceptance of the truth of Scripture without further inquiry, though it is sufficient for salvation, is inferior to a higher degree of understanding, which he calls gnosis.[30] Faith, when it accepts the truths of Scripture, provides the principles and foundation of demonstration, but the demonstration itself consists in the understanding of Scripture, and for that philosophical wisdom is necessary. This latter is not for everyone, of course, and Clement is willing to accept the Gnostics' distinction between "the simple" and a spiritual elite, without denying salvation to the former, however. The Christian "Gnostics" of Clement have access to the "mysteries" of Scripture because they can penetrate to its deeper philosophical truths, whereas most of the faithful must remain content with symbol and parable.

Most of Clement's thinking about theology is found strewn across a work he called *Stromata* or *Carpets*.[31] It is not an unnatural distribution, perhaps, since from Philo onward the compatibility of speculative theology and divine revelation was principally demonstrated in the exegesis of Scripture, and it was the sequence of the sacred writings that provided the form within which both Jewish and Christian theologians worked. No Christian had undertaken that exegesis on the same scale and with the same penetration as Philo until Origen, Clement's successor in the nascent Christian school in Alexandria, took up the work. Origen could do the same kind of philosophical analysis of Scripture as his Jewish antecedent, but as a Christian he added typology, the foreshadowing of events in the New Testament by the Old, a method

[30] On this question, see S. Lilla, *Clement of Alexandria: A Study of Christian Platonism and Gnosticism* (London: Oxford University Press, 1971).

[31] English translation in Vol. II of *The Ante-Nicene Fathers* (1885; reprint Grand Rapids: Eerdmans, 1951), pp. 299-567; selections in Bettenson, *Early Christian Fathers*, pp. 168-184.

already popularized by the Gospels themselves. Origen was, in addition, a considerable textual scholar.[32]

On the Philonian model, every Christian theologian had necessarily to be an exegete. But Origen was more. He was the first Christian to put his hand to systematic theology by arranging his material in the logical order of an academic school treatise—he may have attended the Platonic Academy in Alexandria—rather than in that dictated by the order of Scripture. The result was *On First Principles*, a vast statement of the truths of Christianity derived from Scripture but stated and argued in theological form.[33] Thus in speaking of the Father, Jesus the Logos, and the Holy Spirit,[34] Origen describes each as a separate "essence" or "substance" (*ousia*) and "individual" (*hypostasis, hypokeimenon*), and characterizes the Trinitarian unity as "consubstantial" (*homoousios*).[35]

None of this terminology had the slightest scriptural justification, of course, but was borrowed from the common philosophical vocabulary of the time, and its use by Origen, his precursors, and his immediate successors guaranteed that it would set the terms of the debate to follow. Jesus had indeed said "I and the Father are one," but what was one to make of a text like "the Father is greater than I"? Was *homoousios* an adequate description of either relationship? For Origen there never was a time when the *Logos* was not; for some others, among them Arius, a cleric of Alexandria, that notion was a betrayal of the implication of Sonship: the Lo-

[32] *P. R. Ackroyd and C. F. Evans, eds., *The Cambridge History of the Bible* (Cambridge: Cambridge University Press, 1970), I, 454-489: "Origen as a Biblical Scholar."

[33] Translated by G. W. Butterworth, *Origen: On First Principles* (1963; reprint New York: Harper Torchbook, 1966); selections in Bettenson, *Early Christian Fathers*, pp. 185-282.

[34] On the evolution of the Holy Spirit in Christian thought, see J.H.D. Kelly, *Early Christian Doctrines*, 4th ed. (London: Black, 1968), pp. 83-137, and Wolfson, *Church Fathers*, pp. 155-256.

[35] See Wolfson, *Church Fathers*, pp. 270-280, 317-321; and Bettenson, *Early Christian Fathers*, pp. 230-243. On the early history of *homoousios*, G. L. Prestige, *God in Christian Thought* (London: SPCK, 1952), chapter 10.

gos was, like the rest of creation, generated, and thus Jesus was God by courtesy, as it were.

Arius' motives may have been impeccable—to protect the absolute unity of God in a monotheistic faith—but the result was to reduce Jesus to what appeared to many as a demigod, and so apparently reintroduce a kind of polytheism.[36] Nor did it help to turn (the first of many such well-intentioned turnings) to *homoiousios*, "of a similar substance," as a compromise. Pandora's hope chest had been opened, and it turned out to contain a rich dowry indeed. Out of it flowed not only *homoousios* and *homoiousios*, but "nature," "substance," and "person," and more; some of them Greek and some Latin; some philosophical terms and some borrowed from Roman law; each intended to clarify and move forward Clement's apparently modest proposal of a simple scriptural faith illumined by secular understanding. Gnosis, as it turned out, was as an elusive and divisive goal for Christian theologians as it had been for the Greek philosophers before them.[37]

The solution to the problem of reconciling Athens and Jerusalem was, in the end, Rome—the old Rome on the Tiber and the new Rome at Constantinople. If the theologians could not reason to a consensus, as they sometimes could, the empire intervened by convoking a council. The first Council of the Great Church was convened by Constantine at Nicea in 325 C.E. to deal with the Trinitarian problem raised by Arius, and they recurred with some regularity in the following centuries. An ecumenical council, one at which all the bishops of the Church or their legates were in principle present, was a curious blend of a judicial process, an academic debate, and a political effort to make the episcopal Apostolic tradition

---

[36] Kelly, *Early Christian Doctrines*, pp. 223-231; Wolfson, *Religious Philosophy*, pp. 126-157.

[37] The best guides to this troubled theological terrain are A. Grillmeier, *Christ in Christian Tradition* (London: Sheed and Ward, 1965), where the emphasis is theological, and W. Frend, *The Rise of the Monophysite Movement* (Cambridge: Cambridge University Press, 1972), with a more detailed historical background.

speak, if not with one voice, then at least in harmony. Documents were submitted in evidence, and the relevant passages of Scripture were assembled and scrutinized. Within, the bishops prayed, debated and caucused; without, various pressure groups demonstrated, at times violently, and lobbied for their favored position.

The Council of Nicea produced a creed or short statement of belief that embodied its decision and served to define and canonize what the assembled Fathers understood as the "catholic" position, that is, a form of orthodoxy common to the entire Church.[38] It set down as well a series of anathemas condemning in explicit detail positions that it regarded as heretical. Thus came into being at Nicea what Wolfson has called the "statutory Catholicism of Christianity . . . to take the place of the consentaneous catholicism that had fought and won its victory over Gnosticism."[39]

We cannot judge whether Rabbi Tarphon held the alleged conversation with the Christian philosopher Justin mentioned earlier, but such conversations must surely have occurred in the earliest days of Christianity, and must equally surely have broken off as parent and offspring moved further apart.[40] There was not, at any rate, a course of Jewish theology parallel to the broadly swelling stream of Christian speculation. While Christianity moved first tentatively and then boldly into the world of Greco-Roman learning and established its intellectual credentials there, the bloody sequel of the Jewish revolts of 70 and 135 C.E. rendered Hellenic accommodation not merely suspect but dangerous to many Jews. What had come into Judaism from the Greeks before those events remained lodged within Jewish mystical specu-

[38] On the term "catholic," see Wolfson, *Church Fathers*, pp. 495-496, and on the evolution of creeds, J.N.D. Kelly, *Early Christian Creeds*, 2nd ed. (London: Longmans, 1960), and J. Stevenson, *Creeds, Councils and Controversies* (London: SPCK, 1966).

[39] *Church Fathers*, p. 578.

[40] See H.-J. Schoeps, *Jewish-Christian Argument: A History of Conflict* (New York: Holt, Rinehart and Winston, 1963), and N. de Lange, *Origen and the Jews: Studies in Jewish-Christian Relations in Third-Century Palestine* (Cambridge: Cambridge University Press, 1976).

lation, but we have already seen how the rabbis kept that side of Jewish piety well concealed beneath the all-enveloping garment of the Law.[41]

The difference ran very deep. Pharisaic and rabbinic Judaism was conservative in nature. Its goal was fidelity to a tradition, and the instrument of that fidelity was the Law: Torah and Talmud. Its distinctive institution was not the synagogue, the house of prayer (*bet ha-tefilla*)—all religions have such—but the *bet ha-midrash*, where the sole occupation was the loving study of Scripture and particularly the Law.[42] Christianity, on the other hand, was innovative in the literal sense of that word. Metamorphosis, reform, is a Pauline term used to describe the Christian process of "putting on the new man," and the idea remained fundamental in the early Church.[43]

When he talked about "renewal," Paul meant the working of Jesus' redemptive act and of divine grace. This notion might have remained entirely within the Church's sacramental system, but the Greek intellectuals who became Christians were as much interested in the wisdom (*gnosis*) of Scripture as they were in the operation of grace. The truth of Scripture became the issue between the Christian intellectual and his pagan counterpart.[44] Scripture was the Christian's "philosophy," and already by the time of Clement the corollary had emerged: Christianity and Greek culture were rival forms of education (*paideia, morphosis*), each with its own claim to reforming the human spirit.[45] It was the Christians' license,

[41] See Chapter VII above.

[42] See the passages quoted in C. G. Montefiore and H. Loewe, *A Rabbinic Anthology* (New York: Schocken pb., 1974), pp. 116-173.

[43] See G. Ladner, *The Idea of Reform: Its Impact on Christian Thought and Action in the Age of the Fathers* (New York: Harper Torchbook, 1967).

[44] The debate can be treated most clearly in Celsus' *True Discourse* and Origen's response on behalf of Christianity: H. Chadwick, *Contra Celsum* (Cambridge: Cambridge University Press, 1953).

[45] H. I. Marrou, *A History of Education in Antiquity* (New York: Mentor pb., 1964), pp. 419-438; and W. Jaeger, *Early Christianity and Greek Paideia* (London: Oxford University Press pb., 1969).

contested at times both within and without the Church,[46] to expropriate the entire Greco-Roman intellectual heritage from Homer to Plato and Aristotle, from Cicero to Vergil and Seneca.[47]

The discussion and assimilation of Greek speculative theology by Christianity took place in the great urban centers of the Mediterranean littoral in the third and fourth centuries of the Christian era. By the fifth century, paganism itself and the world that produced it was dying, and by the sixth century had all but expired. Its literary legacy was preserved by a few scholars and Christian clerics.[48] Christianity had meanwhile penetrated deep into the hinterland, to the haunts of the "pagans," the agricultural peasantry (*pagani*) who were the last holdouts against the new creed.

In the Near East the hinterland was also the home of developed regional cultures that had also to some extent escaped the full force of the Hellenization process. Here among the Copts or native Egyptians and the Syriac-speaking Arameans of the Fertile Crescent, Christianity took on a different, only partially Hellenized form. Syriac Christianity, for example, had deep roots in the older Semitic religions and the literary culture of the Near East.[49] Its theology and exegesis, though characterized as "Antiochene" and typified in the work of such Hellenized intellectuals as Paul of Samo-

[46] See T. R. Glover, *The Conflict of Religions in the Early Roman Empire* (1909; reprint Boston: Beacon Press pb., 1960); and A. Momigliano, ed., *The Conflict of Paganism and Christianity in the Fourth Century* (London: Oxford University Press, 1963).

[47] See C. N. Cochrane, *Christianity and Classical Culture: A Study in Thought and Action from Augustus to Augustine* (London: Oxford University Press pb., 1957).

[48] A.H.M. Jones, *The Later Roman Empire*, 3 vols. (Oxford: Blackwell, 1964), abridged as *The Decline of the Ancient World* (London: Longmans pb., 1975); P. Brown, *The World of Late Antiquity* (London: Thames and Hudson pb., 1971); L. Reynolds and N. Wilson, *Scribes and Scholars* (London: Oxford University Press, 1968).

[49] The history of Syriac Christianity is still to be written, but its major center at Edessa is tolerably well known: J. B. Segal, *Edessa: The Blessed City* (London: Oxford University Press, 1970).

sata, Theodore of Mopsuestia, and Theodoret of Cyrrhus, are not altogether distant reflections of Judaism and Jewish Christianity.[50] And whatever Muhammad knew about Christianity, it almost certainly derived from this Syro-Aramaic form.

It seems paradoxical that though we do not know a great deal about institutions of Christian higher learning in the Hellenic metropolis, possibly because many Christian scholars went to secular universities,[51] we possess considerable information on the chief Syriac Christian *bet ha-midrash*, which was located first at Edessa and then across the Persian frontier at Nisibis.[52] It was devoted almost exclusively to exegesis, for which the students learned a bare minimum of Greek logical analysis, though not the demonstrative method appropriate to speculative theology. And its labors unfolded entirely in Syriac: Greek propaedeutics, the exegetic models of Theodore of Mopsuestia, and the text of Scripture itself were all studied in Syriac Aramaic.[53]

Though the products of the Syriac Christian schools were more haggadic than halakic in nature, masters and students there were by no means disinterested in either theology or its Greek antecedents. These latter interests survived into Islam, and kindled similar interests on the part of Muslim intellectuals. More, the Syriac Christians of Iraq served as the primary agents for the transmission of the Greek philosophical and scientific legacy into Islam, where it had the some-

[50] J. Daniélou, *The Theology of Jewish Christianity* (Chicago: Regnery, 1964), pp. 21-33; Grillmeier, *Christ in Christian Tradition*, pp. 177-178, 338-360; Frend, *Monophysite Movement*, pp. 83-91; *Ackroyd and Evans, eds., *Cambridge History of the Bible*, I, 489-509.

[51] See H. I. Marrou, "Synesius of Cyrene and Alexandrian Neoplatonism" in Momigliano, ed., *Conflict of Paganism and Christianity*, pp. 126-150; and the early career of Augustine described by Peter Brown, *Augustine of Hippo* (Berkeley and Los Angeles: University of California Press pb., 1969).

[52] A. Vööbus, *History of the School of Nisibis* (Louvain: CSCO, 1965).

[53] F. E. Peters, *Allah's Commonwealth* (New York: Simon and Schuster, 1973), pp. 308-324.

what same effect as it previously had upon the Jews and Christians.

The Kalam

Christian theology had begun with a generation of second-century scholars who were learned in both Roman law and the wisdom of the Greeks, and so could defend Christians' rights to legal and intellectual toleration in the Roman world. Islam had little need for that kind of apologia. Though Islam was the newcomer in the family of religions, it was Judaism and Christianity that were the tolerated religions in the recently conquered Near East. Islam did, however, require intellectual defense against far more sophisticated Christian theologians like John of Damascus (d. 749), who was a skilled dialectician and well versed in the Qur'an and Islamic traditions.[54] Though the Muslim sources are very sparing on the details of these early debates, and trace the origins of their own theological speculation to purely internal and often political developments in Islam, a case can be made that here in Christian-Muslim religious polemic in the first century of Islam the seeds of Muslim theology were sown.[55]

If such a case can be made, however uncertainly, on an issue like free will and predestination, there were other discussions that took place within the Islamic community in the first century of its existence that have the appearance of being generated by the internal dynamic of Islam: questions concerning the nature of the community and its leadership.[56]

[54] D. Sahas, *John of Damascus and Islam* (London: E. J. Brill, 1972).

[55] So M. Seele, *Muslim Theology: A Study of Origins with Reference to the Church Fathers* (London: Luzac, 1964); contra, W. M. Watt, *Free Will and Predestination in Early Islam* (London: Luzac, 1948), and *The Formative Period of Islamic Thought* (Hawthorne, N.Y.: Aldine, 1973), pp. 88-99. For a survey of the question, see H. A. Wolfson, *The Philosophy of the Kalam* (Cambridge: Harvard University Press, 1976), pp. 58-63.

[56] J. Wellhausen, *The Religio-Political Factions in Early Islam* (1901; revised translation New York: American Elsevier, 1975), and W. M. Watt, *The Formative Period of Islamic Thought* (Chicago: Aldine, 1973), pp. 9-179; see Chapter III above.

The arguments put forward by both parties to those debates were certainly religious, since they appealed to the Qur'an and the traditions for their authority, but the argument was not yet theological in the formal sense of discursive and systematic reasoning on the Greek model.

In choosing this Greek-devised definition of theology, which serves so well in describing certain aspects of Christian thought and an occasional Jewish thinker like Philo, one does little justice to the complexities of halakic reasoning, which occupied the intellectual energies of so many of the learned and the pious in both Judaism and Islam, where the type of the scholar was the lawyer and not the theologian. *Halaka* and *haggada* divide between them the mind and heart of post-Exilic Judaism, as we have seen, and the same may fairly be said of Islam. They are the mode of the Qur'an itself,[57] as well as of the majority of the Muslim thinkers who addressed themselves to belief and practice toward the end of the eighth Christian century.[58]

Among their opponents, the early Muslim lawyers were accustomed to distinguish between "partisans of *hadith*" and "partisans of *kalam*" as two extreme positions whose adherents were unwilling to be drawn into the Shafi'ite consensus. The first, the "traditionists," opposed the sanctioning of local legal usages and preferred to rely as closely as possible upon the Qur'an and those *hadith* reports of the Prophet whose history we have already inspected. The second rejected the *hadith* reports in favor of using their own powers of research (*nazar*) and intellectual application (*ijtihad*) on the revealed Qur'an.[59] This occurs in a legal context, and though the traditionists continued to make their principal case within the domain of jurisprudence, the partisans of *kalam* found other,

[57] See J. Wansbrough, *Qur'anic Studies* (London: Oxford University Press, 1977), passim.

[58] See Chapter IV above.

[59] On the "hadith folk," see J. Schacht, *The Origins of Muhammadan Jurisprudence* (London: Oxford University Press, 1953), pp. 253-257, and for "partisans of *kalam*," ibid., pp. 258-259.

more congenial terrain for their preoccupations. They acquired another name as well, that of Muʿtazilites.[60]

Kalam means literally "speech,"[61] but we know too much about its history and development to regard it simply as that, or even as an elliptic Arabic translation of the Greek *theologia*. At first *kalam* may have appeared as such inasmuch as it seemed to oppose scientific investigation (*nazar*) to unquestioning acceptance (*taqlid*). When, however, a genuine philosophical tradition appeared in Islam and generations of Muslims and Jews had an opportunity of observing the difference between it and *kalam*, the true nature of the latter became manifest.[62] *Kalam* is probably best translated, then, as "dialectical theology" in that it began not from the first principles of reason but from commonly held opinions. Nor did it proceed in the strict syllogistic method prescribed by Aristotle in his *Analytics*, but invoked the shorthand, persuasive arguments described in the *Topics*.[63]

In the eyes of the philosophers, *kalam* was at best a defensive and apologetic weapon and at worst a misleading replica of wisdom. But it was in fact some kind of theology, in that it attempted to explain and argue its positions on God and the universe instead of simply asserting them. Muslim lawyers had been using that type of *ijtihad* in legal reasoning, but where the Muʿtazilites broke new ground was in applying analogy and the like to nonhalakic and even nonqurʾanic questions such as substance and accident, cause and effect,

---

[60] The original meaning of the name is best rendered as "neutral" in the seventh-century debate over the claims of ʿAli to the caliphate-imamate: Watt, *Formative Period*, pp. 215-217.

[61] Wolfson, *Kalam*, pp. 1-2.

[62] On the later Muslim understanding of *kalam*, see Wolfson, *Kalam*, pp. 3-42, and for Maimonides' sketch of its history, ibid., pp. 43-57.

[63] On these distinctions, commonly drawn by critical philosophers, see the passages from al-Farabi (d. 950), *Enumeration of the Sciences*, translated in R. Lerner and M. Mahdi, eds., *Medieval Political Philosophy* (Ithaca: Cornell University Press pb., 1972), pp. 27-30; and Averroes (d. 1198), *Decisive Treatise* in G. Hourani, *Averroes on Harmony of Religion and Philosophy* (London: Luzac, 1961), pp. 33, 92.

matter and spirit.[64] This is familiar ground for us, who have observed the progress of Greek philosophy into the vitals of Jewish and Christian religious discourse, but was exceedingly alien to the "partisans of *hadith*," who knew nothing of such concepts and found them threatening to the scriptural heritage of Islam. The Mu'tazilites were not Greek rationalists, of course; they began with the generally admitted premises of the Qur'an. But they extended those premises beyond both the problematic and the conceptual currency of the Qur'an into a view of the physical world that they felt accorded well with their view of God's omnipotence, and into a distinction between God's essence and His attributes that they felt safeguarded the spirituality and simplicity of the Godhead.[65]

If the concepts of the Mu'tazilites appear familiar, we are at a loss to explain how these transparently Greek notions got to eighth-century Basrah and Baghdad. These "kalamists" (*mutakallimun*) were not Greek intellectuals converted to a new faith, but Arabs who antedate most of what we know of the translation movement in Islam. What we do know is that the same Caliph who sponsored and supported the beginnings of the translation movement, al-Ma'mun (813-833), was also a staunch supporter of the Mu'tazilite point of view, and made an effort—a rather rare effort in Islam—to define it as orthodoxy and to force the traditionists and their leader, Ibn Hanbal, to accept it as such.[66] The translation movement was an extraordinary moment in the history of Islamic civilization. In the brief span of perhaps two centuries between 800 and 1000 C.E., most of the basic texts of Greek philosophy and science were translated, sometimes from Greek, sometimes from Syriac, into Arabic, in what were finally

[64] On the early Mu'tazilites, see Watt, *Formative Period*, pp. 180-252, and Peters, *Allah's Commonwealth*, pp. 180-208.

[65] On the limits of the problematic of *kalam*, see A. J. Wensinck, *The Muslim Creed* (1932, reprint London, Frank Cass, 1965), pp. 58-83, and Wolfson, *Kalam*, pp. 72-79.

[66] W. M. Patton, *Ahmed ibn Hanbal and the Mihna* (London: E. J. Brill, 1897); Peters, *Allah's Commonwealth*, pp. 163-170.

refined into sophisticated versions of Plato and Aristotle, Ptolemy, Euclid and Galen, many of their later Greek commentators, and a great number of pseudonymous exemplars of such occult sciences as alchemy and astrology.[67] Thus were laid down the foundations of the imposing structure of Arab science and of a philosophical tradition that would both intimidate and fertilize the nascent pursuit of *kalam*.

The received version of philosophy (*falsafah*) in Islam was not unnaturally Greek in its origins, methodology, and problematic.[68] It was also predictably eclectic in the manner of late antiquity, and its more theologically inclined contributors such as Plotinus and Proclus were disguised, as they often were earlier for the Christian reader, by anonymity or pseudepigraphy. But disguised or not, and whether called "first philosophy" or "metaphysics," Islam possessed a theology, or rather another theology, to set beside the Qur'anic portrait of God and that newly fashioned by the Mu'tazilite masters of *kalam* (*mutakallimun*).

The very first master of *falsafah*, al-Kindi, a younger contemporary of Ma'mun, set out a series of disturbing positions: a God who created by emanation rather than a single, willed act; a universe filled with the workings of natural causality; and most ominously, the existence of a human rational wisdom that ran parallel to the Sacred Wisdom of revelation.[69] In Kindi human wisdom, to which the lawyers had

[67] Peters, *Allah's Commonwealth*, pp. 266-331. There is a generous selection of these texts in English in F. Rosenthal, *The Classical Heritage in Islam* (Berkeley and Los Angeles: University of California Press, 1975).

[68] The standard work on Islamic philosophy, Majid Fakhry's *History of Islamic Philosophy* (New York: Columbia University Press, 1970) is admirably straightforward and clear, and there is a briefer but masterful synthesis of *falsafah* (and *kalam*) in Muhsin Mahdi's contribution to the new *Encyclopedia Britannica*: "Islamic Theology and Philosophy."

[69] Al-Kindi's major philosophical treatise, which is not as "theological" as its title might suggest, has been translated and commented upon by A. Ivry, *Al-Kindi's Metaphysics* (Albany: SUNY Press, 1974); cf. R. Walzer, *Greek into Arabic* (Cambridge: Harvard University Press, 1962), pp. 175-205, and Peters, *Allah's Commonwealth*, pp. 428-440.

granted some small autonomy under the rubric *ijtihad*, was given direct access to God: what the Prophet had gained without toil by God's gift the philosopher could also attain by laborious intellectual struggle. It was a generous if somewhat grudging concession to philosophy, but another was willing to go further. The physician and philosopher al-Razi (d. 925) not only granted the philosopher access to a knowledge of God; he denied it to the prophets of revelation: philosophy was the only wisdom.[70] This was apostasy and disbelief (*kufr*) pure and simple, and though not many other philosophers were willing to go as far as al-Razi, the dangers of the rationalist position were manifest. *Falsafah* cannot be said to have had a brilliant career in Islam, despite the efforts of such men as Farabi and Avicenna to reconcile faith and reason in a more sophisticated manner than Kindi, and with far greater Islamic sensibilities than those displayed by Razi.[71]

Unlike Kindi, Farabi (d. 950) was unwilling to write off prophetic revelation as a separate and independent means of attaining enlightenment. Farabi approached the question from the distinctive angle of political philosophy, distinctive not with regard to his mentor Plato, of course, but in the light of the history of later Greek philosophy, which betrayed no interest in political philosophy.[72] Farabi's ideal state was to be ruled by a man who combined both intellectual and practical enlightenment, the qualities of the philosopher and the prophet. The true prophet, according to Farabi, was someone who could take the truths he shared with the philosopher by reason of surpassing intellect and convert them, through

[70] Fakhry, *Islamic Philosophy*, pp. 112-124; Peters, *Allah's Commonwealth*, pp. 440-445.

[71] The entire debate is surveyed, not very satisfactorily, by A. J. Arberry, *Revelation and Reason in Islam* (New York: Macmillan, 1957).

[72] On this aspect of Farabi's thought, see E.I.J. Rosenthal, *Political Thought in Medieval Islam* (Cambridge: Cambridge University Press, 1962), pp. 122-142, and the generous selections from Farabi in Lerner and Mahdi, eds., *Medieval Political Philosophy*, pp. 22-94. How Farabi integrated his philosophy is best illustrated in the texts translated by M. Mahdi, *Alfarabi's Philosophy of Plato and Aristotle* (Ithaca: Cornell University Press pb., 1969).

his imaginative faculty, into the figured truths of a revelation like the Qur'an or the concrete realities of a law like the shari'ah.[73]

What Farabi said of the "prophet" was true of all prophets, and there was no attempt to defend the unique quality of Islamic revelation.[74] Christian philosophers and theologians had inherited the notion of a historical "presence" or parousia from their Jewish messianic background. The parousia was where the twin arches of the Greeks' human wisdom and the Jews' revealed and prophetic wisdom converged on Jesus. Islam had its own messianic tradition in the figure of the Imam—both Farabi and Avicenna were Shi'ites and so well within that tradition—but the intellectual bases of imamite theology, which were beginning to be put down in Farabi's own day in the tenth century, were cyclic on a Gnostic model rather than linear-historical on a Jewish one, and so showed little interest in historical process.[75] Maimonides, who otherwise stood so close to Farabi, could and did make a case for the unique character of the Mosaic revelation.

Ibn Sina, whom the West calls Avicenna (d. 1038), could explain no less than Farabi both the need and process of prophecy-revelation[76] and wrote a special treatise On the Proof of Prophecy.[77] The process could be devised easily enough within the capacious categories of Greek cognitive theories, with which Avicenna and Farabi were both well acquainted,

[73] Peters, Allah's Commonwealth, pp. 498-514; R. Walzer in *Armstrong et al., Later Greek and Early Medieval Philosophy, pp. 652-669, and Walzer, Greek into Arabic, pp. 206-219.

[74] The dangers of this position in a religious society, dangers well understood in the Platonic tradition to which Farabi belonged, are underlined by L. Strauss, Persecution and the Art of Writing (Glencoe, Ill.: Free Press, 1952).

[75] *M. G. Hodgson, The Venture of Islam (Chicago: University of Chicago Press pb., 1974), I, 381-384; Peters, Allah's Commonwealth, pp. 592-617.

[76] See especially F. Rahman, Prophecy in Islam (London: Allen and Unwin, 1958), pp. 30-91.

[77] Translation in Lerner and Mahdi, eds., Medieval Political Philosophy, pp. 112-121; cf. ibid., pp. 98-111, and A. J. Arberry, Avicenna on Theology (London: John Murray, 1951), pp. 42-49.

but the need for revelation, if the same truths were available to unaided human reason, was quite another matter. The philosophers fell back on familiar Platonic and Gnostic ground: not everyone was capable of reflective reasoning, and it was for the great mass of the unphilosophical that God, the God of the ignorant and the learned, chose to reveal His truths through a prophet.

The argument is not unlike that found among Sufis and other mystics in pursuit of private revelation: the Law is not for them; it is for the masses. Avicenna could savor that line of reasoning, since he was not much removed from the mystical stance in his own later philosophy. Many of the Greeks in the Platonic tradition had argued that discursive reasoning had its limits, and that the final knowledge of God was the result of an intuitive leap to God, a moment of illumination that was for Plotinus the climax of what he called "the flight of the alone to the Alone."[78] That moment took on great importance for Avicenna. Illumination (*ishraq*) or gnosis (*ma'rifah*) does not loom large in Avicenna's philosophical encyclopedias like the *Book of Healing* or his *Book of Scientific Knowledge,* but his later mystical treatises make it clear that this intuitive union with the Divine was central to what he was beginning to conceive of as a kind of esoteric philosophy.[79]

The distance between Avicenna and the Mu'tazilites of scarcely two centuries earlier is almost immeasurable. They began with the Qur'an; he with the first principles of reason. Their reasoning was dialectical; he had full command of the Aristotelian scientific logic. They had fed on some ill-digested philosophical material from disguised sources; Avi-

[78] *Armstrong et al., *Philosophy*, pp. 258-263.

[79] There are selections in English in H. Corbin, *Avicenna and the Visionary Recital* (New York: Pantheon, 1960). One of them, "Hayy ibn Yaqzan," is the narrative of an allegorical voyage to a mystical "Orient." The theme was reworked by a Spanish Avicennan, Ibn Tufayl (d. 1185), and is translated with commentary by L. E. Goodman, *Hayy ibn Yaqzan by Ibn Tufayl* (New York: Twayne, 1972).

cenna had educated himself on the entire range of Greek philosophical science.[80] But even the Mu'tazilites' modest movement in the direction of a rationalizing theology had gotten them in trouble with the traditionists, who regarded it as a dangerous innovation, particularly after Ma'mun's official support was withdrawn by his successors.

Traditionism, unquestioned reliance upon the Qur'an and the *hadith* reports from the Prophet, was a popular movement and the genuine voice of Islamic piety. The followers of Ahmad ibn Hanbal had no less hesitation in taking to the streets of Baghdad and voicing their opposition to innovators than did the fifth-century Christian monks of Alexandria, Antioch, or Constantinople.[81] But even as they did, forces of reconciliation were at work. Tradition credits the first step to al-Ash'ari, who was a contemporary of Farabi but was neither a philosopher nor in the end a *mutakallim*. He was a traditionist who was willing to vacate some of the more virulent anti-intellectualism of the Hanbalis and to accept at least some Mu'tazilite positions.[82] But he could not and would not embrace a Mu'tazilite universe governed by the laws of natural causality or their version of God divested of His eternal, Qur'anic attributes.[83] Ash'ari's universe was an occasionalist one of atoms and accidents in which God, a Qur'anic God of the traditionist type, intervened directly, everywhere, and at all times.[84]

Ash'ari did not entirely convince the Hanbalis, nor did the

---

[80] See Avicenna's autobiography, translated and annotated by W. E. Gohlman, *The Life of Ibn Sina* (Albany: SUNY Press, 1974).

[81] *Hodgson, *Venture*, I, 389-392.

[82] Two of Ash'ari's major works are available in English: W. C. Klein, *The Elucidation of Islam's Foundations* (New Haven: Yale University Press, 1940), and R. J. McCarthy, *The Theology of al-Ash'ari* (Beirut: Impr. Catholique, 1953).

[83] See Wensinck, *Muslim Creed*, pp. 83-101.

[84] The debate between the Ash'arite "occasionalist" theologians and the philosophical naturalists continued well into the thirteenth century; see Wolfson, *Kalam*, pp. 466-600, and M. Fakhry, *Islamic Occasionalism and Its Critique by Averroes and Aquinas* (London: Allen and Unwin, 1958).

strict traditionists for their part prevent a version of Ash'arite *kalam* from winning a place in the spectrum of Islamic orthodoxy as a legitimate instrument for explaining and defending revelation and the traditions.[85] The opportunity for showing the usefulness of *kalam* as a dialectical weapon was provided in the eleventh century by the rise of Isma'ili Shi'ism, which rested its convictions upon the infallible teaching (*ta'lim*) of an Imam, but which was in fact suffused with the models and methods of Greek philosophy. Sunnism's defense was taken up by al-Ghazali (d. 1111), a professor of jurisprudence in Baghdad who sought to convict not only the Isma'ilis but also the philosophers who were their inspiration.[86] He did so not by falling back on traditionist arguments, which would have been rejected out of hand by his opponents, but by infusing *kalam* with sufficient rigor to meet the opposition on their own ground.[87] The philosophers, chiefly Farabi and Avicenna, were taken on in *The Incoherence of the Philosophers*,[88] and the Isma'ilis in a whole series of polemical treatises. Ghazali was by no means a theological reactionary. He expropriated into his version of *kalam* far more of Avicenna than Ash'ari could conceivably have dreamed of, and he accepted and glorified a form of Sufism whose intellectual foundations ran deep into Neoplatonism.[89]

[85] *Hodgson, *Venture*, II, 323-325; Peters, *Allah's Commonwealth*, pp. 585-592, 680-690.

[86] Ghazali has described his own spiritual and intellectual quest for truth and certainty in his *Deliverer from Error*, which has been translated by W. M. Watt, *The Faith and Practice of al-Ghazali* (London: Allen and Unwin, 1967), pp. 19-85. A great deal has been written on Ghazali, but one might begin with W. M. Watt, *Muslim Intellectual: A Study of al-Ghazali* (Chicago: Aldine, 1963), and for the theological background, F. Shehadi, *Ghazali's Unique Unknowable God* (Leiden: E. J. Brill, 1964).

[87] *Hodgson, *Venture*, II, 180-188; Peters, *Allah's Commonwealth*, pp. 690-707.

[88] Most of which is translated, together with Averroes' counter refutation; see n. 102 below.

[89] See Chapter VII above.

Avicenna and Ghazali are central figures in later Islamic theology. Ghazali's critique of Avicenna's cosmology and of the Greek cosmology that lay behind it made it forever suspect among the *mutakallimun*. But in following Avicenna onto the path of illuminationism, Ghazali opened to his successors the royal road to theosophy.[90] Traditional *kalam* is not distinguished after Ghazali and Fakhr al-Din al-Razi (d. 1209).[91] Indeed, traditionists such as the Spaniard Ibn Hazm (d. 1064) and the Syrian Ibn Taymiyyah (d. 1327) show a great deal more intellectual vigor in attacking the rationalist tradition than the *mutakallimun* in defending it.[92]

And yet the final triumph belonged to *kalam*. One cannot always calculate the traditionist response, since it more often defended itself with polemic than with dogmatic statements. Christianity, as we have seen, defined and redefined itself in a series of credal statements, and in the positive dogma and negative anathemas issued by the councils. Islam had no comparable conciliar structure, and its closest approximation to a creed in the sense of a baptismal formula is the simple *shahadah*: "There is no god but The God and Muhammad is His Envoy."[93] By the mid-eighth century, however, longer statements in the form of a creed (*'aqidah*) began to appear anonymously in legal circles. Wensinck, who has studied them,[94] has noted that they have nothing to do with the two basic elements of the *shahadah*, which are the affirmations required of the individual Muslim, but address themselves to current religio-political disputes. Thus the ten articles of the so-called Fiqh Akbar I take their stand against Kharijites, Shi'ites, and the partisans of free will, and so probably date from around 750 C.E., when these issues were current.[95]

A century and a half later, the "Testament of Abu Hani-

[90] See Chapter VII above.

[91] See Fakhry, *Islamic Philosophy*, pp. 354-358.

[92] Ibid., pp. 347-354.

[93] On the origins and function of this formula, see Wensinck, *Muslim Creed*, pp. 1-35.

[94] Ibid., pp. 102-247.

[95] Text ibid., pp. 103-104.

fah" had grown to twenty-seven articles.[96] It reflects the Mu'tazilite controversy about the createdness of the Qur'an, where it takes a strongly Hanbalite and traditionist stance in opposition, and is markedly more adventuresome than its predecessor in attempting to define faith and to adjudicate between the relative importance of faith and good works.[97] Technical *kalam* vocabulary also makes its first appearance. A third document, the Fiqh Akbar II, completes the evolution. This late tenth-century creed shows clearly the penetration of *kalam* into traditionist thought. Like its predecessors, it is not a declaration of what one must believe to be a Muslim but is rather a not very systematic Ash'arite statement of position on the theological arguments of its day: the corporeality of Allah, the allegorical understanding of Scripture, and the attributes of God.[98]

All these so-called creeds were manifestly not documents to live by but somewhat sectarian statements on problems troubling the early lawyers and *mutakallimun*. Many of the points were still in contention at the time of composition, but if one moved forward to the period of Ghazali (d. 1111) and beyond, when a consensus of sorts had developed in Sunni Islam, the Muslim creeds have much the same appearance as a Christian catechism, that is, of highly stylized, albeit abbreviated and simplified treatises of scholastic theology. Duncan Macdonald has translated three such in his *Muslim Theology, Jurisprudence and Constitutional Theory*:[99] the catechism inserted by Ghazali himself in his *Revivification of the Sciences of Religion*; the *Articles of Belief* of Najm al-Din al-Nasafi (d. 1141); and the *Creed* of al-Fudali (d. 1821).[100]

[96] Text ibid., pp. 125-131.

[97] See Chapter V above.

[98] Text in Wensinck, *Muslim Creed*, pp. 188-197. It includes as well the first intimation that there might be semantic problems ahead when the question of the Qur'anic attributes of God came to be discussed in Persian and other nonqur'anic languages; see ibid., pp. 236-237.

[99] 1903; reprint Lahore: Sh. Muhhammad Ashraf, 1964.

[100] Ghazali's catechism = Macdonald, *Muslim Theology*, pp. 302-312; Na-

However "philosophical" it had become, *kalam* found little favor among the ever-thinning strain of philosophers in Islam. Ibn Rushd or Averroes (d. 1198), the most cogent Aristotelian produced in Islam,[101] wrote his *Incoherence of the Incoherence* to refute Ash'arite *kalam* in general and Ghazali's sophisticated defense of it in particular.[102] Nor did he spare Avicenna in the process. The universe was not the product of a divine emanation, as Farabi and Avicenna thought it was, because earlier philosophers had misunderstood Aristotle; nor was it composed of atoms linked only by God's will, as the *kalam* maintained in a misguided effort to defend God's omnipotence. Efficient and final causality reigned everywhere, from God, the First Cause, to man, the moral agent.[103]

In another, briefer work, *The Decisive Treatise*,[104] Averroes turned from the *mutakallimun* to a defense of philosophy against what was in twelfth-century Spain a far more powerful body of antagonists, the lawyers. Ghazali's works had been burned in public when they arrived in Spain for the first time; even relatively mild versions of Ash'arite *kalam* aroused the Spanish jurisprudents, who were fiercely attached to Maliki traditionism. But by the beginning of the twelfth century there were new religious and political stirrings among the North African Berbers. In 1121 c.e., one of them, Ibn Tumart, was proclaimed Mahdi or "the Rightly Guided One" who would unite all men in the observance of Islamic Law and so pre-

---

safi: ibid., pp. 313-322; Fudali: ibid., pp. 323-370. Nasafi's *Articles of Belief* and its classic commentary by Taftazani (d. 1390) has also been translated by E. Elder, *A Commentary on the Creed of Islam* (New York: Columbia University Press, 1950).

[101] On his career and works, see Fakhry, *Islamic Philosophy*, pp. 302-325.

[102] It has been translated, together with the appropriate sections of Ghazali's *Incoherence*, by S. Van den Bergh, *Averroes' Tahafut al-Tahafut*, 2 vols. (London: Luzac, 1954).

[103] On Ghazali's denial of causality and Averroes' defense of it, see Fakhry, *Islamic Occasionalism*, pp. 56-138.

[104] Translated by G. Hourani, *Averroes on the Harmony of Religion and Philosophy* (London: Luzac, 1961).

pare them for the End Time. His Berber followers, who were called "Unitarians" (al-muwahhidun; in English, Almohads), eventually ruled over all of North Africa from Tunis to Morocco and the southern half of Spain, and created a new religious and intellectual climate that permitted the work of Ibn Tufayl and Averroes, while it forced into exile the theologian Maimonides.

The paradox of the divergent fates of Averroes and Maimonides simply repeats a greater one in the mahdism of Ibn Tumart. He, a Sunni of the Sunnis, borrowed the Shi'ite ideology of the infallible Imam to complement his role as Mahdi. He and his followers followed the strictest principles of Zahiri law,[105] forced conversion upon Jews and Christians, and at the same time took up theological positions associated with Mu'tazilite and Ash'arite kalam, and, in the case of Averroes, encouraged a reconciliation between shari'ah and falsafah; or to state it in Averroes' more modest way in The Decisive Treatise: is the study of philosophy permitted or even obligated by the Islamic Law?

The answer was, of course, yes: the Qur'an commands a study of God's purpose in the universe, and that is the goal of philosophy. The principal objection to this smoothly argued conclusion is raised immediately. Philosophy, which lays its own independent claims to truth, has often been at odds with the truths of revelation. The differences, according to Averroes, are only apparent, and arise from two different modes of expression, the figurative, metaphorical language of Scripture and the scientific language of philosophy. Thus the solution lies where it had always lain from Philo onwards, in the allegorical exegesis of Scripture. Averroes even pressed the point: it is the philosophers and not the mutakallimun and the lawyers who are uniquely qualified to interpret Scripture, since they and they alone possess a true understanding of its "real," that is, philosophical meaning.

---

[105] *J. Schacht, Introduction to Muslim Law (London: Oxford University Press, 1964), pp. 63-65; cf. I. Goldziher, The Zahiris, Their Doctrine and History (1884; revised translation, London: E. J. Brill, 1971).

The lawyers were unconvinced by Averroes' *Decisive Treatise*, and after him there was no Muslim to speak so broadly and boldly for the rights of the philosopher vis-à-vis the lawyer on the one hand and the *mutakallim* on the other; Averroes' voice continued to echo in Christian Europe and not in the Dar al-Islam.[106] But there were other voices, speaking in somewhat different accents, that continued to raise the issue of reason and revelation in the Arabic-speaking world. The chief of them was that of the Jewish physician, philosopher, and talmudic scholar Moses Maimonides (d. 1204), whom Almohad persecution had driven from Spain to a long and successful career in Egypt.

Maimonides came in the midst of a long tradition of Jewish theology in the Middle Ages. The practice of speculative theology begun by Philo and so suddenly abandoned was taken up once again under Islam by the Gaon Saadya ibn Yusuf (d. 942). Learned in both the Scripture and the mystical tradition,[107] Saadya was the first Jew to follow his Muslim Mu'tazilite contemporaries into the *kalam*. The result was the first systematic treatise on Jewish theology, the Arabic *Book of Beliefs and Opinions*.[108] There is no mistaking who Saadya is and what he is about. In his preliminary discourse he assures his readers that his task is primarily to confirm the truths of revelation and to clear up doubts, not to establish new truths. Truth, he explains, arises generally out of the senses, reason, and intuition to which he, as a member of "the community of monotheists," adds a fourth: authentic

[106] Gilson, *Christian Philosophy*, pp. 387-409, and *Reason and Revelation in the Middle Ages* (New York: Scribners, 1938), pp. 37-66.

[107] Among his other works, Saadya was responsible for the first translation of the Bible into Arabic, and wrote a commentary on the Book of Creation.

[108] The Arabic original has been translated into English by S. Rosenblatt, *Saadia Gaon: The Book of Beliefs and Opinions* (1948; reprint New Haven: Yale University Press, 1967), and there is a partial translation by A. Altman in *Three Jewish Philosophers* (New York: Meridien pb., 1960). On Saadya's theological positions, see J. Guttmann, *Philosophies of Judaism* (New York: Schocken pb., 1973), pp. 61-73.

tradition or revelation. An entire treatise of the work is devoted to a defense of the validity of prophecy in general and of the Torah in particular, and another to the redemption of Israel.[109]

Saadya, it is clear, was not a philosopher on the Greek model but a theologian of the type developing within all three of the monotheistic religions of revelation. They all hastened to acknowledge that revelation was the primary source of truth. But though revelation was originally verified by miracle, it could be shaken by interior doubts and attacks from without, and so stood in need of the support of rational arguments. All the *mutakallimun* would agree on those propositions, and though they might differ on the necessity of rational understanding—Clement would take a more forceful position than Saadya, for example—they all cast philosophy to play Hagar to Scripture's Sarah.[110]

Even in Saadya's lifetime other Jews were discovering the attractions of *falsafah* as an autonomous discipline without the manacles of a bondswoman. But it was primarily in the vigorous new Jewish centers in Spain that scholars began the serious pursuit of philosophy.[111] The century between Ibn Gabirol (d. 1050 or 1070) and Ibn Ezra (d. 1167) witnessed a remarkable development of Jewish Neoplatonism. It even found its own Ghazali in the person of Judah Halevi (d. 1141), whose *Khazari* or *Kuzari*,[112] though cast in the form of a debate among a philosopher, a Muslim, a Christian, and a Jew in the presence of the king of the Khazars, had much the same intention as Ghazali's *Incoherence of the Philosophers*, to give the lie to the philosophers' claims to arrive at the truths

[109] Rosenblatt, *Beliefs and Opinions*, pp. 137-179, 299-322.

[110] Wolfson, *Church Fathers*, pp. 97-101.

[111] Guttmann, *Philosophies of Judaism*, pp. 89-120.

[112] English translation by H. Hirschfeld, *Judah Halevi's Kitab al-Khazari*, rev. ed. (London: Routledge and Sons, 1931), and *Kuzari: An Account of the Faith of Israel* (New York: Schocken pb., 1966); partial translation in *Three Jewish Philosophers* (New York: Meridien pb., 1960).

that only revelation, here specifically a Jewish, biblical revelation, could provide.[113]

The response from philosophy ignored Judah Halevi, though not the problem he presented. Maimonides' *Guide of the Perplexed* is an apologia for philosophy and the role of reason in religious discourse, but it is much more besides, as Leo Strauss' introduction to the English translation makes obscurely manifest.[114] Averroes and Maimonides shared a common conviction that Aristotelianism was a more rigorous and truthful account of God and the universe than the prevailing Neoplatonism, and a common "political" concern about the fate of the uninstructed believer who was caught among the unenlightened traditionism of the lawyers, the half-learned arguments of the *mutakallimun*, and the hard truths of philosophy. Averroes was less cautious in his expression but more prudent in his proposals. Allegorical exegesis, for example, ought not be broadcast among the ordinary believers.[115] Maimonides was more cautious in the involuted *Guide*, but more willing to provide guidance for the ordinary Jew in other contexts.[116] In both the introduction to his *Mishneh Torah* (see Chapter IV above) and his *Commentary on the Mishnah* (*Sanhedrin* X, 1), Maimonides set down the thirteen fundamental propositions of Jewish belief in the dogmatic form of orthodoxy rather than in the more traditional halakic mode of orthopraxy.[117] "Naked faith" was no more satisfactory for Maimonides than it had been for Clement or Origen.

The *Guide* is at least in part intended to help the Jewish believer move from simple talmudic piety to an affirmation

[113] Guttmann, *Philosophies of Judaism*, pp. 120-133.

[114] English translation of the Arabic original by S. Pines, *Moses Maimonides: The Guide of the Perplexed* (Chicago: Chicago University Press, 1963). On Maimonides' career and work, see Guttmann, *Philosophies of Judaism*, pp. 152-182.

[115] Hourani, *Harmony*, pp. 32-37, and translation, pp. 63-71, 76-81.

[116] See Leo Strauss' Introduction to Pines, *Guide*, and the translator's own remarks, pp. cxvii-cxxiii; cf. n. 21 above.

[117] Guttmann, *Philosophies of Judaism*, pp. 154, 178-179.

of those propositions by patiently explaining the allegorical exegesis of Scripture, particularly those passages that might suggest that God is corporeal. But it was also designed to guide the more sophisticated student around the perplexities raised by the *kalam*. The *mutakallimun* are dangerous because they pretend to explain. They are, in fact, dialecticians rather than philosophers and their arguments are riddled with errors, as Farabi had pointed out two centuries earlier. And yet Maimonides will not blindly follow the philosophers. In a revealing passage he shows no hesitation in setting aside Aristotle's demonstration for the eternity of the universe as unproved; and since it is an open question, to follow without benefit of formal proof the teaching of Scripture "which explains things to which it is not in the power of speculation to accede."[118]

Maimonides had confidence in the power of prophecy and its promulgation in a revealed Scripture, and devoted a long section of the *Guide* (II, 32-48) to explaining and defending it. But unlike his mentor Farabi, whose arguments he followed here, Maimonides was willing to make a case, as Saadya had done, for a special Jewish revelation and to set Moses apart from the other prophets. Thus Maimonides was committed to defending the rational and philosophical basis of the Torah, a task to which Farabi had never to address himself with respect to the *shariʿah*.[119] The philosophy of the Scriptures is, of course, concealed; its natural science lies within the "Work of the Beginning" and its divine science in the "Work of the Chariot," and the explanation of these two themes, which were the favorite points of departure for Jewish mystics and the subject of frequent cautionary remarks by the rabbis,[120] is the alleged program of the entire *Guide*.[121] Having indicated by these programmatic remarks that Scrip-

---

[118] *Guide*, II, 17 = Pines, p. 294.

[119] On Maimonides rationalization of Torah and Talmud, see Chapter IV above.

[120] See Chapter VII above.

[121] Introduction to Parts I and III = Pines, *Guide*, pp. 5-9, 415-416.

191

ture contains both a physics and a metaphysics, Maimonides can proceed to disengage these two sciences from the errors of the *mutakallimun* and their reconstitution on the basis of his own Aristotelian convictions.

Ghazali and Maimonides, one arguing for *kalam* and one against, had much the same effect on their successors. A purely rationalist philosophy, whether from Aristotle or from al-Razi, remained unacceptable to the adherents of a revealed religion, and even the accommodations of a Farabi, on Avicenna, or an Averroes could not conceal the fact that they prized philosophical over religious wisdom, Athens over Mecca, and could make no case for the unique status of the latter. Maimonides, on the other hand, could and did make such a case for Jerusalem and so "rationalized" the Law by the skillful application of a political philosophy, which the Muslim philosophers could not.[122] But the Islamic Law was "rationalized" nonetheless, not by the philosopher Farabi but by the *mutakallim* Ghazali.[123]

Ghazali and Maimonides both argued that the conclusions of human reason did not have the final word in the process of understanding; many of them were faulty even in their own terms. Nor could human reason be ignored. Post-Ghazali *kalam*, Jewish, Christian, or Muslim, could no longer afford the luxury of being dialectical rather than totally demonstrative: if it was going to be the handmaiden of Scripture, it must at least be an honest woman.[124]

Christianity had little difficulty in constructing a "sacred theology," which is *kalam*. The early Christian Fathers had an immediate and profound knowledge of Greek philosophy and did not have to reckon with a highly specified "tradition." Indeed, later Greek philosophy had itself developed into a species of *kalam* for the benefit of sacred books like

---

[122] Pines, *Guide*, pp. lxxxix, xcviii–cxxiii.
[123] See Chapter IV above.
[124] On post-Ghazali *kalam* in Islam, see Wensinck, *Muslim Creed*, pp. 248–276.

the Chaldean Oracles.[125] Between Justin and Origen the project was for all practical purposes complete, and if it had to be repeated in the twelfth century, it was because European Christian scholars had to rediscover Greek philosophy, now accompanied and complicated by the cumulative problems of Muslim *kalam*.[126] And it seems likely that the development of a Jewish *kalam*, which was begun so auspiciously by Philo, would have proceeded as rapidly as the Christian version had it not been aborted for a time by what was essentially a political confrontation with Hellenism and the consequent ascendency of traditionist rabbis.

The first Muslim *mutakallimun* appeared well after the lawyers had established themselves as the paramount arbiters of Islam. Again, their discovery of Greek rationalism was piecemeal and imperfect, and they presented the results of their speculation to a public that judged them alien to both their religious and their cultural heritage, which in fact they were. Then suddenly the whole range of Greek philosophy was made available in translation to the Muslim intellectual. The arrival of a full-blown *falsafah* in Islam after the first steps toward *kalam* had been taken revealed the intellectual weakness of the latter, and confirmed the suspicions and fears of the traditionists who could now inspect the past of the new tradition and peer down the road to its future. Neither view was very comforting.

[125] Peters, *Harvest of Hellenism*, pp. 676-679, and *Allah's Commonwealth*, pp. 291-293.

[126] See F. Van Steenberghen, *Aristotle in the West* (Louvain: E. Nauwelaerts, 1955) and Gilson, *Reason and Revelation in the Middle Ages*.

Epilogue: Sacred History

THE historian is interested in origins, in the working of cause and intelligible effect on the slippery ground of human behavior. With the tools of comparative linguistics and archeology he pursues the origins of Judaism in the ancient legal and epic traditions of the Near East, in the Code of Hammurabi or the tablets of Ebla. What precisely were the charges upon which Jesus of Nazareth was tried and executed, and under whose jurisdiction? The identity of Muhammad's Jewish or Christian teachers is sought with an iron persistence, despite the equally iron conviction that we will never know.

The queries of the secular historian will continue to be pressed, with little effect, perhaps, on the continuing history of the objects of his study. These same religious communities are also interested in history, and have been so from the beginning—not in the rationalist's enterprise, to be sure, but in another view of the past that has been exalted or reviled under the name of "sacred history."

Sacred history, like its secular counterpart, is committed to meaning and understanding, to a human understanding of God's meaning. In the Greek view, God created the world and then permitted it to evolve along the course of the natural causes He had sown within its genes. Nothing could be more remote from the thinking of these three revelational religions, for whom God not only created the world, but continues to act in and upon it, and who will in the end judge it.

It has always been thought so, and Jews, Christians, and Muslims have long collected and preserved evidence of God's providential plan for His creation. The Greek was impressed by the orderly progression of the seasons, the regular and

194

majestic movement of the heavenly bodies: "the heavens themselves proclaim the glory of God." Such thinking is not entirely alien to revelation, and Jesus could indeed point to the paradigm of the lilies of the field, and Muhammad too frequently cited the natural signs that God's hand lay upon the universe. But of far greater interest to Moses and Jesus and Muhammad was God's special care of His own people, a care manifested by an intervention in history on their behalf.

If a miracle is the suspension of the operation of the natural causality so meditated by the Greeks and their European successors, then sacred history is a record of the miraculous, not merely of the prodigious—like the descent of manna in the desert, or the transformation of water into wine, or the sundry other acts whereby God identifies and confirms His prophets—but of an entire divine economy whereby God undertakes to instruct and guide His people toward an end that He himself had decreed. For all three religious communities, God's intervention manifests itself in two chief ways: in the revelation of His truth, whether as message, admonition, or covenant, and in His ongoing "political" guidance to the community of believers, His governance of that frail ark through the turmoil of the other "nations," the *gentes*, "Gentiles," as the Jews called them; the "unbelievers" (*kafirun*) of the Muslims.

For Jew, Christian, and Muslim alike, the history of revelation and the history of the community are the twin foundations of their sacred history, but it is the concurrence of the matter of that history that binds them forever together. The sacred history of the Jews cares nothing for Hammurabi and knows nothing of Ebla; it is rooted in Abraham and the events of Sinai. For the early Christians, Jesus too would have been incomprehensible without Sinai and the Prophets, and the Gospels have as part of their agenda a demonstration that Jesus fulfilled what was uncontrovertibly part of that revelation, the messianic promise. As Jews, the Evangelists simply assumed the authenticity of that revelation and that

195

promise; Muhammad could make no such assumption: he was constrained to unfold God's earlier revelations and to demonstrate to a pagan, not a Jewish, audience that his Book and his experiences on Mount Hira were a continuation of what had begun on Sinai. It fell to the successors of the Prophets, the Sons of Israel, the Christian *ekklesia* and the Muslim *ummah*, to trace for an eternal remembrance the history of the community in its social and political context.

Each community validated the revealed covenant of its predecessors, even as it departed from it in the name of a new revelation that represented both the continuation and the transendence of what had gone before. The Israelites who gathered with Moses at the foot of Sinai affirmed the truth of what had been announced to Abraham and the tribal patriarchs, and read it into the record of Scripture; indeed, the sacred history of the Jews begins with creation itself. And though there were those who had misgivings, the early followers of Jesus affirmed, like Jesus himself, the experience of the Covenant. There was, the Christians agreed, a New Covenant, but the new was inexplicable without the old, and so the sacred history of the Jews, the history of both the Law and the community, became the holy past of the Christian movement.

Christianity was a revolution in Judaism in that it announced not simply a reform of the Law but its effective abrogation. It instructed the new Christians, more and more from among the Gentiles, that the Law, its study and observance, both linch-pins of what rabbinic Judaism defined as a Jew, was neither obligatory nor indeed praiseworthy. Christians of strict or even regular observance were not distinguished by their voluntary embrace of the rabbinic ideal but by the pursuit of an asceticism that was radically alien to the world of the Talmud.

Islam too validated God's earlier revelatory interventions into human history—the Sacred Books of the Jews and the Christians were true Scripture—but Muhammad claimed neither the perfection nor the abrogation of those revelations of earlier times. Rather, the Qur'an itself suggested without undue emphasis on the question that those other "Peoples of the Book" had misread or misunderstood or misinterpreted the words that God had entrusted to their safekeeping: a view somewhat closer to Jesus' own than to Paul's understanding of the past of Judaism. Jesus quarreled with the Pharisees and Muhammad with the "Jews," but Paul took on the function and intent of the Law itself.

If in the sequel Jesus was or appeared to be a Jewish revolutionary, Muhammad was an Israelite fundamentalist. He knew the history of the prophets, with whom he closely identified himself, but he had no interest in their Books and so none in the messianic mission of Jesus, who reverted to the role of prophet in the Qur'an. As a result, none of those Books—Torah, Psalms, and Prophets—become part of the devotional life of the Muslim, as they had for the Christian. Muhámmad proposed not to reread the older Scriptures with the new eyes of an enlightened faith, but to return to the source, the "natural" pre-Torah religion of Abraham, the father of all believers.

Muslim and Jew come together in the figure and symbol of Abraham, a Jew before the Torah, a Muslim before the Qur'an, the father of both Isaac and Ishmael, the former the tribal ancestor of the Sons of Israel, the latter of all the Arabs. This was the biblical genealogy, and it was not disputed by Islam. Where they did disagree was on the fulfillment of the promise to Abraham, whether it came to term in the Israelites or the Arabs.

There are in fact two Abrahams in the Qur'an, the well-known figure from Genesis, embroidered here and there with what appear to be Jewish legendary *midrash*; and another Abraham, the product of some other sensibility, who emigrated to Arabia with his wife Hagar and his son Ishmael to settle in Mecca, where he built the Ka'bah, the "House of God," and instituted most of the ritual practices of the later Islamic pilgrimage.

Both Abrahams are the creations of sacred history, and the

historian stands mute before one or the other. His silence is no great loss, perhaps, since the Muslims' and the Jews' perception of the past owes nothing to the secular historian but is grounded in God's own word; all the history that either requires is spelled out in the Bible and the Qur'an.

But even sacred history is no stranger to polemic. The historian may note that the Abraham associated with Mecca appears in the Qur'an only after Muhammad's first confrontation with the Jews of Medina, and so the invocation of Abraham may have been a response, a retort to the Jewish rejection of Muhammad's own prophethood. It is certainly so in Paul. Both Paul and Muhammad claimed Abraham as a believer before the fact. In both instances the "fact" was the Law or its symbol in circumcision. For Paul, Abraham's faith before circumcision made him the prototype of all believers, circumcised and uncircumcised, Jew and Gentile. For Muhammad, Abraham's belief separated *islam*, submission, from the Law that codified it. Thus Abraham, by his faith (according to Paul), or by his submission (according to Muhammad), undercut Jewish claims to exclusivity.

Paul's appeal to Abraham is made almost in passing in his letter to the Romans, and the Patriarch looms not nearly so large in Christianity as he does in the Jewish and Muslim understanding of the past. It is the person and the acts of Jesus that are crucial to Christianity, and it is precisely Jesus who separates the typology of Christianity from that of both Judaism and Islam. Both Muslim and Jew are covenantors for whom the path to holiness lies in fidelity of heart and observance to that covenant. The Christian is asked not so much fidelity as faith, faith in Jesus who is, in his own person, the New Covenant. Jew and Muslim measure their fidelity by a deeply considered and articulated body of *halakoth*, behavioral norms that are the touchstone of orthopraxy; the Christian measures his faith by the instruments of orthodoxy, creeds, and definitions. The archetypical figure in traditional Judaism and Islam is the legal scholar, the rabbi or

198

'alim; in traditional Christianity it is the priest, the mediator who, like the Arch-Mediator Christ, bridges the gap between the human and the divine.

By his dual nature and his redemptive death and resurrection, Jesus sanctified matter and set in train the Christian system of sacraments that replicate the Messiah's own conciliation of the domain of the spiritual and of the material. In Judaism and Islam the only bridge thrown across that great abyss is revelation itself, the Word, the Book. The anomaly of Christianity for both Muslim and Jew is that the Word became flesh, not in the sense that the Torah or the Qur'an was expressed in human speech, but in the more radical understanding that the Word became man. Jesus was his own Scripture.

The Christian view gave rise to consequences alien to the sensibilities of the other two: the doctrine of the Trinity and its implied repudiation of monotheism; a priesthood that is both the infallible interpreter of the Christian tradition and the sole dispenser of sacramental grace; the Eucharistic sacrifice wherein flesh becomes the Word on every altar in Christendom; the veneration of saints and images. Muhammad was merely a man, asserts the unanimous Muslim tradition, a servant of God, and the Jew has never thought it worth declaring that self-evident fact in the case of Moses and the Prophets. Jesus is both God and man, professes the Christian, and we can only be saved through and by the Christ.

Viewed in this light, Islam looks like a return to traditional Judaism in the face of an aberrant Christianity. Or it would, if the Qur'an did not appear to be directed to a pagan and Jewish audience rather than a pagan and Christian one. But we do not know about that and many other things besides. The secular historian wishes he understood more about the politics of messianic expectation in the first century, about the fate of Jewish Christianity, about the extent and quality of Judaism in Arabia on the eve of Islam, about the types of

199

Christianity with which Muhammad came in contact before and during the period of his prophethood, about the authenticity of the traditions ascribed to Muhammad. The Jew, the Christian, and the Muslim rest content, however, with sacred history and the Word of God.

Glossary

THE following technical terms appear in the text transcribed from Arabic (A), Greek (G) and Hebrew-Aramaic (H). All transcription systems are unsatisfactory for those who read the original languages, and probably baffling for those who cannot. The ones used here make no special claim in that regard. Those who know the originals will doubtless recognize that I have preferred to cling to the certainties of spelling rather than try the slippery way of pronunciation, and it is for this reason that some readers who expect to find *yeshiva*, for example, will be confronted with *yeshiba* instead. Again, I have attempted to keep diacritical marks to a minimum, on the same grounds that few will be either deceived or uninstructed by their omission. Where entries appear in the form *halaka/halakot*, the first member is the singular, the second the plural. Quotation marks enclose the literal meaning of a term wherever that seemed useful.

Ab Bet Din (H): junior member of the "pair" who collegially presided over the Sanhedrin or Great Assembly.

adab (A): appropriate way of acting; etiquette.

agape (G): "love"; the nonliturgical community meal celebrated by the early Christians.

ahkam (A): "judgments," esp. of God; binding prescriptions of Muslim Law.

ahl al-hadith (A): "partisans of *hadith*-reports"; traditionists; see *hadith*.

ahl al-kalam (A): "partisans of dialectical reasoning"; see *kalam*.

allegoria (G): "other-referent"; a sense of a text different from the literal or apparent meaning; see *ta'wil* and *batin*.

amida (H): "standing"; the series of benedictions that constitute the central part of the synagogue service.

amir (A): commander; *Amir al-Mu'minin*: "Commander of the Faithful."

amora/amoraim (H): "speaker"; the rabbis whose comments on the Mishna constitute the two *gemarot*.

anachoresis (G): "withdrawal," esp. the Christian "withdrawal from the world" for religious motives; cf. Eng. "anchorite."

anamnesis (G): "remembrance"; the recollection of Jesus' redemptive passion and death as part of the Christian liturgy.

anaphora (G): "lifting up"; the central part of the eucharistic liturgy; the "canon" of the Roman mass.

Apocrypha (G): "hidden"; those religious writings excluded from the official canon of Scripture.

'aqidah (A): creed, statement of Muslim beliefs; cf. *symbolon*.

baraita (H): "additional material," esp. additional to the contents of the Mishna; see *tosefta*.

barakah (A): "blessing"; the special favor or divine grace possessed by the "friends of God" and esp. the Sufi master; see *wali, murshid, silsilah*.

batin (A): "concealed"; the sense of Scripture concealed beneath the literal meaning of Scripture and accessible only to the adept; see *ta'wil*.

Bene Yisrael (H): "Children of Israel"; Israelites; Jews.

berit (H): covenant, esp. the Covenant concluded between Yahweh and the Bene Yisrael.

bet din (H): Jewish law court; the "Great *Bet Din*" was the Sanhedrin, the chief legislative and judicial body of post-Exilic Judaism.

bet ha-knesset (H): "house of assembly"; congregational meeting place; the synagogue.

bet ha-midrash (H): "house of study"; school for the study of Jewish Scripture and Law; see *midrash, yeshiba.*

bet ha-tefilla (H): "house of prayer"; the synagogue as a liturgical center.

catechesis (G): instruction, esp. the instruction prior to Christian baptism; cf. Eng. "catechism."

Dar al-Harb (A): "Abode of Conflict"; those lands not under Muslim political control.

Dar al-Islam (A): "Abode of Islam"; the territories under Muslim political control.

dhikr (A): "recollection," esp. of God; the external repetition of His name in a rythmical manner; a Sufi devotional exercise.

Diaspora (G): "dispersion"; the Jewish communities outside of Eretz Yisrael.

eidos/eide (G): archetype; idea.

ekklesia (G): congregation; church; an individual Christian community or the total body of Christians who constitute the "Great Church"; cf. Eng. "ecclesiastic."

epiklesis (G): "invocation"; the calling upon the Holy Spirit to sanctify the sacrificial offering in eastern Christian liturgies.

episkopos (G): "overseer"; the head of a Christian community with responsibility for their faith and morals; bishop; cf. Eng. "episcopal."

episteme (G): knowledge, esp. discursive knowledge; also the contents of that process, science; see *'ilm* and cf. Eng. "epistemology."

Eretz Yisrael (H): "the land of Israel": the land promised to the Israelites in the Covenant; in law, Palestine and adjacent areas where the *halakot* had to be strictly observed.

erub/erubin (H): "mixture"; by extension, the domain within which Sabbath activity was permissible; a tractate of the Mishnaic Order of *Sabbath* devoted to that question.

euangelion (G): "good news," namely, of Jesus, a Gospel; the literary work embodying such, esp. the four canonical Gospels attributed to Matthew, Mark, Luke, and John; cf. Eng. "evangelical."

eucharistia (G): "thanksgiving"; the sacrificial liturgy of the Christians commemorating and reenacting the redemptive death of Jesus; the Eucharist.

falsafah (A): "philosophy," esp. the methods and content of Greek philosophy transposed into Islam.

fana (A): annihilation of self, the state antecedent to the mystic's union with God.

faqih/fuqaha (A): jurisprudent; one skilled in the interpretation of the *shari'ah*; see *fiqh*.

fasiq (A); a sinner; a Muslim who has violated the Islamic Law, usually in some grave manner.

fatwa (A): an advisory judgment on a case of Islamic Law rendered by a competent authority; a *responsum*; see *mufti*.

fiqh (A): jurisprudence; the science of interpreting the *shari'ah*; see *faqih*.

gaon/geonim (H): "eminence"; the heads of the great Jewish law schools under Islam and the chief authorities of the Jewish communities in Babylonia and Palestine during that period.

gemara/gemarot (H): "completion"; an Aramaic commentary on the Mishna by the rabbis of either the Babylonian or the Palestinian academies; see *amora*.

geniza (H): storeroom, esp. one attached to a synagogue, where texts and documents were preserved.

gezera/gezerot (H): a legal enactment that extended or specified a rabbinic *halaka*.

gnosis (G): "knowledge," esp. the hidden knowledge of the adept, which guarantees salvation; see *hikmah*.

habura (H): table-fellowship; a common meal shared by those who had common standards of ritual purity.

hadith (A): a report purporting to transmit the words or the deeds of Muhammad on the authority of his contemporaries.

haftara (H): a passage of about ten verses from the Prophetic Books whose recitation followed that of the Torah in the Sabbath synagogue service.

haggada/haggadot (H): homily; exegesis of Scripture in the form of expositional homilies that emphasized the moral and ethical content of the text.

hajj (A): pilgrimage, esp. the pilgrimage to Mecca incumbent upon all Muslims.

halaka/halakot (H): a binding legal enactment of the rabbis that was either derived from Scripture by exegetical means or appealed for its authority to the "tradition of the Fathers."

hasid/hasidim (H): "pious"; a term used of 1. early religious supporters of the Maccabees and so the forerunners of the Pharisees; and 2. a number of groups of medieval Jewish pietists, but particularly 3. an eighteenth-century eastern European movement of popular mysticism.

205

hegoumenos (G): leader or superior, esp. of a Christian monastic community; an abbot.

herem (H): "taboo"; "unholy"; permanent expulsion from the Jewish community; cf. Eng. "harem," the taboo section of a Muslim household, the women's quarters.

hesychia (G): tranquillity, quietude in the mystic's contemplation.

hijrah (A): "emigration," esp. Muhammad's emigration from Mecca to Medina in 622 c.e., a date that marks the beginning of the Muslim era; cf. Eng. "hegira."

hikmah (A): wisdom; the highest level of understanding; in particular the illuminative, intuitive wisdom of the mystic, the Gnostic, or the theosopher.

hiyal (A): "devices," esp. legal devices or fictions used to avoid the violation of the direct letter of the law.

homoousios (G): "of the same substance"; cf. *homoiousios*, "of a similar substance," both used of Jesus in reference to the Father.

hyponoia (G): "under-meaning," the latent sense of a text, which must be elicitied by allegorical exegesis; see *allegoria*.

'id (A): festival, holy day; particularly *'id al-fitr* at the end of Ramadan and *'id al-adha* during the *hajj*.

ijma' (A): consensus; the consensus of legal scholars of one center or school, but eventually understood to be the consensus of all Muslims.

ijtihad (A): "personal effort"; the application of everything from common sense to sophisticated legal reasoning to the explication of a text.

'ilm (A): knowledge, esp. discursive, demonstrative knowledge and its contents; science; see *episteme*.

imam (A): leader; prayer-leader. Imam: the charismatic leader of the Muslim community; in the Shiʿite view, a descendent of ʿAli who is so designated by his predecessor.

iman (A): faith; belief; the internal acceptance of God and the Prophet's mission that finds its external expression in the *shahadah*; see *muʾmin*.

ishraq (A): "illumination"; the intuitive understanding of the mystic or certain of the philosophers; see *hikmah, maʿrifah*.

islam (A): "submission," namely, to the will of God; see *muslim*.

isnad (A): the chain of authorities on whose authority a *hadith* is transmitted.

ittihad (A): identity, union, esp. the mystic's union and identification with God.

jamaʿah (A): community, esp. the Islamic community viewed as a unity; see *ummah*.

jamiʿ (A): place of assembly, esp. assembly for liturgical prayer in Islam; a mosque, esp. the mosque designated for the Friday congregational prayer; see *masjid*.

jihad (A): "striving"; striving in the way of God in either the internal or the external forum; in the latter, "Holy War."

jizyah (A): poll-tax, a financial obligation upon all non-Muslim residents of the Dar al-Islam.

kafir (A): an unbeliever; one who has not submitted to the will of God; a pagan; see *kufr*.

kalam (A): "speech"; dialectical theology, characterized by its starting from commonly accepted assumptions, its use of dialectical rather than demonstrative reasoning, and its employment as an instrument for the defense of Scripture; see *mutakallim*.

karamat (A): spiritual blessings, esp. those given to the "friends of God"; see *wali*.

kenoma (G): "emptiness"; the lower material and sensible world of the Gnostic; see *pleroma*.

kerygma (G): "preaching"; the mode of discourse that has shaped the Gospel narratives.

ketubim (H): "writings"; a division of the Bible that includes the Psalms, Proverbs, etc.

khalifah (A): "successor"; the successor of Muhammad as the head of the community of Muslims; see Imam, the preferred Shi'ite term to describe the same office; cf. Eng. "Caliph."

kharaj (A): land-tax; a financial obligation upon the non-Muslim residents of the Dar al-Islam.

khutbah (A): sermon, esp. the sermon delivered at the Friday congregational prayer in the *jami'*; see *minbar*.

kohen/kohanim (H): priest; celebrant of the Jewish sacrificial liturgy.

koinobia (G): community, esp. a community of Christian ascetics sharing a common life or rule; cf. Eng. "cenobite."

kufr (A): disbelief, paganism; see *kafir*.

logos/logoi (G): word, speech, reason, human or divine, the latter sometimes personified; the mode of discourse constructed upon discursive reason; pl: the discrete manifestations of reason inherent in the universe; cf. Eng. "logic."

madrasah (A): school for the advanced study of the *shari'ah*.

Mahdi (A): "the guided one"; an eschatological and messianic figure in Sunni Islam.

ma'rifah (A): knowledge, esp. the intuitive knowledge characteristic of the mystic or Gnostic; see *hikmah*.

masjid (A): "place of prostration": shrine; mosque; see *jamiʿ* and cf. Eng. "mosque."

mawla/mawali (A): client; non-Arab convert to Islam.

mazalim (A): courts of appeal and special jurisdiction.

metamorphosis (G): "re-formation," esp. of one's moral and spiritual life through grace.

midrash/midrashim (H): "study," esp. the study of Scripture; exegesis and the works devoted to such.

mihrab (A): a niche in the mosque wall indicating the direction of Mecca and so the orientation of prayer; see *qiblah*.

millet (A): a semi-autonomous community within the Dar al-Islam, usually constituted on religious grounds from among the "Peoples of the Book" but with distinctive ethnic overtones.

minbar: raised pulpit near the *mihrab* of a mosque; the place from which the *khutbah* is delivered.

minim (H): heretics, possibly the Jewish Christians, mentioned in talmudic sources.

Mishna (H): the corpus of legal and other matter compiled by the rabbis of the second and third century C.E., and esp. the authoritative final redaction of such by Rabbi Judah ha-Nasi; see *tanna*.

mithal (A): example, symbol, esp. the symbol of the Muslim Gnostic.

mitzva/mitzvot (H): "commandment"; a legal prescription explicitly found in Scripture.

morphosis (G): "shaping," "forming"; education; see *paideia*.

muʾadhdhin (A): "caller"; a public summoner to prayer in Islam; cf. Eng. "muezzin."

mufti (A): one who is competent to render an opinion on a case of Islamic Law; see *fatwa*.

mu'min/mu'minun (A): one who has faith, a believer; a Muslim; see *iman*.

murshid (A): spiritual guide or master; the Sufi director of novices, who possessed a particular charisma or grace (*barakah*); in Persian, a *pir*.

mushaf (A): copy, codex, redaction, esp. of the Qur'an.

muslim/muslimun (A): "one who has submitted," namely, to the will of God; a Muslim.

mutakillim/mutakallimun (A): a theologian, one skilled in *kalam*.

nabi (A): prophet, the recipient of a divine revelation; see Nebi'im.

Nasi (H): "leader," "ruler," "prince"; the senior partner of the "Pair" and the chief officer of the Sanhedrin or Great Assembly; later, the "Patriarch," the chief representative and acknowledged head of the Jewish communities of Palestine and the Roman Diaspora.

nazar (A): investigation or research, esp. by rational or scientific methods; see *ijtihad*.

Nebi'im (H): "the Prophets"; that part of the Bible which includes the prophetic writings.

nidduy (H): temporary suspension from the Jewish community.

notzrim (H): early Jewish term for Christians.

paideia (G): education and its content, esp. its literary content; culture; see *morphosis* and compare *adab*.

paradosis (G): "handing on or over"; tradition, esp. the Christian tradition of the teachings of Jesus passed down the line of the "Apostolic succession."

parasha (H): one of the fifty-four consecutive sections, one for each week of the lunar year, into which the Torah is divided for recitation at the Sabbath synagogue service; see *seder, pesiqta.*

parousia (G): "advent" or "presence," esp. of the Messiah in either the historical present or the eschatological future.

peshat (H): the plain or literal sense of a Scriptural passage; see *zahir.*

pesher/pesharim (H): commentary on Scripture, esp. those composed by the Qumran sectaries; see *midrash.*

pesiqta (H): That portion of the Torah and the Prophets read in the liturgical celebration of special Sabbaths and holy days; see *seder, parasha, haftara.*

petiha/petihot (H): "opening"; the verses chosen from the "Prophets" or the "Writings" by the synagogue preacher to introduce his homily.

pistis (G): faith, acceptance; see *iman.*

pleroma (G): "fullness" or "Perfection"; the upper spiritual world of Gnosticism; the abode of God and the Aeons and the spiritual home of the divine part of man; see *kenoma.*

presbyteros/presbyteroi (G): "elder"; the collegial heads of the Christian community; later, the subordinates of the bishop; the Christian priesthood, the celebrants of the eucharistic liturgy and the ordained ministers of the sacraments.

qabbala (H): "that which is handed on," esp. the esoteric knowledge of the Jewish Gnostic traditions; cf. Eng. kabbala.

qadi (A): the government-appointed judge who was the Caliph's delegate in adjudicating cases falling under the jurisdiction of the *shari'ah.*

qiblah (A): "orientation," esp. for prayer; the direction toward Mecca marked in the mosque by the *mihrab*.

qiyamah (A): "resurrection," esp. the spiritual resurrection of the Isma'ili End Time.

qiyas (A): analogy, esp. legal reasoning using the analogical method to define or extend legal enactments; a type of *ijtihad*.

Qur'an (A): "recitation"; the collected revelations given by God to Muhammad through the agency of the Angel Gabriel and the text in which they are written down; the Muslim Scripture; see *mushaf*.

qutb (A): "pole"; the spiritual master of each generation.

rasul (A): "envoy" or "apostle" of God to man; the Prophet Muhammad.

Resh Galuta (H): the Exilarch; the head of the Jewish communities in the Iranian empires in pre-Islamic times; an office parallel to that of the Nasi in Roman jurisdiction and antecedent to the *geonim*.

salat (A): prayer, esp. the liturgical prayer obligatory on every Muslim five times daily.

sama' (A): "hearing"; a Sufi ritual performance of acts like chanting and dancing in preparation for the ecstatic state; see *dhikr*.

seder/sedarim (H): One of the six "Orders" into which the Mishna is divided; also used of the one hundred fifty-four sections into which the Torah is divided for liturgical recitation in the Sabbath synagogue service across a three-year cycle; see *parasha, pesiqta*.

sefira/sefirot (H): "numbers," hence, elemental principles; in the kabbala the primary emanations of God that constitute the *pleroma*.

212

semika (H): "ordination"; the Nasi's formal delegation of his judicial powers to others.

shahadah (A): "witnessing" or professing, esp. the Muslim profession of faith and its formulaic expression: "There is no god but The God and Muhammad is His Envoy"; see *iman*.

Shari'ah (A): the Islamic Law in general; in particular those enactments whose authority is derived from 1. the Qur'an, or 2. the *sunnah* of the Prophet, or 3. the consensus of the community of Muslims, or 4. the legal reasoning of jurisprudents.

Shema' (H): Deuteronomy 6:1, beginning with the phrase "Hear (*shema'*), O Lord"; in a liturgical sense, the prayer constructed around that passage.

Shi'ah (A): "party" or "partisans," esp. the party of 'Ali and his descendents; those who supported the 'Alid claim to the caliphate-imamate; Shi'ites.

shirk (A): "association," esp. of others with the unique God; polytheism.

silsilah (A): "chain": the line of past masters through whom the spiritual enlightenment of a Sufi order passed; see *barakah*.

siyasah (A): "polity"; the discretionary political powers of the Caliph.

sofer/soferim (H): scribe, esp. the professional scribe of post-Exilic Judaism who was also a student and exegete of the Law.

suf (A): woolen cloak worn by early Muslim ascetics; cf. Eng. "Sufi."

sunnah (A): "custom," "customary practice," esp. the customary practice of the Prophet as reported in the *hadith*; cf. Eng. "Sunni."

surah (A): a chapter of the Qur'an.

symbolon (G): ritual formula; creed.

synaxis (G): "gathering, assembly" esp. for a religious service; a Christian prayer-meeting on a synagogue model that was later incorporated into the eucharistic liturgy as a part preliminary to the *anaphora*.

tafsir (A): commentary, esp. scriptural commentary; originally, perhaps, the explication of the "plain sense" of Scripture; see *zahir*.

ta'lim (A): "teaching," esp. the authoritative and infallible *magisterium* of the Imam; see *imam*.

Talmud (H): The Hebrew Mishna of Rabbi Judah ha-Nasi accompanied by either its Palestinian (Talmud Yerushalmi) or its Babylonian (Talmud Babli) Aramaic commentary (*gemara*).

Tanak (H): acronym for Torah, Nebi'im, and Ketubim; that is, the Bible.

tanna/tannaim (H): "repeater" or "reciter"; the generations of second- and third-century rabbis whose enactments and discussions are preserved in the Mishna.

taqlid (A): acceptance on the authority of another.

taqqana/taqqanot (H): legal enactments whose object was to create new institutions for the improvement of the religious, social, or economic conditions of the Jewish community.

tariqah (A): "way," esp. the "way" of the Sufi, and eventually any one of a number of institutionalized "ways" that constituted the Sufi orders.

ta'wil (A): allegorical exegesis; the explication of obscure or "concealed" (*batin*) passages in the Qur'an.

ta'ziyah (A): dramatic reenactment of the martyrdom of the Prophet's grandson and 'Ali's son Husayn.

theologia (G): scientific discourse about God, characterized by its proceeding from the first principles of reason and its use of the demonstrative method; see *kalam*; also, mystical contemplation of God; see *theoria*.

theoria (G): speculation, contemplation, esp. the mystic's contemplative knowledge of God; see *theologia, ishraq*.

targum (H): "translation," esp. the Aramaic translation, frequently of a haggadic nature, of the Bible.

Torah (H): the Law; a term used generically of Jewish religious Law or specifically of the first five books (the Pentateuch) of the Bible, where the terms of the Covenant between God and the Israelites are set forth within the narrative framework of early Jewish history.

tosefta/tosafot (H): "addition" or "supplement"; 1. a tannaitic collection of materials parallel to but posterior to the Mishna; and 2. the plural refers most frequently to a collective commentary on the Talmud that is commonly included, together with Rashi's commentary, in standard editions of the Talmud.

'ulama (A): "the learned"; the Islamic "rabbinate" whose prestige derived from their mastery of the religious sciences; see *faqih*.

ummah (A): the community of all Muslims, so constituted, like those of the Jews and Christians, by their possession of a sacred Scripture.

wali/awaliya (A): "friends," namely, of God; those who possessed special spiritual gifts; Muslim saints; see *karamat*.

waqf (A): land or property whose income was inalienably deeded to the support of pious causes, such as the con-

215

struction of a mosque or *madrasah* and the support of its faculty and students.

yahad (H): community, esp. the community at Qumran.

yeshiba/yeshibot (H): academy; school for the study of Torah and Talmud; see *bet ha-midrash*.

zaddik (H): "just man"; a holy man characterized not only by his observance of the Law but by his asceticism, and at times by his possession of special spiritual powers; a Jewish saint.

zahir (A): the "open," plain, or literal sense of a text, esp. of Scripture, and so the object of *tafsir*.

zakat (A): the tithe obligatory upon all Muslims as an offering to the poor.

zug/zugot (H): "pair"; the two officers, the Nasi and the Ab Bet Din, who presided over the Sanhedrin or Great Assembly of the Jewish community in Palestine.

Index